the Lyle
official
ANTIQUES
review

1976

Edited by TONY CURTIS

Compiled by SHIELA PORTEOUS
Drawings by PETER KNOX
          STUART BARTON
          NORMA TWEEDIE

the Lyle
official
ANTIQUES
review

1976

Acknowledgements

Dowell's, Edinburgh
King & Chasemore
Michael Gorton Design
Tweeddale Press
May Mutch
Stuart Barton
Annette Hogg
Constance Inglis

All photographs and text of the arms were
provided by Wallis and Wallis, 'Regency
House', 1 Albion Street, Lewes, Sussex.

Copyright © Lyle Publications 1975   6th year of Issue

Published by Lyle Publications Glenmayne Galashiels Selkirkshire Scotland

Printed by Apollo Press, Unit 5, Dominion Way, Worthing, Sussex.

Preface

In common with many other businesses, the antiques trade seems, during the present period of monetary depression, to be surviving on a day-to-day basis, waiting for better times to come. Being adaptable and acute by nature, however, most professional dealers are managing to maintain the previous year's level of earnings, but it is clear that inflation is hurting, and the level of joviality when dealers meet is nowadays somewhat subdued.

The increased price of petrol has had its effect, too, causing many dealers to cut back on their buying runs. The resultant drop in healthy competitive buying in shops slowed the overall movement of goods. On the other hand, inflation has dropped the value of many an income to the point where more goods from private sources are being forced onto the market. This is, naturally, a source of frustration to many dealers whose capital may be tied up in slow-moving stock, and who probably have fewer regular and reliable buyers than they had a year or two ago.

Junk, for want of a better word, seems to be selling well, however, as are the top-quality, investment pieces, but middle-quality goods seem to be hovering in a limbo of uncertainty.

Due to the fall of the pound, our goods are now cheapening in comparison with those of many other countries. In consequence, a number of European dealers (notably German & Dutch) have been showing enthusiasm at the present state of affairs, as have the growing number of British dealers who have taken the initiative and loaded up their vans for quick trips across the water.

One of the more favourable effects of the situation has been the formation of a number of Trade Associations. Although these are not particularly influential at present, they will, I am sure, have gained sufficient strength within a year or two to assert some influence on the powers that be in order to safeguard dealers themselves and our future heritage. And "future heritage", lofty a phrase as it may sound, is, I consider, what the Antiques Trade is all about. Despite the common assumption outwith the trade that dealers are concerned more with profits than ethics (and this is, unfortunately, true of a small minority), the vast majority are dealers primarily because they have a love of antiques and wish to preserve things of beauty for future generations.

Looking optimistically ahead, we know from experience that bad times are replaced by good — let's hope it will be sooner rather than later.

TONY CURTIS

CONTENTS

ADVERTISERS INDEX

Woburn Abbey Antiques Centre

The largest Antiques Centre under one roof in England, with over 40 independent shops and 50 established dealers, some of whom are members of the B.A.D.A., is situated in the magnificent South Court of Woburn Abbey.

We are pleased to offer the dealer and private collector a wide range of Antiques: Clocks, Porcelain and Glass, Paintings, Prints, Furniture, Jewellery, Georgian Domestic Silver, later silver, Bronzes, Works of Art etc., at competitive prices.

ALL ITEMS ARE VETTED BY A COMMITTEE OF ESTABLISHED DEALERS TO ENSURE THEIR AUTHENTICITY.

Within one hour's drive of London via M. 1, Exit 12 (signposted Woburn Abbey). Trains from St. Pancras to Flitwick can be met by prior arrangement. Dealers admitted free and their park entrance refunded at the Antiques Centre. Visiting dealers' car park adjacent to the Antiques Centre.

OPEN EVERY DAY OF THE YEAR
Including Sundays and Bank Holidays

Easter to October 10 − 6 p.m. November to Easter 10 − 5 p.m.

WOBURN ABBEY ANTIQUES CENTRE, WOBURN ABBEY, BEDFORDSHIRE. MK 43 0TP

Telephone Woburn (052525) 350.

CAMBRIDGESHIRE

Somersham Antiques

97 HIGH STREET SOMERSHAM CAMBRIDGESHIRE
Tele. Somersham 487 (STD. 04874)

Showrooms Open 9.30a.m. — 5.30p.m.
Monday — Thursday — Friday — Saturday.
Evening & Sunday viewing by
appointment.

**Dolls and Toys on viewing by
appointment only.**
We normally maintain a good
assortment of antique Copper and
Brass items.
Country furniture, Pine Period
Pieces, Shipping lines, Trade items,
All normally stocked. Phone or
send SAE for current Photo list.

WANTED

As specialists in pre-1930 China &
Wax Head Dolls we are able to pay
top prices for rare or unusual
examples.
Phone or write with details for our
offer. We are often able to value
over the phone or by return of post.
We are willing to call at your home
or shop anywhere for worthwhile
examples. Distance No Object.
Never undervalue your dolls: obtain
our expert offer. Many People are
amazed at what we will pay.

Antique and Quality Secondhand Items.
Always in stock — Always Wanted.
Large Furniture Showroom. Worth a visit.
Somersham. Approx. Miles From;
Chatteris..................................... 5 miles
Ely & A 10....................................10 miles
Cambridge...................................15 miles
St. Ives...................................... 5 miles
Huntingdon & A 1.....................10 miles
Peterborough............................15 miles
Include SOMERSHAM on your buying trip.

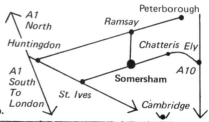

18

CHESHIRE   ESSEX

DYFED

19

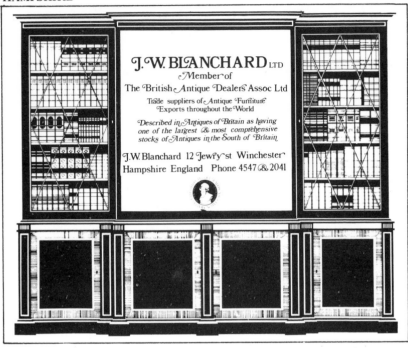

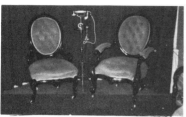

21

LANCASHIRE

LEICESTERSHIRE

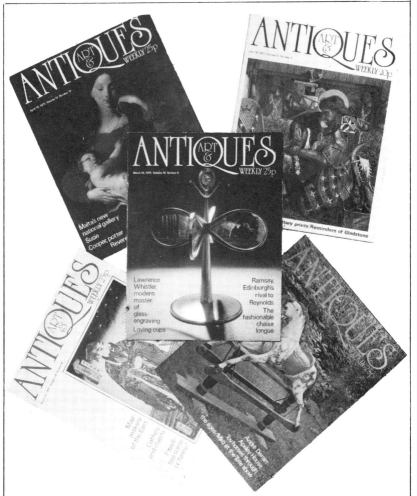

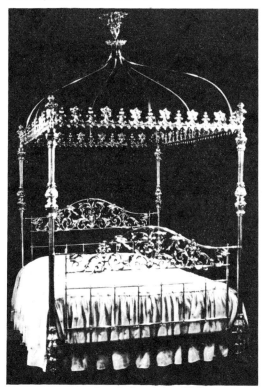
27

28

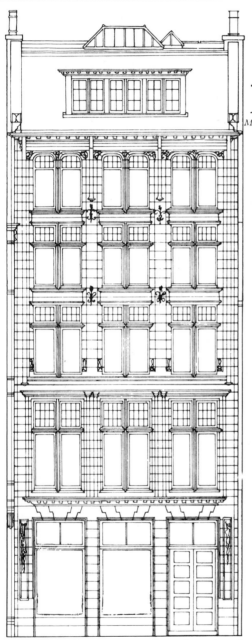

30

Henry Spencer & Sons

This pair of Royal Worcester vases painted by Harry Davis and bearing the date symbols for 1911 realised £1,400 in one of our specialist sales of porcelain. The sale included sixty lots of Royal Worcester which totalled over £10,000.

Many of the drawings throughout this book illustrate the varying types of items which pass through our salerooms and which we value for Insurance and Estate Duty Purposes.

Free brochure of our services and charges on request.

Offices and Salerooms

20, THE SQUARE, RETFORD, NOTTINGHAMSHIRE DN22 6DJ.
Telephone RETFORD 2531 and 3768 (10 lines).

Members of the Society of Fine Art Auctioneers.

32

Laughton of Farnham

WILLEY MILL, WINCHESTER ROAD, (A31), FARNHAM, SURREY.
Tel. Farnham 21422/23480 (any time) Open Mon to Sat (other times by appointment).

40 Miles West of London 7 Miles off M.3.

We were going to show you a photograph of our stock but it changes so quickly we feel that as Willey Mill was mentioned in the Doomsday Book it is more permanent.
Any restoration can be undertaken in our own workshops by craftsmen, prior to delivery.

One of the LARGER stockists in Surrey The country Dealer who keeps the Quality up and the Prices down.
We cater particularly for the EXPORT market and the TRADE.

Always in stock at realistic trade prices: a good selection of desirable **early oak and walnut, Georgian mahogany,** and a comprehensive selection of **Victorian furniture and collectors' items** including tables, sets of chairs, bookcases, bureaux, pedestal desks, chests of drawers, clocks, porcelain, paintings, sporting prints, brass and copper, button back chairs, settees and chaise longues.

We like to buy privately and unrestored and will purchase immediately single items or complete contents.

The Antique Centre Guildford

Surrey

22 Haydon Place & 25 Chertsey Street
Telephone 67817

OPEN TUESDAY, THURSDAY, FRIDAY and SATURDAY 10 a.m.—5.30 p.m.

With
TEN DEALERS

showing a wide range of the 17th, 18th and 19th century, especially collectors' items, silver, jewellery. Also Victoriana and Militaria.

Situated off North Street adjacent to the Surrey Advertiser Building.

Worldwide Removals.

Export Packing.

Specialists in Antiques.

Container facilities available to many destinations.

Direct road van deliveries to Europe.

Large Depositories.

Martell's of SUTTON Ltd.

71-74 Westmead Road SUTTON Surrey
and at
01-642 9551 East Grinstead, Sussex
Telex: **946305**

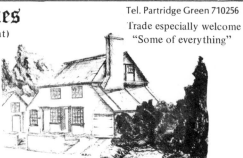
34

ADRIAN ALAN LTD

WAREHOUSE AT 5–6 UPPER GARDNER STREET BRIGHTON SUSSEX.
Open 9a.m. – 6p.m. BRIGHTON 25277.

*In our warehouse we have large and varied stocks of English and Continental
Furniture from all periods, Clocks, Bronzes, Barometers, Sextants and
Telescopes.*

ADRIAN ALAN ANTIQUES
51, UPPER NORTH STREET BRIGHTON SUSSEX
Brighton. 0273 – 25277
Evening:. 0273 – 7366/5

36

PROFILE ON

BRITISH ANTIQUE EXPORTERS

There are a great many antique shippers in Britain but few, if any, who are as quality conscious as Norman Lefton, Chairman and Managing Director of British Antique Exporters Ltd., of Newhaven, Sussex. Twelve years experience of shipping goods to all parts of the globe have confirmed his original belief that the way to build clients' confidence in his services is to supply them only with goods which are in first class saleable condition. To this end, he employs a full-time staff of over 40, from highly skilled packers, joiners,

cabinet makers, polishers and restorers, to representative buyers, valuers and executives. Through their knowledgeable hands passes each piece of furniture before it leaves the B.A.E. warehouses, ensuring that the overseas buyer will only receive the best and most saleable merchandise for their particular market.

As a further means of improving each container load, Mr. Lefton asks customers to return detailed information on each item included in every shipment. "We buy for our customers" he explained, "and this feedback of

Restorers busy bringing pieces up to first class saleable condition.

Roll top desks, Wooton desks, Chippendale, Windsor and barley twist chairs, clocks, Oriental furniture and porcelain are a speciality of the House of British Antique Exporters Ltd. They are bought in any condition, repaired on the premises and shipped in first-class saleable state to overseas buyers.

Wooton desk.

information is the all important factor which guarantees the success of each future container. By this method we have established that an average £4,000 container will, immediately it is unpacked at its final destination, realise in the region of £6,000 to £8,000 for our clients selling the goods on a quick wholesale turnover basis."

In any average twenty foot container, B.A.E. put about six really good pieces, some twenty quality pieces, twenty run of the mill items and as many as four to five hundred smaller pieces of Bric-a-Brac, all in eminently saleable condition.

Based at the south coast port of Newhaven — a few miles from Brighton and on a direct rail link with London, (only 50 minutes journey) the company is ideally situated to ship containers to all parts of the world. The showrooms, restoration and packing departments are open to overseas buyers and no visit to purchase antiques for re-sale in other countries is complete without a call at their Newhaven premises.

Packed ready for containers.

40

SUSSEX

TELEPHONE

NEWHAVEN

(STD CODE 07912)

5561

BRITISH ANTIQUE EXPORTERS LTD.

WE ALWAYS BUY & SELL

	GEORGIAN	VICTORIAN	1900–1930
BUREAU BOOKCASES	✓	✓	✓
SETS 4, 6 OR MORE CHAIRS	✓	✓	✓
BRACKET CLOCKS	✓	✓	✓
CALENDAR CLOCKS		✓	✓
DINING TABLES	✓	✓	✓
SIGNED GLASS			✓
HALL STANDS		✓	✓
WASHSTANDS	✓	✓	✓
'S' CURVE ROLL TOP DESKS		✓	✓
PAIRS SEVRES VASES		✓	
CLOISONNE		✓	
WOOTON DESKS		✓	
SIGNED FURNITURE	✓	✓	✓
WELSH DRESSERS	✓	✓	✓
STAINED GLASS WINDOWS	✓	✓	✓
LIMOGE CHINA			✓
ORIENTAL FURNITURE		✓	
IMARI/CANTON PORCELAIN		✓	

NEW ROAD INDUSTRIAL ESTATE, NEWHAVEN, SUSSEX

TELEPHONE: NEWHAVEN (07912) 5561

BRITISH ANTIQUE EXPORTERS Ltd.

50

SUSSEX

Christopher GEORGE Antiques

*CUSTOMER SERVICE

*We offer a complete Container service to the trade.

*All restoration work, polishing and packing carried out on our own premises.

WORKSHOP & WAREHOUSE

5 Trafalgar Ct Trafalgar St Brighton

phone

559191
500481
692468

*We have finance available for containers.

you can trust us

wanted..

- GRANDFATHER CLOCKS
- MUSIC BOXES
- ORIENTAL FURNITURE
- BRONZES
- ARMOURY
- SILVER
- JEWELLERY
- PLATE
- FURNITURE
- COPPER
- BRASS
- OIL PAINTINGS
- GLASS
- CHINA

Antiques of all descriptions!

WE PAY THE HIGHEST AND FAIREST PRICES

LICENSED GUN DEALER

HARRIS & SON

BRIGHTON 29947

40-41 Castle Street · Brighton · Sussex

54

SUSSEX

WE INVITE YOU TO VISIT OUR SHOPS & WAREHOUSES WHERE YOU CAN VIEW THE LARGEST STOCK OF ANTIQUES IN THE SOUTH OF ENGLAND
ANTIQUE DEALERS' ENTIRE STOCK PURCHASED

DIRECTORS
DAVID HAWKINS · CAMILLA ANN HAWKINS

3 NEW ENGLAND ST. (HEAD OFFICE)
BRIGHTON
TEL. 27409
21009

We have a wide variety of antique, reproduction, and second-hand furniture, porcelain, pictures, clocks, and miscellanea, which we keep in three large warehouses and two shops covering nearly 100,000 square-feet, all in the Brighton area.

We already export extensively to the Continents of Europe and the United States of America, Australia, Canada and South Africa, and are acknowledged as being one of the largest exporters in Europe.

Catering as we do for the Export Market we offer a complete service tailor-suited to the individual customer's requirements, including liason with customers' shipping agents, and facilities for packing and delivery world-wide.

We would be pleased to welcome you to Brighton, which is only one hour from London, and can assure you that your visit will be both pleasant and profitable.

Please do not hesitate to write or telephone for an appointment.

57

Two invaluable guides to the antiques and art trade in Great Britain, Europe and the USA.

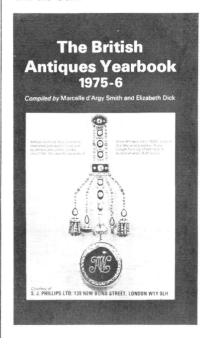

The British Antiques Yearbook 1975-6

The comprehensive guide to the art and antiques trade in the British Isles and Eire. Details of over 4000 dealers and restorers. Further information on antiques fairs, packers and shippers, auctioneers, associations, magazines and fine art book publishers. Route maps and street plans and a specialists index.

Price £6 (£6.50 including postage)

1000 pages

The International Antiques Yearbook 1975

Similar in format to the British edition, this book is a guide to the antiques and art trade in Europe and North America. There are almost 9000 detailed descriptions of dealers, together with sections on packers and shippers, auctioneers, international fairs and a specialists index.

Price £6 (£6.50 including postage)

984 pages

Both editions are available at leading bookshops or direct from the publishers (at £6.50 per copy including postage):

ANTIQUES YEARBOOKS, 29 MADDOX STREET, LONDON W1R 9LD

73

DEALS ON WHEELS

MICHAEL SEDGWICK

The collectors' market in antique cars established itself between 1961 and 1965, with the 'great leap forward' occurring in 1968, the year of the memorable Smith Auction at Cross-in-Hand, Sussex. (One journalist headed his report: 'All Barriers to Belief Suspended!!') Since then discernible patterns have been emerging.

Two factors are peculiar to the motor-car market. This first is a clearly defined relationship between a vehicle's 'usability' and its sale value, and the second a marked differential in the price a given model may fetch in different countries.

The first development has been in evidence since 1969, and may in part be ascribed to growing congestion and a tightening of Construction and Use Regulations which limit the practical use of the older cars on the highway. While so far the restricted-number-plate schemes operated in parts of the U.S.A. and Australia are purely concessional, there remains the risk that they may become compulsory for all users of even pre-1940 cars, and this is now having its effect on the value of Brass Age Antiques. Exceptional prices are still being recorded: £12,000 was paid for a 1904 Gladiator tonneau in 1973, representing a 55% rise on the 'highs' of 1968. It is, however offset by an actual fall in the mean price of less exceptional specimens.

The pattern of enthusiasm has changed. Up to 1968, the snob value of vehicles eligible for the R.A.C.'s London-to-Brighton Run (i.e. those built before 1 January, 1905) was formidable, and a *four-seater* Brighton car was a safe winner. The differential, indeed, between a dated 1904 model and its identical 1905 twin could be as much as 30%.

A similar drop can be seen in the 1905-18 category. Such cars are also affected by the 'utility' factor, though the fall is more recent, starting in 1970 and gaining momentum ever since. As an indication of how this slump is outrunning even saleroom 'form', predicted prices for three fine cars offered by Christies in July, 1974 were £12,000 for a 1905 Tourist Trophy-type Arrol-Johnston, £6,000 for a 1906 single-cylinder Cadillac, and the same price for a 1910 16-20 h.p. Hotchkiss. Actual high bids were, respectively, £9,000, £2,800, and £4,500, representing shortfalls of between 25% and 55%.

It can be argued that certain models continue to run counter to this pattern, with up to £30,000 still being paid for pre-World War I Silver Ghost Rolls-Royces, or about 250% up on 1968. These are, however, the exceptions that prove the rule: the Old Masters of the new cult. Among later Old Masters one can number any original *open*-bodied Rolls-Royce, the Model-J Duesenberg, all species of supercharged Mercedes-Benz, the old-school Bentley, and the better and faster Bugattis. Here the steady upward movement continues; but with one proviso — authenticity. Bentleys used to be worth around £1,000 per litre of cylinder capacity: £3,000 a litre seems fair in 1974, but a rough original is a better bet than a superbly-reconditioned hybrid. Only recently £7,500 was paid for a 1928 4½-litre that had not turned a wheel since 1946 — and looked it!

As for the curious price-differentials that occur between different countries, these are more easily illustrated by 'second-division' cars. If a 1955 Gullwing Mercedes-Benz (one of the new generation of collectables) rates £6,000-£6,500 in whatever currency it is sold, open-bodied Packard Eights of

1931 4½ litre, four-seater Bentley. £17,000
(Christie's)

the mid-Classic (say 1928-34) period are a trickier proposition. £7,000 plus is safe in the U.S.A., but £3,800 would be big money in Western Europe, and in Britain, where American cars have a very limited following, £3,000 might be hard work for any auctioneer.

A further new pattern is emerging from a mixture of economic stringency and the increasing selectiveness of buyers. Since 1972 observers have become aware of the existence of two 'sound barriers' in the price structure – the first between £5,000 and £7,000, and the second around £15,000. The lower barrier represents the limit to which an amateur, one-car man will normally venture; the higher one marks the point at which the true collector, be he private individual or museum owner, starts wondering if he really wants this particular vehicle. In either case, only exceptional specimens in their class penetrate this invisible wall, and if, say, a top-class 4½-litre Bentley is not still attracting three bidders at the £12,000 mark, it is doomed to peter at £14,000.

It is, of course, the £5,000 barrier that is of paramount interest in 1974. The five-figure prices get the publicity, but precious few cars in fact approach £15,000. At the July, 1974 Christie Sale,

Model - A 24 H.P. Roadster, 1928. £2,083
(Christie's)

The Rixon Bucknall 1956 Jaguar 3½ litre special 2 - seater, finished 1967.
Reg. No. R.B. 1903.　　*(Christie's)*　　£3,800

over 50% of the entries realised bids of £5,000
or less, as against a mere 9.5% that penetrated
the upper end of our range. And while a slump
is detectable in those rarefied atmospheres, one
can discern a marked upward movement towards
the £5,000 level. More important, this rise in prices
centres round the later cars, with little progress being
made in the 1919-25 sector, where hard-to-find
beaded edge tyres and brakes on the rear wheel
only serve as effective deterrents to the ambitious.

Two classic instances of how this upward trend
works can be seen in the Derby Bentleys of 1933-40
and the overhead-camshaft M.G. Midget (1929-36).
Both are easy to find, both have earned international
recognition, and both can be used on the road.
Seven years ago a good saloon Bentley was worth
£850, and a drophead coupé (true tourers are very
rare) around £1,150. Today it is well-nigh impossible
to find a sound specimen of even the regular Park
Ward saloon for less than £3,000, and the combination of pretty coachwork and a good mechanical
history can push the price up another £2,000. As
the model has a modest appetite for low-octane fuel,
this trend may well continue. As for the M.G. — a

car once despised by the *aficionados* — this presents a frightening picture.

Go back to 1967, and a fair prediction for a P-type of 1934-36 would run from £200 for a fair one up to £400 for a first-class specimen. By the end of the 1960s a good (but not exceptional) 1936 PB had been auctioned for £700, and in 1972 a similar one went to £900. In German-speaking countries, where the marque is held in immense affection, one now thinks in terms of £1,500, and though some of this inflation may be explained away by the strength of the Deutschmark and the Swiss Franc in relation to sterling, we are still left with an appreciation of 100% in the first five years, not to mention 45-50% in the second period (1972-74). Even more significant is a 'run' on the less popular M.G.s as the classic o.h.c. designs vanish out of reach. That the selfsame 1929 14-40 h.p. two-seater appreciated at auction from £1,000 to £2,800 between 1971 and 1974 undoubtedly stems from the paucity of surviving examples of this type, but how to account for £1,000 and more paid for good examples of the still-common TC 1946-49) or TD (1950-53) species? Much less for the inflated figures asked for the big Wolseley-based pushrod cars of the immediate pre-war years, renowned for unsporting gear ratios and endemic woodrot. There is even a growing interest in such youngsters as the MG-A, introduced at the 1955 London Show, though in England, at any rate, this has always been a rarity; well over 90% of all As were exported.

With all these factors considered, we can now approach perhaps the most significant trend of all to emerge from the past five years — the increasingly high prices paid for post-World War II thoroughbreds, or Milestones, as our American friends now term them. In 1967 the owner of a 3½-litre Delahaye of the late 40s was lucky to realise £400; by the end of 1973 a Type 135 at £1,500 was a bargain, and at the 1974 Dallas Auction somebody actually paid close on £8,000 for an outstanding specimen.

Why? Such cars are not antiques in any sense, and have only recently been retired from the transportation role. They present no challenge even to a young driver nurtured on disc brakes and automatic transmissions. Stylistically, they are often transitional nightmares; for all the functional beauty of the original Jaguar XK120 fixed-head coupé and roadster, one must also contemplate the half-timbered Town and Country Chrysler of 1946-48 (a great favourite in America) and some of the slab-sided extravaganzas perpetrated on Rolls-Royce chassis *circa* 1949. Spares are not always obtainable off the shelf, especially in the case of Lost Causes like the Facel Vega, and many Milestones present maintenance problems far beyond the relative simplicity of 1920s or 1930s models.

Sundry factors govern this new boom. First of all, the younger generation of buyers no longer regard Bentley, Bugatti or Deusenberg as their *beau ideal.* Such cars were already collectors' pieces (and priced out of reach) when their enthusiasm was first kindled. To a thirty-year-old, a 1955 Gullwing Mercedes-Benz already belongs to yesteryear. Better still, many Milestones incorporate much of today's statutory equipments (e.g. screenwashers and double-dipping headlamps) and thus require no modification or prostitution before they can be run regularly on the road. It is significant that the collection of post-war machinery originated in the U.S.A., the birthplace restrictive legislation, spreading first to the E.E.C. countries, where similar ideas now obtain. In Britain, where ideas are more 'liberal', the Milestone has taken longer to attract a following.

Already the new class has its established recruits — post-war T Midgets, the Gullwing, the early

Rolls-Royce 20.25 H.P. four passenger drophead coupe, 1933.   £6,667
(Christie's)

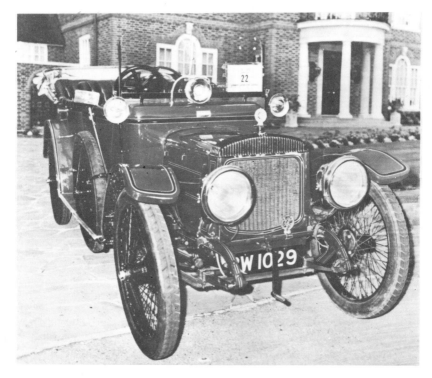

A 1911 Daimler Silent Knight, open 4-seater tourer, Reg. No. BW 1029.
£9,600   *(Christie's)*

Four-door convertible Phaeton, 33.8 H.P., 1930.   £208,333
(Christie's)

XK Jaguars, and (in America) the two-seater Ford Thunderbird of 1955-57. Others are on the move; consider the case of Italy's Lancia Aurelia Granturismo, a £350 item in 1970. An indifferent specimen made £985 at Geneva in 1974, which indicates an appreciation of something like 400% in our period. Less probable still is the saga of the Mercedes-Benz 300 four-door cabriolet, by no means a sports car (it was once a favourite with presidents of emergent republics). No specialist auctioneer would have looked at such a machine in 1968, and £500 would have been a high price in 1970-71. As a rare species, it rates a cool £1,000 at the beginning of 1974 — but how wrong could the wiseacres be? Within three months, two came up for auction in two different countries, and their mean price was — £2,600!

This is a clear case, like the M.G. affair, of 'runners-up' attracting bidders without means to aspire to the more favoured variants of a given make. As the true Milestones approach the sound barrier, we may well see an increasing number of the lesser breeds at top-grade auctions. This is already happening in America and on the Continent, and each British sale reveals a higher post-1945 content.

As a final illustration of what is happening, consider an up-and-coming 'collectable'. No, nothing hand made, but the 2.3-litre Sunbeam-Talbot (later plain Sunbeam) 90 made in sizable quantities between 1951 and 1957. Already the rare Alpine roadster has passed the £1,000 mark without a single recorded appearance at a European specialist auction. Good saloons and dropheads currently rate £600-£700, but how soon will these, too, cross their Rubicon? And may we predict that the time may soon come when any car of any standing will pass immediately from £50 'banger' status to that of a collectable?

COMMERCIAL VEHICLES

The collectors' market for commercial vehicles is a difficult one to assess, largely because commercials, unlike cars, tend to be 'put out to grass' (literally) once their useful life is over. The result is that there is no 'market' such as one encounters in the world of the pleasure automobile. Enthusiasts find rusting relics in yards or fields, rebuild them, run them in rallies, and then pass them on to fellow enthusiasts through clubs whose anti-inflationary attitudes serve as a check on prices.

Further, the number of people physically equipped to take on a double-decker Leyland Titan or a chain-driven articulated Scammell are few indeed. In Britain, the limiting factor to truck collection might be expected to be snobbery (one cannot run a four-ton Albion at Prescott) or fuel bills (a big petrol-engined fire engine of the 1930s does 8 m.p.g.). In fact it is space; hence there are few such vehicles offered at auction, and few price trends to observe.

Four such trends have, however, been observed. The first concerns the car-based light commercials, which present few storage problems, and have appreciated some 130% in the last four years. The second reveals a mounting interest in later vehicles, though curiously this has little to do with mounting inflation in the earlier classes. It is the logical effect of a tendency to acquire vehicles for preservation as they come off service.

At the moment the effective life of a 'bus is about twenty years, and that of a heavy truck around twelve, but these life-spans are bound to decrease as regulations tighten, and one can thus predict that high prices will soon be obtained for commercials

1924 Fowler steam roller. £800
(Christie's)

of the 1946-55 period that have led sheltered lives. It is also more than likely that collectors may be eager to snap up original petrol-engined vehicles in the 2-3-ton class, in view of the ever-growing trend towards diesel power in all but the smallest categories.

Also worth watching is the hearse, a fringe-commercial, and almost invariably using a car-type chassis. Until 1967 it was possible to acquire a hearse-bodied 20-25 h.p. Rolls-Royce of the 1930s in good running order for less than £200. Mechanically this would have been a better proposition than a high-mileage sports saloon at five times the price, but there was no concealing the origins of the coachwork, and not many people fancies an off-beat station wagon-cum-caravan. Now, however, the replica-body industry is well established, and one finds £1,500 and more being asked for Rolls-Royce hearses. But for the antipathy shown by American clubs to replica coachwork, a similar boom would have occurred across the Atlantic, where the mortician's favourite transport in the 1930s was a Packard or a Cadillac.

Finally, there are the Old Masters of the 'heavy' world, the steam traction engines (steam wagons like the Foden seldom come on the open market). The traction-engine cult is over twenty years old,

An 1898 Merryweather Horse-drawn steam fire engine, built by William Rose of Manchester, and supplied to the grandfather of the present owner at Shadwell Park. £2,200

(Christie's)

and an established hobby; hence by 1967 £3,000 was the going figure for a straightforward road engine, with £7,000 and more being paid for the Showman's type. The steam roller, thanks to its lower degree of 'roadbility' and even more leisured performance, could, however, be bought for under £1,000. Now, however, rollers are on their way up, while at the 1974 Christie Auction £8,250 was paid for an Aveling and Porter road engine. Since such a figure places the vehicle on the far side of the first sound barrier, it is only a matter of time before someone pays £4,500 for a roller.

MILITARY VEHICLES

Here we encounter perhaps the sole sector of the historic road vehicle market which has yet to 'move'.

It is imperative to stress that we refer to World War II and later military types, for the earlier ones are so infrequently encountered that there are no guide-lines for a price structure.

Further, the larger and more specialised vehicles, such as tanks, are hardly collectable in the ordinary sense, being unusable on the road. requiring heavy transporters, and consuming fuel at an alarming rate. More manageable specimens (Jeep, MW and OY Bedfords, Dodge Weapons Carrier and Command Car) survived in minor armies many years after they were retired from the strength of the ex-combatant countries, while those that entered civilian life often ended up on farms or as garage breakdown trucks, in which occupations they were frequently found as late as 1965. At that time Canadian Military Pattern Chevrolets and Fords were still common sights. Further, the Military Vehicle Rally is a phenomenon of the 1970s, though collectors did exist before that time. The laws of supply and demand, however, applied; few people wanted the vehicles, and both complete ones and spares were plentiful.

As yet the military vehicle fraternity are a close-knit group with the will to resist inflation. Genuine rarities (e.g. the Bantam-built Jeep that preceded the familiar Willys and Ford variants) will command high prices, but relatively few people know a rarity when they see it. Museums as yet confine their interest to a few 'representative' types, usually light-weights like the Jeep and the VW Kübelwagen. So far no late-type militaries have been seen at specialist auctions, while the vehicles now coming into preservation, such as the 1-ton 4 x 4 Humber range, have been obtained at war-surplus sales. High prices, if they come, will result from the exhaustion of existing sources of 'surplus', and the disappearance of W.D. vehicles from truck breakers' yards.

BICYCLES AND MOTORCYCLES

Bicycle prices have shown no major movement during the past five years. Demand is small and specialised, and while boneshakers and very early species of tricycle can and will make more than £350, they were doing so in 1967. Most 'collectors' bicycles are of pre-1900 vintage, and were established as historic before the present wave of high prices came into force.

Motorcycles present a rather different case, though the small amount of space occupied by such vehicles in a collection is partly offset by the type of person who collects them; he is usually a user rather than a would-be investor. There have, however, been substantial rises, and in ten years the price of a pre-1914 flat-twin Douglas has risen from the 1964-65 norm of £120-£140 to £450 and more: £550 was actually paid for such a machine at a 1973 auction. As with the cars, the big jump dates from 1968, when prices of Veteran motorcycles doubled within eighteen months. They seem, however, to have levelled off since then.

In the Vintage field machines are more plentiful as well as being better suited for regular riding, and

A 1923 Norton H S/V racing motor cycle, Reg. No. EN 1741. £230
(Christie's)

rises have been proportionately greater. In 1962 an expert was heard to observe that 'anyone who pays more than £50 for a 1920s touring bike wants his head examined', and £30 would buy most reputable species in good running order. Even in 1965 £120 was considered ridiculous for a 1928 Sunbeam, while a mint 1920 Harley Davidson combination caused a sensation when it fetched £205 at auction. Run-of-the-mill Royal Enfields and B.S.A.s sold at £40-£60.

Thereafter, as in all other sectors, the 1968 boom took over, and by the end of that year £105-£110 was par for a Vintage motorcycle; this has since doubled approximately, with over £300 being paid for outstanding specimens, usually original combinations or bikes with a sporting flavour.

There are other parallels with the car, notable a growing interest in later models. That this took longer to be significant is due to the fact that until very recently the motorcycling fraternity recognised new equivalent of the Vintage Sports Car Club's post-Vintage Thoroughbred category. Hence up to the early 1970s only such makes as Brough Superior, Scott and Vincent in post-1930 form held their price, such as it was. Early 'thirties Broughs in good order could still be had for under £100 in 1970.

The demise of the classic British motorcycle, and the flooding of the market with Japanese bikes helped encourage the collection of these later Thoroughbreds, and the influence of nostalgia is clear to see. In 1969 no specialist auctioneer would have looked at a shaft-driven Sunbeam S7/S8 of the 1946-57 period. The first one thus offered seemed very expensive at £85 in 1972, but this figure went up by 80% in two years. Nor was this the limit, for at Dallas in 1974 £230 was paid for a similar machine. At this particular auction, incidentally, the mean price of seven post-war British motorcycles was a high £395. Admittedly these included a brace of racing Nortons and a Vincent (that most-fancied of breeds) which went to an incredible £750; they also included a Silent LE Velocette (£30 worth?) which passed the £150 mark. When one considers that the number of makes of full-sized British motorcycles dwindled from 17 in 1961 to five in 1971, one can also detect the influence of that affection for Lost Causes that governs the choice of many a collector in this country.

BOTTLE COLLECTING

An embossed Victorian whiskey bottle, black glass. £15

A Green Warners Safe Cure. A year ago, £10, Today's value, £40/£50.

During the last two years bygone bottle collecting and digging has become the fastest growing hobby in Great Britain, and many Commonwealth countries. Every week literally hundreds of people join the ranks of Britain's fast growing army of bottle collectors. The rise in popularity in this once rather obscure pastime is due to the fact that it is almost certainly the only form of antique collecting where the collector can by digging his bottle out of a long forgotten rubbish dump, still build up a respectable and often very valuable collection for the cost of a few hours' work with a fork and spade.

The bottles most sought after by collectors are in the main the mass-produced ones of the late Victorian and early Edwardian eras, although there are also many specialist collectors who collect 18th and early 19th century bottles. This is a very specialised field, and the price of a single bottle can often run to several hundred pounds. These bottles have in fact been collectors' pieces since the 19th century.

Over 95% of collectable bottles are recovered from long-forgotten rubbish dumps. The variety of heavily embossed glass and toned saltglaze stoneware, to be found in these dumps is almost inexhaustible. Britain's bottle-collecting fraternity do not in fact only collect bottles – digging old dumps reveals a wealth of other collectable relics – coloured and black and white potlids, clay tobacco pipes with decorated bowls and German and French bisque dolls' heads.

This sudden interest in these artifacts has resulted in an almost unprecedented rise in prices. In many cases a rise of 500% in a year is not uncommon, and all the signs are that this trend will continue through 1975. Anyone considering buying antiques for investment would be well advised to give bottles a lot of thought.

It is estimated that there are now in the region of 50,000 bottle collectors in Great Britain and that during 1974 at least £2,000,000 worth of bottles and other relics were recovered from beneath the ground. Many of these found their way to the very lucrative Australian and U.S. markets. Strangely though, despite all these bottles and relics being

A Prices Patent Candle
Co. cough medicine
bottle. Cobalt blue
Registry marked.   £30

A true Daffy's Elisar
Cure All.   £28

An example of a Hiram
Codds marble stoppered
bottle in cobalt blue.
                Up to £100.

An unusual variation on the octagonal glass ink.   £3

found, supply just cannot keep up with demand, especially where the rarer pieces are concerned.

Late in 1972 the British Bottle Collectors' Club was formed and it still is the only club of its kind in Great Britain, having many members both here and throughout the World. Regular meetings, sales, auctions and digs are now held in most parts of the country and the club also runs an advisory and valuation service for members and produces four quarterly bottle news magazines a year. Membership costs £1.50 yearly and is obtainable from the National Secretary, 19, Hambro Avenue, Rayleigh, Essex SS6 9NJ.

Bottles most popular with British collectors fall into four categories: –

1. Mineral water, beer and other beverage bottles.
2. Quack medicine and 'Cure All' bottles.
3. Glass and stone ink bottles.
4. Poison bottles.

Most collections start with a mineral water bottle, the most popular being Hiram Codd's marble-stoppered lemonade bottle, and the transfer-printed stone ginger beer bottle. Especially sought after are coloured varieties of the Codd bottle. A year ago they could be bought for £5-£8. Today the green and amber varieties change hands at £30-£50 and cobalt blues at £100.

Two years ago stone ginger beers sold for 20p each. Today they run from £1.50 to £8 for a coloured-shouldered variety.

The patent medicine/quack cure category also shows an indication of some staggering increases in value. A year ago a Warners Safe Cure Bottle, green in colour could be bought for £10-£12. Today you may be lucky enough to pick one up for £20, but most are changing hands at £40-£50 on the overseas market.

The variety of both stone and glass ink bottles to be found is vast, ranging from a simple eight-sided

Three different ginger beer shapes, the centre one with blue lip.
Left & Right: £2 each. Centre: £7/£8.

Bow fronted embossed poison bottle in cobalt blue.   £3/£4

variety to the most sought after of all, the cottage ink, so called because it was moulded in the form of a small cottage with doors and windows. Until recently these were considered to be worth between £5 and £10. Now, because of demand, they average around £40 and certain very rare examples go to overseas collectors at around the £250 mark.

Poison bottles too are becoming a very specialised category. Most valued are cobalt blue varieties. A good example of a cobalt blue Victorian poison bottle embossed 'Not to be taken' can fetch £3-£4 whereas a year ago they were rated at only a few pence. At the other end of the scale, a blue poison bottle shaped rather like a submarine or in the figural form of a skull and crossbones, is considered so rare that the price would be negotiable between buyer and seller.

Needless to say all would-be buyers now have to contend with reproductions that are finding their way into the antique shops. Most experienced collectors can recognize these and the British Bottle Collectors' Club has a record of many of these fakes.

S.F. BARKER — National Secretary, British Bottle Collectors' Club.

COLLECTING NATURAL HISTORY ITEMS

HISTORY OF COLLECTING

The infinite variety of natural objects has long provided the widest field of interest for the collector. Their particular fascination extends equally to the amateur enthusiast who appreciates them for their beauty or curiosity, and to the specialist for whom they are the basic material of scientific study.

While intellectuals of earlier centuries undoubtedly amassed cabinets of curiosities, more or less at random, systematic collecting began with the growth of scientific exploration which was such a feature of the 16th century. A wealth of material, brought back from the far corners of the known world, inspired the leading scientists of the day to record and classify these new wonders. The development of printing helped to promote the study of all aspects of natural history but books remained, for a long time, the prerogative of the few.

Until the late 18th century the study of natural history was still a little-understood diversion for a wealthy minority. Indeed, the legendary Lady Glanville nearly had her will set aside when her family claimed that collecting insects was evidence of insanity!

With improvements in education, communications, and travel, the 19th century was the great age of the Natural Historian. Many of the well-known authorities and collectors of this time were Clergymen or Doctors; members of a new middle-class with money and leisure to pursue their interests. Most of the finest collections from this period now form the bulk of the material in the larger Natural History Museums of the world. We are particularly fortunate that in the British Museum (Natural History) are some of the most important of these, including the vast number of animal specimens collected for the late Lord Rothschild. In consequence collectors from all over the world visit London, to study this wealth of material, in great numbers every year.

COLLECTING TODAY

The modern collector is much more scientific in approach than his 19th century counterpart. The mere amassing of large numbers of specimens serves no useful purpose. Collecting is no longer an end in itself; a modern collection should be a point of reference for a particular study.

In recent years many adverse environmental changes have put pressure on rare animals and plants, the numbers of which, in some cases, have been drastically reduced. The collector who takes a true interest in the object of his study should not contribute to this pressure and all naturalists should be in full accord with the measures that have been taken by many countries to protect these endangered species. Controlled collecting can be compatible with conservation but one must accept that restrictions may be essential to preserve threatened wild life and ensure its continuance for future generations.

A large Ammonite in Matrix. £48

MINERALS AND FOSSILS

Over the last few years there has been a greatly expanded interest in the study and collection of mineral specimens. At the simplest level the purchase of a tumble-polisher for stones enables anyone to reveal the true beauty of seemingly-ordinary seaside and garden pebbles. Small specimens of the more exotic minerals can be obtained from specialist dealers, often at very modest prices. Larger examples of attractive crystalline formations are now much in demand for interior decoration and consequently costs are rising. Points to look for are good shape and colour with well-formed unbroken crystals. Goedes, which are stones split to reveal an internal cavity with crystalline growth, are particularly attractive and sought after. Fine large examples are now £20-£30. Polished slabs of beautifully-marked minerals such as Agate can generally be obtained at £5-£10, while small crystal groups of semi-precious stones such as Tourmaline, Garnet and Amethyst can be purchased for a few pounds more. Good specimens of rarer minerals, such as Arsenopyrite or Wolframite, may command several hundred pounds.

Meteorites are of particular scientific interest and even quite small iron examples may be £20-£30, but volcanic glass Tektites can generally be picked up for a pound or two.

Fossils are the petrified remains of creatures existing millions of years ago. The term covers everything from impressions of fern leaves found in household coal, to complete skeletons of Jurrasic dinosaurs. The latter, familiar to every schoolboy, may be valued in thousands of pounds and are generally destined for the world's museums. Even incomplete examples can only be the province of the wealthiest collectors. Some delicate creatures, such as insects, are very rare in fossil state and specimens of these are likely to prove expensive. However, shells and fish offer an enormous range to the fossil enthusiast. Well-preserved examples of fish, even a hundred million years old, may be only £10-£15, but here, as in everything, quality counts and perfect specimens of rarer groups may be four or five times as much.

Fossil shells are very easily obtained. The local quarry may yield examples of the commonest forms, and even from dealers an interesting collection can be built up without ever spending more than a few pounds on a specimen. The large Ammonites, resembling a tightly-curled ram's horn, have always been popular and are the source of the popular legend in which St. Patrick drove all snakes from Ireland. The price of large examples (anything over six inches in diameter) has more than doubled in recent years, sometimes exceeding £100.

With all fossils the condition and extent of the Matrix (the material in which the fossil is embedded) has a considerable bearing on the value of the specimen.

Artefacts such as bone knives and flint arrow heads should be mentioned in passing under this heading. These are much more numerous than is generally supposed and good examples can be obtained· quite cheaply. The beginner should be warned, however, that fakes abound.

SHELLS

The beauty and variety of shells cannot fail to arouse admiration and interest and few of us as children have not made a collection on seaside holidays. The warmer oceans of the world yield beautiful examples which can be purchased from shell dealers from a few pence to several pounds. Many of the most glamorous are not expensive and are widely used as decorative items in bathrooms or

'Glory of the Sea'. cone shell.   £230

on coffee tables. Examples of these are the Abalone or Mother of Pearl shell at about £2 or the handsome pink-flushed Queen Conch at a similar price.

Some collectors specialise in a particular group and one of the most popular of these has long been the Cowries. Their smooth ovoid shape is patterned or coloured in a great variety of stripes and spots and while a few are very rare indeed most can be obtained for under £1. To this group belongs one of the famous of all shells, the deep yellow Golden Cowrie Cypraea aurantium, a measure of wealth in some Pacific Islands; good specimens commanding anything from £50-£100. Even rarer are some of the beautiful Cone shells. A specimen of Conus gloriamaris – The Glory of the Seas, was sold recently for £230.

Shells grow by developing progressive layers, thus enlarging in size. Growth series, showing examples of the same species in progressively larger sizes, are particularly sought after by the serious conchologist (shell collector).

INSECTS

Collecting insects, especially butterflies, has long been one of the most popular hobbies and it is easy to see why this is so. Butterflies are among the most beautiful objects of natural creation, and in most countries it is possible to make a collection for a very small outlay. The basic equipment needed to collect and preserve butterflies can be made at home or purchased from entomological dealers. The latter can also supply specimens from other countries, most of which cost less than 50p – much less if the collector is expert enough to buy them unmounted.

'Abbe Allote's Birdwing' Butterfly.   £750

Except in the case of great rarities only perfect condition specimens are of value to the specialist and, as with all natural history items, the data giving the locality where the specimen was found is of great importance. Generally speaking the more striking butterflies from less-travelled parts of the world (e.g. the jungles of Brazil or New Guinea) command the highest prices and a few may be worth several hundred pounds. Some of the rarest species are protected by law restricting their breeding or capture. One of these is the Paradise Birdwing Ornithoptera paradisea from New Guinea which ten years ago could be obtained for about £30-£40. A fine male example today could be three times as much. The most expensive butterfly sold was a specimen of Abbe Allote's Birdwing Ornithoptera allotei, also from New Guinea, which reached £750 at auction a few years ago.

Complete collections, from various regions, sometimes come in to the hands of antique dealers who generally fall into one of two errors regarding them. Either they imagine that, because the collection is old, all the butterflies must be now extinct and therefore valuable (hardly any butterflies have become extinct!) or else they only value the cabinet in which the collection is housed, and throw the contents away! This is very sad since although in practice older collections of specimens may have almost no value if they have not been properly maintained, they might possibly contain one or two rarities which only a specialist could identify.

As a general guide, if a collection is contained in a cabinet of drawers, it may well be worth while asking a specialist to look at it, whereas glazed wall cases of brightly coloured specimens are usually of no interest to the collector, since valuable species are seldom treated in this way.

While the interest in moths and other insects is somewhat less some of the rarer species, particularly the larger beetles, may be worth several pounds. It should be pointed out that glamour and rarity do not necessarily go together — some of the most dazzling insects are very common and obtainable for a very small outlay.

BIRDS' EGGS

The position with birds' eggs is somewhat different to that of the previous categories, since many countries have stringent regulations regarding their collection and sale. This is necessary since the existence of very rare species may well be threatened by unscrupulous egg collectors; many birds producing only one or two young in a season. Nevertheless it remains a fact that some people do collect eggs, relying on collections formed in the past as a major source. It must be emphasised that the sale and purchase of egg collections is illegal in Britain but in practice these are sometimes sold as cabinets 'only' and the eggs transferred at no cost — a somewhat doubtful proceeding.

Fossil eggs, which do not come under the scope of the law, are sometimes offered for sale. The egg of an Aepyornis, an extinct flightless bird at one time inhabiting Madagascar, was sold recently for a record price of £1,000.

COLLECTORS' CABINETS

These have already been mentioned under insects but similar types are designed to house collections of eggs or mineral specimens. Insect cabinets have shallow drawers with glass lids; those for eggs and minerals are deeper and generally without glass. Some of those made in the late 19th and early 20th century are beautifully constructed and may contain anything from ten to fifty drawers. The finest examples have locking panelled doors to exclude dust and for these prices of £6-£8 per drawer are not unusual. Natural history dealers generally find that the demand for these cabinets today exceeds the supply, since so many have been used for other purposes such as keeping prints, medals or coins.

Good quality 10 drawer insect cabinet. £70

STUFFED BIRDS, MAMMALS AND REPTILES

Stuffed birds, game heads and skins were beloved by our Victorian ancestors, but in the period between the wars a radical change in public taste took place and these were among the first objects to be discarded. By the time the wheel had gone full circle, countless thousands must have ended their days on the rubbish heap. In the last ten years the enormous revival of interest in the old and curious has produced dramatic effects in some fields. the best example being the steadily rising prices of vintage cars. Interior decorators, set designers, and 'trendies' everywhere now scour the attics and junk shops for fine examples of the taxidermists' art. I can recall a country sale in the early 1950s when a huge collection of stuffed birds and animals was bought by a local builder for fifteen shillings *for the glass in the cases*! Today these would fetch at least £10 per case and Peregrine Falcons and similar rarities four or five times this amount.

Once the pride of every army officer serving in India, tiger skins went through a similar dull period. Again in the 1950s I left a perfectly splendid example behind when we moved our London house; such a skin at the time was worth only a few pounds. The average price of the most recent ones we have sold is £200. Good examples are now hard to obtain. Two years ago we saw them being offered for sale openly in Delhi but their export is banned. Skins of other large carnivores are similarly expensive; those of the Polar Bear reaching £1,000.

Extinct species are naturally much in demand with collectors and museums. The North American Passenger Pigeon Ectopistes migratorius, whose

A fine condition tiger skin with well-mounted head. £200

numbers once darkened the sky, cannot be obtained for less than £100 while last year three and a half times this amount was paid for a pair of Huia, Heterolocha acutirostris from New Zealand, extinct since the early years of this century. The highest price paid for any stuffed bird was £9,000 for a specimen of the famous Great Auk Pinguinus impennis. This sale had an amusing sequel. So much publicity was given to it that some people saw themselves holding a fortune in stuffed birds. Shortly after this event I visited a house to see quite an ordinary glass dome of brightly-coloured Tanagers and Hummingbirds (today's value about £30-£40) for which I was asked £1,000! When I gently pointed out the error and offered £25, the owners became quite abusive, waving newspaper cuttings to substantiate their valuation! Incidentally, these domes of birds can be very attractive but look carefully for the depredations of mites or museum beetle, and take care before buying one with a broken dome – these are now hard to obtain and expensive.

Mounted trophy heads, antlers and tusks are enjoying a similar vogue but stuffed reptiles and fish (most of which are in very attractive bow-fronted cases) are less popular and can still be obtained for a modest outlay.

Mounted specimen of the extinct Great Auk. £9,000

WHERE TO LOOK

There are a large number of natural history dealers in Britain and Europe, most of whom specialise in one or two aspects of the subject. The best of these are staffed by experts who will always advise the beginner to collecting. Dealers also frequently offer mixed lots of items which can be a very economical and interesting way to begin a collection.

Antique and bric-a-brac shops may sometimes have stuffed birds and shells while the local auction rooms may also be worth a visit. The days of the large exclusively natural history sales are sadly no more. Sothebys were the last firm in Britain to hold them regularly and last year they reluctantly decided to discontinue them; far from reflecting lack of interest this was simply because selling paintings and fine furniture proved more profitable. These sales had their heyday at the turn of the century when the famous firm of Stevens of Covent Garden held Natural History sales on virtually every day of the year!

GENERAL ADVICE

Whatever aspect of natural history you decide to study and collect the following points should be observed to derive the greatest satisfaction and reward from this hobby.

Condition is of the greatest importance and little can be done to restore the beauty or value of damaged specimens. Nevertheless only a foolish collector would pass over the opportunity of purchasing a greatly desired rarity with small defects – the chance may not occur again in a lifetime.

If your collection is to retain its value and prove a worth-while investment it must be properly maintained. This involves the provision of adequate containers and (for perishable material) the use of chemical preservatives at regular intervals.

The most important collections are not haphazard but are pursued on scientific lines. Often an enthusiast begins by collecting in a random fashion but will later specialise in a fairly narrow field. He may study and collect only specimens from a particular region or family group, in which he can become expert. much of the pleasure in owning a collection is in knowing as much as possible about the contents.

To get to know your chosen subject thoroughly and thus avoid errors of identification and judgement is essential. Most libraries have a good selection of reliable natural history works which should be your constant study – there is no short cut to obtaining this knowledge.

Where possible learn about your subject at first hand and in the field. Contact with others of similar interest can greatly assist you. Magazines and Societies abound for most aspects of collecting and older hands are usually generous with helpful advice.

Whatever you choose to collect if you follow these basic precepts you will have a never-failing source of interest in this most rewarding of pastimes.

by Paul Smart F.R.E.S.
Line drawings by Chris Samson F.R.E.S.

INVESTING IN ORIENTAL CARPETS

by David Jeans

Traditionally, in the east, Oriental carpets have always performed a dual role:

Firstly, as furnishings they have been used not only as floor coverings but also wall hangings, divan covers, and decoration generally. In Turkey and Iran in particular they satisfy an aesthetic need which, in the west, paintings have fulfilled.

Secondly, in countries where governments and currencies were unstable they performed the function which stocks and shares used to perform here — a reserve of wealth to fall back upon in bad times.

As an investment in present day Europe and America they similarly should fill both roles — for those who take household furnishings seriously they may combine profit and pleasure.

OLD OR MODERN?

Oriental rugs — whether originating in Iran, Turkey, Caucasia, India or Afghanistan — fall into two main groups: Old, including Antique, and Contemporary.

The value and price fluctuations of old pieces depends, at least in the U.K., upon the vagaries of the better class auction rooms.

If Japanese and American buyers are present in strength their prices hold up; if not they may fall at least temporarily.

The basic value of contemporary pieces is much more objective and stable because it is determined by supplies in the London Wholesale Oriental Rug Market. It is to agents and stock holders (sometimes referred to as 'importers') in this market that the principal artist craftsmen and the workshops in the producing countries send the cream of their output for world wide distribution. Over 95% of the rugs, carpets and kelims shipped into the London trade are re-exported all over the world, not only to Europe and U.S.A., but to the South American countries, South Africa, Canada, and more recently to the Arab countries particularly Kuwait and Saudi Arabia.

Thus the prices of contemporary rugs is upheld by two factors: the demand overseas (and if this tends to fall off in one area the importers switch their attention to other more prosperous countries) and the supply.

At the present time demand is growing rapidly while supplies of the finest pieces is showing signs of reduction. Fine Isfahan, Nain, Qum and Turkish Hereke rugs are still as good (though in some respects different) as any made in the last two hundred years. However the latter tend to be over valued because some collectors and museums sometimes confuse ideas of what is good with what happens to be antique. As a result fine contemporary work has been comparatively neglected while attention has concentrated on some types of old rugs on account of their age rather than their aesthetic merit.

Up to three years ago, the carpet investor could reasonably confine his attention to old pieces. Today, in the writer's opinion, he would do well to give attention to the best of the contemporary output before it dries up for ever. It is even possible that the same sort of appreciation will take place as occurred with French impressionist paintings since the beginning of this century.

STUDY THE MARKET

How then to start an investment-collection? Well, for investment purposes one does not buy gold, silver, antiques or paintings through the fashionable retailer. Similarly in the case of rugs, one may buy through reputable auction rooms or, if you visit London, direct through trade channels to avoid the often excess mark up of London retailers. If you intend to use rugs as furnishings you need a wider choice than is usually available in auction rooms, in which case you will do well to find your way into the trade.

First, however, visit a few retailer shops and acquaint yourself with different varieties and the prices asked. Remember that, unlike paintings, the value of a rug is more in proportion to its size and type. This is because the intrinsic value of a rug depends upon months or even years of hand knotting. A fine Qum or Isfahan rug may contain more than half a million minute, hand tied knots per square metre; carrying out this arduous feat is the preliminary necessity for the artist-craftsman before he can give shape to his concepts of design, composition, and colour combination which are also main elements in the final masterpiece. Every hand made rug is different from every other – they fall into types, chiefly according to the traditions of the geographic area in which they are produced, but nevertheless they are as different as one painting is different from another. There are no Picassos in the rug world; it simply is not feasible to execute a masterpiece in half an hour when your concept involves a million hand-tied knots before it is completed.

Secondly, having noted prices asked and the big variations, remember that if and when you want to liquidate your investment you cannot expect to re-sell at the retail price you have just paid, at least until price rises over three or four years have narrowed the margin between the trade price and the retailers' marked-up price. Therefore, when buying for investment set your sights at paying half to two thirds the figure you have seen similar rugs on offer in shops.

Thirdly, consider the types, designs, colours and sizes of rugs which would enhance your home for, to get the best value from your investment it should, like a painting, give you aesthetic pleasure.

Fourthly, at this point you know what you want and the price range you may expect to pay for a good bargain. Now you can start to look around to buy.

HOW TO BUY

Reputable importers are members of The Association of Oriental Carpet Traders of London, and, as such, they undertake not to sell retail or to people outside the trade. Nevertheless they can often be persuaded to do so. You can find their names and addresses in the Yellow Pages of the London telephone directory. The disadvantages of going direct to one or other of the thirty or so reputable importers who constitute the London Wholesale Market are that they tend to specialise in a few varieties of rugs and unless you go to the right one who deals in exactly what you happen to want you may not get much choice and secondly, they are substantial companies which haven't the staff, time or patience to deal with individuals unaccustomed to the trade.

So in fact you have two worthwhile alternatives: trudge round the auction sales — either genuine country-house sales where the entire contents are being disposed of, or reputable auction rooms; or go to one of the London Oriental Carpet Brokers. Their main business is to buy on behalf of their overseas clients in the trade the regular supplies required from the London Importers, but some of them provide a service to collectors or investors who are not in the trade as such. Since prices differ between one importer and another by as much as ±12% for similar rugs, a good broker who steers you to the right importer and enables you to select and buy from his stocks can save you far more than the 5% brokerage which the importer will include in the price quoted to you.

HOW TO SELL

Now – how about re-selling when the time comes – for no matter how good a bargain you may obtain, an investment must be realisable at a profit at some later date?

If you've bought through the trade, you will be able to sell back to the trade in due course. Don't expect to sell back to the same firm from which you bought within six months to make a profit. Trade prices since the war have been free of fluctuations, but they rise slowly and steadily. It may be a year or so before you can sell your piece back to the trade advantageously to yourself and to the importer. Or it may be sooner – for Iran is now enjoying oil wealth, her craftsmen will inevitably be turning away from their traditional occupation towards oil-orientated, better-paying jobs and the supply of fine contemporary rugs may well dry up for ever. The

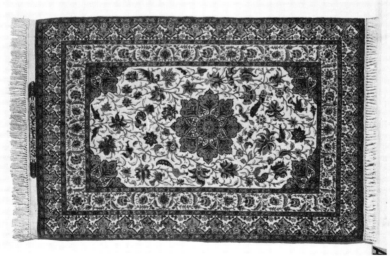

Fine Persian Isfahan rug, 5ft 6ins x 3ft 7ins. £1,800

last of the great hand-craft industries is likely soon to go the way of old master, great architecture and fine hand-made furniture. When that time comes, the London Wholesale Market will seek to buy back contemporary rugs from private owners in U.K. and Europe just as they have long sought to buy in fine antique pieces.

Other ways of realising your investment include advertising in the classified columns of one of the better type daily papers or magazines. Keep the price below that current in retail shops — which you can afford to do if you've bought properly — but high enough to show you a reasonable return.

After all if you live a hundred miles or so outside London not everyone has the time and energy to find their way there to a broker, so you may well be able to sell at a profit in your own locality anytime — so long as you undercut any retailer who serves your area.

If none of these possibilities suit you then ask the advice of your nearest reputable auction rooms as to the reserve you should put on. If they know their business they will give a realistic figure and, since most good auction rooms are attended by buyers from the London trade you should be able to obtain at least a currently competitive price with a good chance of a highly profitable compulsive bid from someone who has fallen in love with the aesthetic appeal of your particular rug and is determined to out bid the dealers.

HOW MUCH? — HOW SOON?

What rate of profit can you hope to make in rugs in the future? No one can answer that. If you are really panic stricken about the prospects of inflation your best bet is to hoard coffee, tea, baked beans or anything else which everyone needs at short notice. But as compared with paintings, antiques, gold and stocks and shares there are many arguments in favour of Oriental rugs.

Comparative figures over long periods are difficult to compile because every rug is an individual work of craftsmanship. Wherever possible each price represents an average of a number of representative pieces and excludes those of either poor or exceptionally good, quality. We would like to acknowledge co-operation of Caroline Bosly, a leading London Oriental Rug Broker, who made available records of rug purchases over several years and the Oriental Rug Information Service, for recent lists of rugs on offer at their showrooms at 18, Green Street, Bath

Best Reported Retail Rug Prices
(equated to rug measuring 5' 3" x 3' 3" = 17sq. feet)
Prices for 1974 and 1975 compiled by courtesy of
The Oriental Rug Information Service, Showrooms, 18 Green St., Bath.

	1971*	1972*	1973*	1974*	1975*
Shiraz, Meshed, Samarkand, Haroun Kashan	32	38	55	65	75
Ardabil, Afshar, Bakhtiari, Hamadan, Gashgai, Serabend	47	55	70	75	100
Kirman	·135	157	160	170	175
Tabriz from	90	110	120	150	160
Sarouk, Khorassan, Kashan	130	140	140	180	200
Bijar	—	225	230	250	260
Town Qum	—	190	200	200	250
Town Qum pt. silk	—	250	300	400	500
Silk Qum	750	900	950	1400	1500
Isfahan — Finest	600	800	875	1300	1300
Nain	600	800	875	1300	1300
Bokhara — Persian	65	90	95	120	140
Bokhara — Mori	34	55	65	75	85
Turkoman Yomud	—	120	125	135	135
Turkoman Tekke	—	160	175	180	185
Afghan — Red	46	60	70	80	85
Golden Afghan (Woven/not washed)	—	—	105	130	140
Daulatabad Afghan	—	80	100	120	140
Herati Belouchi	21	22	24	30	35
Fine Old Belouchi	55	55	60	75	90
Turkish Melas	—	—	78	120	—
Turkish Kula	—	—	92	138	—
Roumanian	46	55	73	80	88
Kelims — Persian	—	50	55	60	75
Shirvan	—	—	120	150	175
Kazak	—	—	75	120	140

*Adjusted for VAT at 8%

Silk Persian Qum hunting rug, 5ft 3ins x 6ft 6ins. £1,500

WHAT TO LOOK FOR

In general it may be said that all hand-made rugs and carpets will appreciate but remember some will probably appreciate faster than others and some are more easily resaleable than others. For instance a fine large Kashan carpet 17' x 10' at £2,500 or so today may double its value in two years time — if you can find a buyer who has a room large enough to accommodate it. Sooner or later you may be sure that it will sell, but smaller rugs which can be used in a variety of rooms or as wall hangings are more readily saleable. Besides, transporting a carpet weighing two cwt to an auction room is not everyone's idea of fun.

So unless you have established a good working relationship with a broker who will sell for you when the time comes, you will do best to stick to smaller sizes — between 5'3" and 7'6" in length.

For investment purposes go for finer pieces, simply because as production of all rugs becomes a thing of the past these are likely to be the first to go.

If you are thinking of silk rugs — particularly splendid as wall hangings — go for the Qum variety in preference to Kashan; you rarely find a poor specimen of a Qum rug but Kashans tend to be more variable. Although Persian Silk Bokharas are very fine, beautiful and excellent rugs in every way and are about two thirds the price of a Qum of similar size, they are not such good investment pieces because the public tend to confuse them with the very silky looking Mori Bokhara rugs from Pakistan. The latter are excellent but are cheaper and must never be confused — in terms of value — with a Persian or Turkish Silk.

To sum up: if you are buying a silk rug, for rapid appreciation, consider the Persian Qum variety. If you want something which will take its share of work and appreciate at the same time, then look at fine Persian Nains, or the finest Isfahan pieces with wool pile knotted in silk warp threads.

At more moderate prices, Turkish Kula and Melas rugs are under priced as compared with the Persian equivalents and, to many tastes, more satisfying.

Finally, even if you make a mistake and pay over the odds because a piece particularly appeals to you, don't be unduly disheartened. The price of all good hand-made rugs has moved up inexorably in the past and there is every prospect it will continue to do so. Your initial learning experience will only

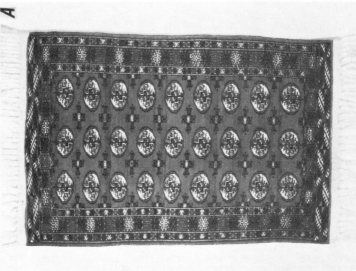

Persian Yamut Bokhara rug, 5ft 1ins x 3ft 4ins.   £185

mean you may have to wait longer for appreciation of your choice. At the present date rugs are imported into U.K. with only minimal import duties and the present rate of VAT at 8% is likely to be an all-time low. If the U.K. stays in the E.E.C. then duties will probably go up to 20%-25% advalorem within the next two to three years. VAT is likely to double and with these increases the value of rugs already bought in the home market will get a bonus boost in addition to that supplied by a growing demand and a diminishing supply.

LONDON CARPET BROKERS

Most brokers do not welcome casual visitors so we recommend a preliminary telephone call to arrange a mutually convenient appointment. The following trade brokers also accept private clients:

Simon Boosey, The Garden House, St. Paul's Walden, Herts. Tel: Whitwell 563.

Caroline Bosly, 18 Vincent Square, Westminster, London, S.W.1. Tel: 01-834 0083. (Descriptive literature on application.)

A.T. Smith, 29 Orchard Avenue, Shirley, Croydon, CR0 8VB. Tel: 01-777 1290.

Oriental Rugs and Carpets Information Service (Mrs P. Blake). (Range of typical varieties on view and for sale at showrooms 18, Green Street, Bath Tel: 0225 4270.)

PLAYING CARDS

MAURICE COLLETT
Kendal Playing Card Sales.

Playing cards have been in use in Britain for over 500 years, or about four times as long as postage stamps. It is strange, therefore, that stamp collectors are considered normal while playing card collectors are regarded as eccentrics. There are, however, many card collectors, and their number is increasing steadily. "The Playing Card Society", based in Britain but with an international membership, exists to further the needs of students of this branch of folk art.

The range of playing cards is quite staggering, and there are specialist collectors within the general theme of the subject. Europe alone has, apart from the "normal" suits of hearts, clubs, diamonds and spades, several completely different suit systems, one in Spain, parts of France and Italy, another in Switzerland, one used throughout the old Austro-Hungarian Empire and Germany, and a version of the Spanish system in large areas of Italy. In Britain we use a design originating in Rouen in the 15th Century.

Playing cards are in use in virtually every country in the world, but in the Far East they bear little resemblance to European cards, not only in shape but in the designs used and the number of cards per pack. Chinese playing cards are similar to long narrow tickets, and the games played are based on Chinese chess, on money or on the game of dominoes. Indian playing cards are circular, with twelve cards per suit. The number of suits range from eight to twenty or more. Shells, peacocks, axes, lotus buds and fishes are just some of the suit symbols used. Japanese cards, called Mekuri-fuda, are small rectangles of thick board, which are hardly recognisable as a derivation of the Spanish-suited cards brought to Japan four centuries ago by Portugese traders.

Apart from their use in games and gambling playing cards have been used for educational purposes, for propoganda, satire, advertising and even as money. Tarot cards, which were developed for the game bearing that name, and which are still used in parts of Europe for their original purpose, have been adopted by the fortune-telling fraternity and invested with all sorts of supernatural powers never envisaged by their makers. Throughout the centuries card designers have produced many beautiful variations of the court cards, with historical personages, national costume, actors and actresses.

For a modest outlay a representative collection of the cards used in various parts of the world can be obtained, and because it is a relatively unknown hobby, it is still possible to build up a collection of older and rarer packs relatively cheaply. Relatives and friends turning out cupboards and attics of their parents and grandparents often unearth forgotten cards of the last century. These may be standard cards that, in those days, still had full-length figures on the court cards, or perhaps some of the Victorian cards that honoured British monarchs, European statesmen, or four of Shakespeare's plays on the courts. Antique shops, jumble sales and the like, may produce packs, and there are a few dealers specialising in cards.

Like all collectable items, playing cards are appreciating steadily. Age is not the main criterion for value. "Full-length" court cards were in use up to about 1880, and packs can still be bought for £5 – £10. Yet the "Cashmere" pack of 1959, given away by a New York firm specialising in Cashmere sweaters, now changes hands at £20 or more. This pack had each of the four suits portraying the four Eastern races connected with the Cashmere woollen trade. De La Rue issued a beautiful pack in 1957, designed by the French tapestry designer, Jean Picart le Doux. The beautiful court cards and attractive number cards were unacceptable to the card-playing public, and the pack was not a commercial success. Though it was on sale up to four years ago it now fetches 5 or 6 times its original price. An American pack, produced in 1963 for the Presidential election, and showing members of the ill-fated Kennedy family, is now eagerly sought by collectors.

Playing cards are made to be used. Old packs showing signs of wear are quite acceptable and even incomplete packs find a home in a collection.

Some people collect cards for their decorative backs, being satisfied with only one card per pack, others specialise in jokers or spade aces. Some deal only in cards connected with transport, with food,, with the theatre and so on. The most elusive of packs was issued for the Coronation of Edward V111, and withdrawn on his abdication. Sold for a shilling or two it now fetches several pounds.

It is more than likely that many readers of this article have the basis of a collection hidden away somewhere in their own house. They may, in fact, still be using cards on which the Ace of Spades say, "Duty Three Pence". In these days of rising taxation it is encouraging to know that the duty on playing cards was abolished in 1960, and this increases the value of packs with Duty Aces.

Left: Queen of Spades from an early 20th century German Rococo pack.
Centre: Queen of Clubs from an advertising pack made for Simpsons of Piccadilly.
Right: Queen of Hearts from a French pack commemorating the Bicentenary of the birth of Napoleon.

Photo by Keith Kirkby.

110

LYLE OFFICIAL ANTIQUES REVIEW is published on the first of November of every year, enabling you to begin each new year with an up to date knowledge of the current trends, together with the verified values of antiques of all descriptions.

We have endeavoured to obtain a balance between the more expensive collector's items and those which, although not in their true sense antiques, are handled daily by the antique trade.

The illustrations and prices in the following sections have been arranged to make it easy for the reader to assess the period and value of all items with speed.

You will find illustrations for almost every category of antique and curio, together with a corresponding price collated during the last twelve months, from auction rooms and retail outlets throughout Britain.

When dealing with the more popular trade pieces, a calculation of an average price has been estimated from the varying accounts researched. As regards prices when 'one of a pair' is given in the description the price quoted is for a pair, for with the limited space we have at our disposal we feel only one illustration is necessary.

ARMOUR

A good, heavy 16th Century fauld. £36

A scarce, mid-16th Century Pauldron, possibly Italian. £52

A scarce, mid-16th Century Pauldron, possibly Italian. £52

A fully articulated arm and shoulder defence from an Italian, late 16th Century, armour. £55

A very fine set of Indo-Persian armour (possibly Lahore, 18th Century). £530

A fully articulated arm and shoulder defence, from a German, late 16th Century, armour. £100

A good, late 18th Century Cavalry trooper's breastplate £38

A good Cromwellian trooper's breastplate. £120

A good Victorian breastplate. £36

A 17th Century German pauldron.   £50

A good Japanese Jingasa.   £60

A good, Indo-Persian circular iron shield, dhal, diameter 18½ ins.   £40

A good, early 19th Century Household Cavalry breastplate.   £50

An Indo-Persian spiked helmet, Kulah Khud   £52

A good pair of late 16th Century Italian breast and back plates.   £205

A good, mid-18th Century Cavalry trooper's breastplate of heavy form.   £52

A good, 17th Century breastplate of siege weight.   £62

An Imperial Russian Cavalry black-japanned curiass and backplate.   £100

BADGES

A rare, other rank's glengarry badge of The Argyle and Sutherland Highlanders.   £40

A Georgian officer's gorget of The Coldstream Guards.
£43

A rare, other rank's glengarry badge of The Black Watch.   £36

A good, Georgian officer's oval shoulder belt plate of The Caithness Highlanders.
£30

A post 1902 officer's silvered plaid brooch.
£70

A Georgian other rank's cast brass oval single breast plate.
£35

A Victorian officer's silver plated 1855-pattern shako badge.
£22

Victorian pre-1881 officer's blue cloth helmet plate.   £52

A Victorian officer's 1855-pattern shako badge.   £28

A post 1902 officer's rectangular single breast plate.   £14

A good, officer's rectangular single breast plate.   £46

An officer's gilt rectangular single breast plate, pre-1855. £46

An officer's Waterloo
period universal-pattern
shako plate.   £36

A Commander in
Chief's Yeomanry
Escort hat badge.   £40

An officer's Waterloo
period universal-pattern
shako badge.   £57

An officer's silver
plated plaid brooch.
£60

A Georgian officer's
universal-pattern gorget.
£50

A fine and rare,
hallmarked silver
(1808) oval single
breast plate.   £56

A Victorian officer's
silvered helmet plate.
£30

Pre-1881 officer's
blue cloth helmet
plate.   £30

Victorian officer's blue
cloth helmet plate.
£26

An officer's shoulder
belt plate, circa 1840-
55.   £42

A William IV officer's
rectangular single breast
plate of the Grenadier
Guards.   £50

A post 1881 Victorian
officer's single breast
plate.   £30

BAROMETERS

A 19th century rosewood and mother of pearl inlaid banjo barometer and thermometer by Green, Glasgow. £90

Mahogany wheel barometer, by Justin Vulliamy, in a case by John Bradburn, 4ft 2ins high. £5,400

George III wheel barometer in mahogany case with boxwood and ebony stringing. £95

18th century mahogany stick barometer by Pyefinch, London, 3ft 3ins. £350

A Georgian mahogany stick barometer with thermometer by Whitehurst & Son, Derby, 3ft 3 3/8ins long. £380

A carved walnut barometer. £5

A Victorian carved oak aneroid barometer and thermometer. £20

19th century 'main top' walnut cased barometer and thermometer. £34

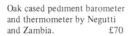

Oak cased pediment barometer and thermometer by Negutti and Zambia. £70

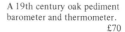

A 19th century oak pediment barometer and thermometer. £70

116

A 19th century rose-
wood barometer and
thermometer.   £35

A 19th century mahogany
pediment barometer and
thermometer, by C. Tochetti,
Aberdeen.   £80

A 19th century mahogany
inlaid wheel barometer and
thermometer, with small
mirror.   £85

An early angle barometer,
by Bathasar Knie.   £280

Mahogany wheel baro-
meter with swan neck
pediment, and ebony
and boxwood stringing,
39ins high, circa 1800.
                      £95

A very fine mahogany
wheel barometer, with
satinwood stringing and
silverised dials, 40ins
high, circa 1825. £110

19th century mahogany
pediment barometer. £46

Early 19th century
wheel barometer by
G. Balsgry, London,
in an inlaid mahogany
case.   £65

Regency period mahogany
wheel barometer and
lygrometer, with ebony
and satinwood stringing,
and swan neck pediment,
circa 1810.   £87

A mahogany inlaid
wheel barometer by
J. Della Torre, Perth.
                     £60

BAROMETERS

Mahogany inlaid wheel barometer and thermometer, inscribed J. Faglioti, Clerkenwell.
£90

19th century mahogany framed pediment barometer by Gardners, Glasgow.   £44

A barometer and thermometer in mahogany inlaid case.   £7

Mahogany pediment barometer by Ramage of of Aberdeen.   £52

A wheel barometer and thermometer in mahogany inlaid case of Sheraton design. £46

Late 18th century mahogany barometer with satinwood inlay.
£65

George III mahogany wheel barometer by N. Barnuka, Bury, circa 1795.   £175

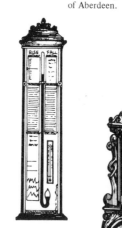

19th century Admiral Fitzroy barometer in an oak case.   £55

An aneroid barometer and thermometer in carved oak case.   £32

Victorian mahogany cased banjo barometer and thermometer. £50

19th century German barometer
clock with an oak case.   £85

A Victorian aneroid circular
barometer in a spelter case,
with three winged figures in
high relief.   £32

Victorian oak cased wall
barometer.   £14

BARRELS

An oak and metal bound
wine cask with tap, 1ft
8ins.   £8

An attractive well bucket,
with wrought swing handle
and decorative riveted
strength bands, circa 1790,
17ins high.   £48

A steel banded oak cider
barrel with hand riveted
joints to bands, 11ins
diam at top, circa 1840.
          £35

Steel banded barrel,
circa 1820, 16ins
high.   £28

Steel banded wooden corn
measure, stamped KP,
circa 1790, 16½ins diam,
14ins high.   £45

Stoneware spirit barrel
with brass tap   £28

A 19th century bronze study of a Roman warrior clutching an old man, who in turn is holding a young child, 22ins high. £360

(King & Chasemore, Pulborough)

"L'Accolade", a fine cast of P.J. Mene's bronze, signed and dated 1865.
£1,550

Early 19th century French bronze bronze cupid, 16ins high.
£240

An Art Deco bronze and ivory group of a horse with a young girl attendant, on an onyx base, 1ft 3ins wide, 1ft 5ins high.
£620

Pair of Art Deco gilded metal figures of dancers, standing on white alabaster plinths, 14½ins high.
£95

An Art Nouveau bronze and ivory figure of a dancer by Demetre H. Chiparus, on an onyx base, 17ins high.   £420

A pair of 19th century, French, bronze busts on marble plinths, 12ins high.
£30

A bronze group of three Dutch boys climbing onto a cart horse, inscribed by E. Martin Foudeur, Paris.
£800

Art Deco figure of a dancing lady by Preiss.
£875

An ingeniously made, mid 19th century Japanese articulated bronze grasshopper.
£38

BRONZE

An Art Nouveau coloured metal figure of a girl and a pillar, on onyx base, 11ins high. £38

An African bronze group of a man and woman seated, 5ins high. £20

Bronze nude study, 'The Sluggard', signed Lord Leighton, 21ins high. £400

A French bronze figure of a pointer with head raised, by P.J. Mene, 8ins high. £370

A fine Queen Anne period apothecary's bronze mortar with unusual decoration of thirteen raised bosses around band, circa 1710, 5ins diam, 3ins high. £25

Heavy sheet bronze vertical wall sundial, the bronze roman numerals soldered onto the plate, 12ins square. £65

A German bronze statuette of Venus de Milano, on an oblong base, stamped J. Waltz, 3ft 7ins high. £195

Gilt bronze sea dragon from the period of the six dynasties, 5½ins. 70,000gns

A large bronze figure of a man tearing apart a tree trunk, after the antique, on square base, 31ins high. £300

A bronze group of a horse and negro boy, on ebonised base, 11ins high. £20

Classical deep green bronze figure of a Satyr on stepped square base of bronze, 12½ins high. £48

A bronze seated female figure, 8ins high.   £17

A French bronze figure of a stretching dog, by E. Fremiet, 3¾ins high.   £230

A bronze study of a slender young woman, 10ins high.
£80

A bronze mythological female winged statuette on ball and square alabaster plinth base, 27ins high.   £80

Cast bronze heraldic plaque of a fighting cock's leg, mounted on an oak shield, 12ins high, 8ins wide, circa 1820.   £38

A fine Art Nouveau bronze and ivory figure of a ballet dancer by Demetre H. Chiparus, on an onyx base, 29ins high.   £840

A pair of French gilt bronze figures, "Une Repitition, par Faure de Brousse', on green onyx and gilt metal bases, 12ins high.   £76

One of a pair of bronze groups of horses and attendants, on rockwork bases, signed Couston, 20ins high.   £190

A bronze classical female head door mount with bas relief vines.   £4

Bronze sundial, engraved 'Cole Fecit', 10ins diam.
£95

One of a pair of bronze groups of prancing horses with figure attendants, on oblong shaped base, 19½ins high.   £170

BRONZE

Nepalese gilt bronze figure of Maitreya, 25½ins high. £3,600

Pair of 19th century bronzes by J. Willis Good. £850

An old Nepalese seated figure of Bhudda with hollow base, 8ins high. £38

An Oriental bronze double handled bottle shaped vase, inset with coloured enamel bands, 9½ins high. £30

An art nouveau bronze of a female dancer poised with an ivory ball balanced on her forearm, signed Jaeger. £200

A good bronze standing figure of an Imperial German Jaeger soldier, 9¾ins high on heavy marbled base. £66

A 19th century Japanese bronze group of two tigers attacking a rhinoceros, 24ins wide. £145

19th century bronze bust with Eastern style headress. £48

A pair of English bronzes depicting race horses and jockeys, 5¼ins high and 5ins high, circa 1840. £165

A Victorian gilt bronze figure of a man on marble base. £24

A bronze group of a satyr and a young woman at play, both seated on a rocky base, 16ins high. £190

(King & Chasemore, Pulborough)

BRONZE

19th century animalea bronze of a greyhound and pheasant. £45

18th century Chinese bronze incense burner. £58

Art Deco bronze and ivory group of a horse with young girl attendant, on an onyx base, 1ft 3ins wide. £620

Ivory and bronze figure 'Invocation' by Preiss. £800

West Tibetan bronze figure of Kubera wearing jewellery, inlaid with silver and stones, 8½ins high. £1,575

19th century bronze of a stag with two does. £120

Semi-nude bronze female figure by E. Drouot, 27 7/8ins high. £160

One of a pair of African bronze figures of a man and woman seated, 13ins high. £46

Pair of 19th century French bronzes depicting cupids at play. £80

An unrecorded 16th century Benin cast bronze of a standing figure. £12,000

An exceptionally fine horizontal sundial in engraved
bronze, the plain gnomen with
original strengthening bars
either side, inscribed 'Cole
Fecit', 10ins diam.   £95

17th century bronze mortar
with the inscription 'William
Boult, 1654'.   £360

19th century bronze of a
dog curiously surveying a
tortoise, by A. Jacquemart.
£80

Pair of bronze and ormolu
candelabra.   £350

19th century bronzed
and gilded spelter figure
of the Duke of Wellington.
£55

19th century horse bronze
of good colour.   £120

A bronzed spelter figure of a
warrior, in armour, 17ins high.
£25

One of a pair of French
bronze figures of warriors
in armour, on circular
bases, signed A. Garrier,
24ins high.   £400

A pair of French bronzed spelter
figures of "Le Prince Noir and
Le Roi Jean", in suits of armour
on circular ebonised plinths,
25ins high.   £55

A large Thai bronze Buddha,
30ins high.   £450

BRONZE

A bronze whippet, signed
P.J. Mene.   £220

A Japanese bronze circular
jar with domed cover and
pierced border, the base
with two chased bronze
dragons, 17½ins high.   £70

Late 19th century bronze
group of a stag standing
guard over a drinking doe.
                    £1,150

Bronze male statuette
'Le Boucheron', signed
Chambard, 34ins high.
                    £200

A large French bronze
equestrian group with
female figure mounted
on a horse, signed on
base, L. Chalow, 32ins
high.   £600

19th century Italian bronze
figure of an athlete, by
Canova.   £210

An Art Nouveau painted
bronze and ivory figure of
a girl wearing a bathing
costume, signed F. Preiss.
                    £480

An art deco bronze and
ivory group by Professor
Poertzel.   £540

An art deco bronze
group by Etling. £100

One of a pair of early Chinese dogs of Fo.   £480

A Japanese bronze oval double handled hibatchi and pierced wood cover and stand, 10ins high.   £8

A cast bronzed dog door stopper.   £22

A Continental bronze figure of a man seated on a rockwork base, signed A. Filepovie, 12½ins high.   £85

A finely modelled bronze figure depicting the actress Isadora Duncan in an art nouveau dress, signed on base 'Jaeger', 18½ins high.   £235

A bronzed spelter equestrian group of a warrior on horseback, on an ebonised plinth base, 18ins high.   £16

Very handsome hollow backed gilded bronze classical figure of a woman on horseback, signed by "Coutan", 20ins high, 17½ins long.   £120

A bronze whippet by P.J. Mene.   £220

An art deco bronze, ivory and onyx ash tray.   £72

BRONZE

A Western United States bronze depicting the shoeing of an immigrant farmer's horse, by Carl Kauba.   £420

A Burmese bronze figure of a Goddess with traces of red gilt decoration, on a square base with four feet, 17ins high.   £26

Fine 18th century green patinated bronze of a lion attacking a horse, mounted on a square stepped Rouge de fer marble base, 8ins high.   £95

A pair of 19th century French bronze cupids with basket of flowers, 14ins high.   £390

A bronze figure of a dancing cymbals player by Pilkington Jackson, signed and dated 1922, 2ft 6ins high.   £150

A pair of French bronze Spewer female figures of "Gaiete and Modestie", on ebonised plinths, 12ins high.   £21

Late 19th century French bronze, depicting a traditionally dressed Nubian woman playing the harp.   £260

A large bronze mythological group of Europa the bull and four other figures, on square shaped base, with deer and boars, 16ins high.   £280

An exotic ivory and bronze figure of a dancer, on a shaped and coloured onyx base, 26ins high, signed Chiparus.   £2,000

Left: A gilt bronze figure of a naked girl, signed E. Mevsel, 18ins high. £28

Centre: A well modelled bronze study of a naked girl, 21ins high. £30

Right: A bronze figure of a naked girl, 19ins high. £32

(King & Chasemore, Pulborough)

BUCKETS & HODS

A 19th century brass coal helmet with swing handle. £12

A 19th century embossed brass, oval coal pail, with double hinged covers and handle. £34

A copper coal helmet with swing handle. £13

A fine polished sheet iron well bucket, with wrought iron swing handle and hook, circa 1780, 16ins high excluding handle. £48

Victorian embossed brass oval stick stand. £15

A copper circular log pail, with brass bands and swing handle. £26

One of a set of four Georgian oyster pails in brass-bound mahogany, 10ins diam. £1,500

A copper coal hod, with brass loop handle. £18

Copper coal skuttle, circa 1800, 20ins long, 18½ins high. £45

An embossed brass grape carrier.   £60

A large, solid copper wash boiler, the side seam and band near base with large copper rivets, circa 1820, 14ins high, 20ins diam. £28

A copper coal pail with swing handle. £18

A fine Georgian copper coal skuttle with brass handle grips, 19ins long, 17ins high. £55

A Victorian brass coal helmet, with swing handle.   £42

Copper helmet shaped coal skuttle, circa 1810 £28

Solid copper wash boiler, with turned over rim, circa 1830, 17ins diam, 13ins high.   £28

Attractive angular shaped copper coal skuttle, circa 1820, 21ins long, 19ins high.   £48

Edwardian inlaid rosewood coal cabinet with a pierced brass gallery.   £20

BUCKETS & HODS

Victorian brass coal skuttle.
£35

A brass bound copper log pail
with swing handle.   £18

18th century helmet coal
skuttle with ebony handle.
£38

Victorian japanned coal depot
with china handle.   £30

George III brass-bound plate
bucket.   £180

Victorian walnut coal depot
with brass handle and coal
scoop.   £18

Dutch copper and brass peat
bucket, circa 1770, 16ins
high.   £87

Edwardian mahogany coal
cabinet on short cabriole legs.
£15

Circular copper coal pail. £22

Mid 19th century Persian penbox decorated with seven large panels of figure subjects.   £1,950

A fine Chippendale period mahogany tea caddy, containing three compartments and secret drawer.   £48

A coromandelwood oblong stationery box with domed cover and brass mount. £17

A French walnut and kingwood oval shaped jardiniere with brass handles and borders, and inset china plaque and liner, 13ins wide.   £88

A Japanese black lacquered cabinet of five small drawers enclosed by two doors, decorated in gilt, 15ins high, 12ins wide.   £24

Hepplewhite mahogany knife box, 8¾ins high.   £45

A small tortoiseshell case with gold filigree inlay.   £52

Mid 19th century Persian penbox decorated with figures.   £750

An Indian coromandelwood oblong box, the hinged cover ivory inlaid with a circular panel of flowers and an elephant, 14½ins.   £14

A fine and rare George II mahogany cockfighting carrying cage.   £650

A mahogany specimen cabinet of six drawers, 16½ins wide.   £40

George I walnut spice cabinet, 21ins high.   £75

An oak bible box, its front and sides carved with two rows of flutings, with a reeded edge to the top, circa 1600.   £165

A 17th century black and gold lacquered casket.   £940

18th century French papier mache writing box.   £82

A George III mahogany and brass oblong box, with brass handles and feet, 12ins wide.   £25

A Victorian rosewood portable writing desk, with mother-of-pearl inlay and carved, beaded borders.   £25

A large Tunbridgeware tea caddy.   £78

An oak desk box with a hinged sloping front above stylised geometric carving, circa 1690.   £85

Mid 19th century French Second Empire ormolu jewel casket, signed C. De Franor, 10ins wide.   £140

Satinwood lady's work box, with ebony stringing and oval key escutcheon, circa 1795.   £35

A mahogany box, with drawer and brass ring handles, on ball feet, 15ins wide.   £26

Sheraton mahogany tea caddy, with satinwood and ivory key escutcheon, on bun feet, circa 1810, 12ins long, 6ins wide, 6½ins high.   £35

Mahogany brass banded chest, the hinged lid inlaid with brass shield, by Edwards, James Street Street, London, circa 1800.   £85

17th century oak bible
box.   £24

A Regency casket-shaped
mahogany tea caddy, on
brass ball feet, circa 1820.
                         £34

A Victorian mahogany and
brass bound portable
writing desk, 16ins.   £15

An Italian ebonised and walnut
cabinet of eight small drawers,
inlaid with ivory and with
parquetry decoration, 2ft 7½ins
wide, 15½ins high.   £150

A coaching tavern post box
of japanned tole ware,
divided into three compartments, 13ins long, 5ins deep,
6½ins high.   £15

French gold and enamel
box, 1¾ins diam. 1,500gns

17th century oak desk,
I.N., 1636.   £75

A small Victorian wooden
casket, with applied plaster
seals.   £14

A fine brass banded mahogany
box, with ivory label showing
maker's name, Arnold & Sons,
West Smithfield, London, circa
1830.   £38

A very rare mahogany cat or
dog kennel with detachable
gable roof, 15ins long, 11ins
high, 10ins wide.   £125

A fine William and Mary table
desk, in yew-wood, 21ins
long, 17ins high.   £345

Tooled leather writing paper
cabinet, with original brass
key escutcheon and lock, by
W. Houghton, Stationer,
Bond Street, 6½ins long. £18

A miniature ivory parquetry inlaid and amboynawood cabinet of drawers with brass carrying handles, 7½ins x 6ins. £40

A very small oak bible-box, its front carved with a stylised tulip motif, circa 1680. £125

An early Victorian mother-of-pearl inlaid papier mache card-case. £25

An officer's document case, in brass-banded mahogany, with flush inset carrying handles, original Bramah lock by Muckleston Patent. £58

An oak bible-box with lunette carving on the front, circa 1700. £45

One of a pair of 19th century mahogany knife boxes, with shaped fronts, 15¾ins high. £140

A Tunbridgeware bookrack. £35

An early Victorian folding backgammon board, made of walnut inlaid with rosewood, satinwood, boxwood and ebony, circa 1840. £45

An English papier mache wall pocket, circa 1830. £28

A pine watchmaker's cabinet, circa 1800, 23ins high, 12ins wide, 7½ins deep. £47

An oak bible-box, showing the Stuart Coat of Arms, retaining the original hand-blocked lining paper. £75

A Victorian rosewood and mother of pearl inlaid cabinet, the hinged top fitted as work box, one drawer fitted with writing slope, 14ins high, 12ins wide. £50

An oak spice cupboard with eight interior drawers, circa 1670. £125

Georgian mahogany knife box, with brass carrying handle. £28

A tortoiseshell card-case, with silver decoration and a diamond-shaped central cartouche. £14

An unusual octagonal jewel box of colomander with satinwood, ebony and kingwood banding, circa 1810. £35

A laboratory microscope slide cabinet, in white painted pine, the glass door giving access to eighteen drawers, circa 1860. £38

A small round gold filigree inlayed tortoiseshell case. £26

One of a pair of Sheraton mahogany inlaid knife boxes with serpentine shaped fronts, 14½ins high. £160

A miniature walnut inlaid bureau, with a drawer, on bracket feet, 17¾ins wide. £72

18th century elm taper box. £29

An Italian black metal casket with hinged cover, 13¼ins wide, 12½ins high. £88

An extremely fine Sheraton mahogany paint box with ebony stringing, containing the original paints and palettes, by Winsor and and Newton, London. £40

One of a pair of mahogany knife boxes with rosewood banding and shaped fronts, 12ins high. £70

CAMERAS

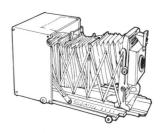

Goerz "Anschutz" camera marketed by Pelling and Van Neck, circa 1918.   £35

Gigantic art studio plate camera in mahogany, on very fine tripod ebonised stand, lens engraved J.H. Dallmeyer No. 27155.
£350

"Trellis" camera by Newman and Guardia, circa 1920, plate size 5ins x 4ins.   £294

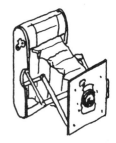

Kodak 4a folding camera, negative size 4½ins x 6½ins.
£63

A mahogany and brass dry plate camera by J. Lancaster & Son, Birmingham.   £48

Kodak folding pocket camera.
£5

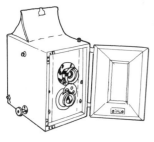

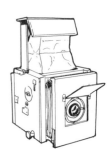

Twin lens reflex, quarter plate camera by Watson of Holborn, circa 1890.   £183.50

A fine dry plate camera, of mahogany and brass with original lacquer, and detachable lens.   £48

A Newman and Guardia reflex camera, circa 1907.   £50

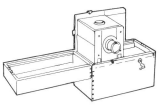

Powell's patent stereoscope camera, 1858.   £1,680

A Sanderson's Patent 19th century dry plate camera with red leather bellows, the mahogany body covered in black leather.   £75

A twin lens reflex 'Pilot' camera, circa 1930.   £115

A Contax 1 miniature camera by Carl Zeiss, circa 1934.   £52

A gigantic art studio 11½ins plate camera in mahogany, the brass cased lens, by J.H. Dallmeyer, on ebonised tripod stand.   £350

McKellens double pinion treble patent camera, circa 1890.   £47

Golden Ernemann high speed press camera, circa 1925.   £273

Late 19th century mahogany and brass half plate camera, by Thornton Pickard, complete with double half plate carrier.   £47

The "Duchessa" miniature plate camera, circa 1920.   £35

CARVED WOOD

Amusing and unique carved wood elephant, with folding sides, enclosing mechanism which operates nodding head, circa 1840, 33ins long, 25ins high.   £285

A pair of barley-twist treen candlesticks with brass sconces, 12ins high.   £8

An unusually large Welsh butter bowl of sycamore wood, circa 1790, 17ins diam.   £28

Venetian boxwood figure of Ladon, the river god, by Andrea Brustalon.   £1,800

A pair of carved wood blackamoor figures, 6ft 5ins high.   £500

A New Guinean ancestral figure, 38ins high.   £170

A Chinese carved wood figure of a sage, fitted for electric light.   £22

A child's rattle in the form of a stylised raven, 13½ins.   £2,700

Painted carved pinewood Brown Trout, mounted on a sea green bevelled board.   £48

A two-sided flat carving of a stylised abstract figure, 55ins high.   £100

142

An Oriental heavily carved teak jardiniere with flowers, fruit and ram heads in relief, on four paw feet, 16ins diam x 11ins high. £65

A pair of decorated lacquered candlesticks, fitted for electric light. £10

Boxwood and ivory group of dentist and patient, German. £860

A 17th century Flemish oak carving of a young woman with a bust of a man at her feet. £170

Late 15th century Netherlandish oak relief of the Entombment, 53.3cm high. £4,725

A New Guinea wooden figure with kaori-shell inlaid eyes and chin. £170

English sportsman's Decoy Duck, circa 1830. £34

An amusing carved wood nutcracker in the form of a grotesque man's head, the jaws cracking the nut, circa 1840. £18

Tsarist period peasant's carved wood model of a sleigh and three horses, circa 1840, 23ins long. £195

A child's rattle in the form of a round mask. £1,900

CARVED WOOD

A circular carved wood tobacco jar. £15

An ornate carved wood Kris stand in the form of a kneeling demon, 12ins high. £105

Boxwood dice-cup. £8

North West Pacific coast wooden club in the form of a seal with bared teeth. £1,600

A Maori wooden mere carved with grotesque figures and masks, 19ins long. £920

Casurina wood club from the Marquesas Islands. £441

A pair of North American Indian carved wooden paddles, 46ins long. £78

A Chinese carved giltwood figure of a kylon, on a carved gilt and red lacquered square shaped stand, 22ins high. £90

19th century carved oak pulpit with fine Gothic carving. £210

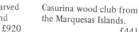

A large carved wood kris stand in the form of a standing demon, 34ins high. £110

Carved wood figure of a jester holding a lamp, 4ft 6ins high. £230

Oriental carved double gourd and cover, 16ins high. £60

A very imposing Chinese lacquer figure of Wen Chang, the God of Literature, dressed as a mandarin, probably of the Sung dynasty, 3ft high. £950

A pair of North American Indian carved wooden paddles, 35ins long. £104

South Sea Islands rootwood war club, 46ins long. £780

A rare South Seas "Kite-" shaped club, 27ins. £26

North West Pacific coast wooden club in the form of a bear embracing a fish. £340

An interesting African, probably Benin, carved oblong wood box, the lid carved with stylised European figure, 5ins x 15ins x 3ins. £60

Early 20th century carved wood figure of a town crier. £1,000

Swiss carved walnut dancing bear, circa 1840, 12½ins high. £68

CASED SETS

A very fine and scarce, .41 ins rimfire Colt Thuer No. 3 Derringer, 4¾ ins, barrel 2½ ins.   £115

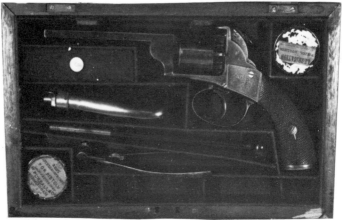

A 5-shot, 100-bore Webley type self cocking percussion revolver, 10 ins, octagonal barrel 5 ins.   £180

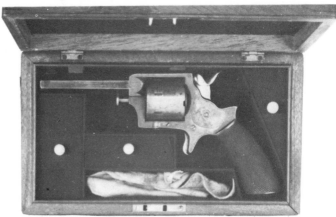

A scarce 6-shot, .32 ins rimfire Tranter's Patent single action revolver, 8¼ ins, octagonal barrel 3½ ins.   £70

A 5-shot, 120-bore, Tranter's Patent double action percussion revolver
No. 14994.T., 8½ ins, barrel 3¾ ins, London and Birmingham proofs.   £350

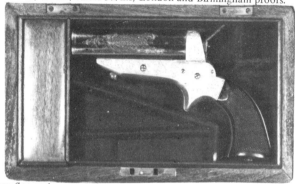

A very fine and scarce, .32 ins Tipping and Lawden four
barrelled 'Presentation' pistol, 5½ ins, barrels 3.1/16 ins.   £140

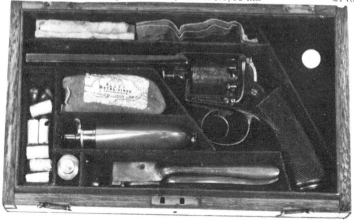

A 5-shot, 54-bore 1851 model Adam's self cocking self cocking
percussion revolver, 12 ins, barrel 6½ ins, London proved.   £340

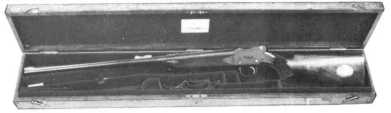

An extremely fine, .303 Martini Sporting Presentation Rifle by Wilkinson Sword Company, 45 ins, heavy tapered barrel with matted top rib, 28 ins. £260

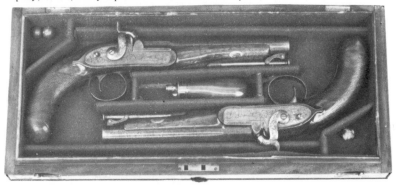

A pair of 16-bore percussion holster pistols by Hewson, 13 ins, quarter octagonal browned twist barrels 7½ ins. £310

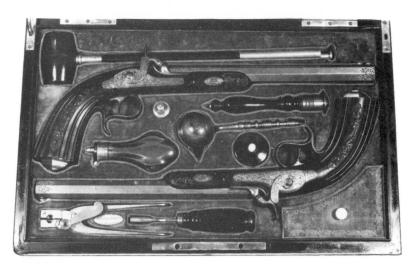

A pair of 36-bore, Cont percussion duelling pistols, 17 ins, octagonal rifled barrels 11 ins. £1,750

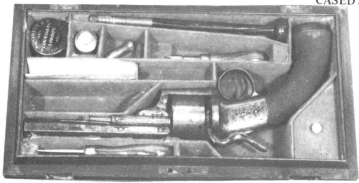

A good, 6-shot, 40-bore open wedge frame single action percussion revolver, 12½ ins, octagonal barrel 6 ins.   £280

A 6-shot, 56-bore open frame bar hammer self cocking Trans percussion revolver, 12½ ins, octagonal barrel 5¾ ins.   £115

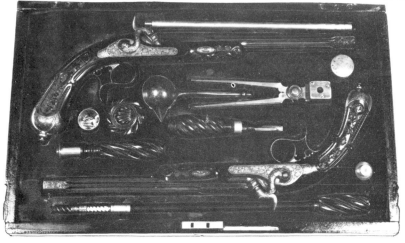

A good pair of 40-bore, Cont percussion duelling pistols, 16½ ins, part fluted rifled blued barrels 10¾ ins.   £1,200

CHINA
BELLEEK

A Belleek lattice work dish
and cover.   £78

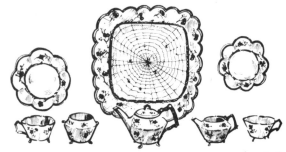

Belleek cabaret set decorated in bronzed gold and gilt.   £160

BOW

19th century Bow
seated Putto. £48

One of a pair of 18th century
quail-pattern Bow octagonal
plates, 4ins diam.   £98

A fine Bow Turkish figure
of a man with fluted bowl,
6ins high.   £270

Blue and white Bow
mug, circa 1760. £75

CAUGHLEY

Caughley porcelain
asparagus server of
Fisherman pattern. £23

Caughley miniature tea
bowl and saucer,
'Fisherman Pattern'. £42

18th century Caughley
fluted teapot, cover and
stand, decorated in
blue and gilt.   £50

A Caughley shell
dish.   £39

COALBROOKDALE

Coalbrookdale plate from a
service which Queen Victoria
presented to the Tsar of Russia
in 1845, 9¾ins diam.   £750

A fine Coalbrookdale plate with
four matching engraved wine
glasses prepared for the Royal
table in 1855.   £520

Coalbrookdale vase decorated
with panels showing peasants
on one side and gentlefolk on
the other, 20½ins high. £360

COALPORT

Large celeste blue Coalport vase with panels by James Rousse, 30¾ins high, 1861 £1,950

Coalport vase and cover with a panel of fruit framed by gilt rococo scrolling, 12ins high, 1900. £360

Coalport vase and cover, painted by R.F. Abraham, 25ins high. £520

A Coalport gigantic tea cup and saucer, decorated with gilt and pastel blue leaf design, circa 1850. £9

19th century English porcelain garniture of three vases in the Sevres manner, probably Coalport. £290

A pair of Corinthian column plated candlesticks. £26

Pair of Coalport rose-pompadour vases and covers, with painted panels of a shepherd and a shepherdess, by William Cook, 1861, 14½ins high. £1,350

Pair of Coalport rose-pompadour vases and covers, painted with gilt-edged panels after Boucher, 1861, 15½ins high. £1,450

CHINA
CHELSEA

Chelsea beaker, Kakiemon, red anchor. £160

Chelsea yellow tiger plate of octagonal form. £150

Chelsea cream jug, triangle mark. £2,400

One of a pair of Chelsea octagonal plates, 8¾ins. £125

Pair of rare Chelsea silver shaped dishes, decorated with exotic birds, circa 1765. £185

One of a pair of large Chelsea circular plates with red anchor mark. £550

A Chelsea scent bottle in the shape of an Oriental lady, circa 1750. £3,000

Chelsea octagonal fable cup and saucer, by J.F. O'Neale, raised anchor. £2,400

Chelsea Derby figure of a young man, patch marks, 5½ins high. £80

Chelsea beaker, Acanthus,
triangle mark.   £880

Chelsea Hans Sloane meat
dish, red anchor.   £720

One of a pair of Chelsea
Botanical plates.   £310

Chelsea strawberry dish,
incised triangle.   £950

A pair of Chelsea figures of a
youth and maiden carrying
baskets richly decorated in
gilt and encrusted with flowers,
7ins high., Gold anchor mark.
£350

Rare red anchor period
Chelsea chocolate cup, cover
and saucer, boldly painted
in polychrome with fruits,
circa 1755.   £75

One of a pair of Chelsea
plates bearing label
Painted by Paul Ferg.
£550

Chelsea Derby figure of
'Summer', 5ins high. £105

Chelsea botanical plate,
one of a pair.   £700

153

CHINA
COPELAND

Copeland pineapple jelly mould, circa 1860.   £18

Blue and white transfer printed small oval dish, impressed Copeland, and number 6, circa 1850, 8½ins long.   £8

An attractive white and gilt Copeland spoon warmer in the form of a large sea shell, on seaweed and coral base, circa 1850, 4½ins high. £28

Copeland Spode teapot. £7.50

A Copeland stoneware 1911 coronation commemorative whiskey flagon with crown stopper, 10ins high overall. £22

19th century Copeland toilet jug.   £12

DAVENPORT

An early 19th century Davenport stone china dinner service of 103 pieces. £430

Octagonal Davenport Longport porcelain dessert plate, circa 1870.   £10

Davenport cup and saucer.   £10

Marked Davenport plate, 10ins diam.   £16.50

DERBY

Pair of Derby candlestick figures, 9¾ins
high. £260

A pair of Derby style figures supporting
candle holds. £95

Late 18th century Derby
female figure. £175

Pair of Bloor Derby figures
depicting Summer and
Autumn, 5ins high. £230

19th century Derby
figure'of Spring. £57

DRESDEN

Part of a 24 piece 19th century Dresden dinner service. £260

19th century Dresden
comport. £25

Potschappel (Dresden) circular punch
bowl, the domed cover having a knop
modelled as two children. £660

19th century four branch
Dresden wall sconce. £60

A Dresden mirror frame, 28ins x 17ins. £170
(King & Chasemore, Pulborough)

An English Delft inkwell, decorated with scattered flower-sprays.   580gns

A Delft, blue and white oval plaque, well painted with a street scene, inscribed in Dutch below, 20ins wide.   £44

17th century Delft posset pot, decorated in blue with an inscription and date, 1651.   £2,100

One of a pair of Victorian Delft vases.   £20

Two of a set of four blue and white Dutch Delft Season plates, 8¾ins diam.   £290

18th century blue and white Delft drug jar, 'V. Galeni', 7½ins high.   £58

English Delft charger depicting William III, 17¼ins diam.   £3,000

Bristol Delft vase decorated with two lion masks and landscapes, 11ins high.   £420

An English Delft charger depicting Adam and Eve, 16¼ins diam.   £1,700

157

CHINA
DOULTON

Stoneware ale barrel tap, impressed "Doulton & Co., Lambeth, London", circa 1869. £18

A Royal Doulton pattern relief moulded lily pattern jardiniere signed M.B., 9ins high. £30

A tall Royal Doulton vase in deep blue and smeared light green stoneware. £29

Doulton jardiniere with near matching stand. £80

A Doulton Burslem blue and white ware jardiniere and pedestal, 3ft 8ins high. £38

Late Victorian Royal Doulton toilet jug. £7

One of a pair of Doulton ware spill vases with flowers and panels of fish in bas relief, 10¼ins high. £16

A pair of Royal Doulton pattern 8814 relief moulded floral design vases, signed E.B., 12½ins high. £35

Doulton vase decorated by Hannah Barlow. £55

EARTHENWARE

An unmarked earthenware coffee-pot, the motto cut through the white slip to the brown clay. £3

A small Victorian earthenware vase, inscribed 'Never too late to mend'. £1

An unmarked pottery hot-water jug. £3

ENGLISH

Vase and cover by John Stinton with highland cattle scene in a mountainous landscape, 1914, 19½ins high. £920

Pair of two-handled vases painted by A. Barker with sheep in a moorland landscape, 1921, 6¾ins high. £280

A Martinware tobacco jar and cover in the form of a bird, circa 1906. £330

A mid 19th century Ashworth's Ironstone dinner service of fifty pieces. £280

Lambeth drinking cup of tin glazed pottery in blue on a manganese ground, 10cm high, 1635. £4,725

English pottery pastille burner, 8¼ins wide. £60

English porcelain sauceboat, circa 1750, 17.1cm long. £1,300

CHINA
ENGLISH

Rodgers pottery sauceboat, with underglaze blue rim, circa 1790. £10

A marked Rogers leaf dish. £9.50

An Aller Vale pottery teapot bearing the legend, 'Ye may get better cheer, But no' wi' better heart'. £3

An attractive stoneware meat platter, decorated in Imari colourings, 18¼ins long, 15¼ins wide. £28

A Lambeth standing salt, 4ins high. £441

A tile from the Watcombe pottery, decorated with leaf and flower swirls. £6

A two-handled loving cup painted by H. Sebright with the date symbols for 1912, 6¼ins high. £190

Pair of vases by Harry Davis with Scottish black faced sheep in mountainous landscape, 1914, 12½ins high. £950

Old stoneware tobacco jar with bas-relief Royal coat of arms with lion and unicorn supporters, circa 1830, 7½ins high. £25

An attractive black transfer Swansea pottery plate, circa 1820, 8¾ins diam. £24

An Aller Vale pottery hat-pin stand, decorated with ship design. £3

A Nantgarw plate with bird decoration. £400

Blue transfer pottery shaped oval dish, possibly Turner, circa 1780, 12¼ins long. £19

A large 19th century Coalbrookdale centre-piece, 18ins high. £145

Rockingham plate from a service made for William IV, 9½ins diam. £980

Chinese Lowestoft cup and saucer, circa 1802. £10

A Goss style Robert Burns cottage. £18

A pot pourri vase and cover painted by James Stinton, date symbol 1908, 7ins high. £250

A Watcombe pottery tile, decorated with leaf and flower swirls. £6

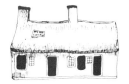

A superb pair of two-handled vases by Harry Davis. £1,400

A fine Ralph Wood Toby Jug, 11¾ins high. £300

One of a pair of Burdett Coutts' plates. £580

A fine Welsh Carmarthenshire pottery jug with snake handle terminating with a swan's head gripping the rim, circa 1840, 8ins high. £18

A very fine example of a Whieldon pottery plate, with raised spotted shaped border, circa 1760. £48

161

Ruskin eggshell pottery bowl, circa 1910.   £45

A Dartmouth pottery jug, inscribed ' No Road is long with Good Company'.   £1

A large 19th century circular jardiniere decorated with a landscape, 29ins high.   £60

A two-handled De Morgan vase, 13½ins high.   £360

A black basalt relief moulded scurier and cover decorated with oak leaves,   £8

A blue and white primrose jardiniere in perfect condition, circa 1790, 14½ins diam. £95

An Adams tray with a black slip ground and applied white classical figures, 9ins x 12ins.   £14

Admiral John Jellicoe jug by Carruthers Gould.   £38

An early English leaf dish.   £140

Porcelain Peace mug of the first world war, 1918.   £5

An unusual pottery cheese dish and cover, with white orange skin body and polychrome raised Japanese stylised flowers, 9ins high.   £37

Early 19th century chemist's honey jar with gilt lettering on Royal Blue band, 10½ins high, circa 1820.   £28

An 18th century blue and white tureen and cover decorated with water landscape and with rabbits' head handles and fruit knop, 13½ins x 8½ins x 8ins.
£90

A 19th century puzzle jug.   £4

A Devonmoor pottery earthenware bowl, with applied and incised decoration.   £8

An orange cow, named "Milk sold here", circa 1850.   £68

Black transfer jug, 'Independent order of Odd Fellows', depicting mother with children, circa 1830.
£14

A large octagonal shaped dish decorated with a fenced garden scene, 15½ins x 11½ins x 2½ins.
£48

A scent bottle in the shape of a girl playing a hurdy-gurdy, circa 1750, 8.2cm high. £2,500

Two plates of a fine set of eleven English porcelain dessert plates.   £210

A Barnstaple pottery jug. £4

A sugar bowl from the Dartmouth pottery, bearing the legend, 'Waste not, want not.'   £1

A rare cream jug, with figure of 'Long Eliza' picked out in coloured enamels, 3¼ins high.
£720

Porcelain George and Mary Coronation beaker, 1911, 4ins high.   £4

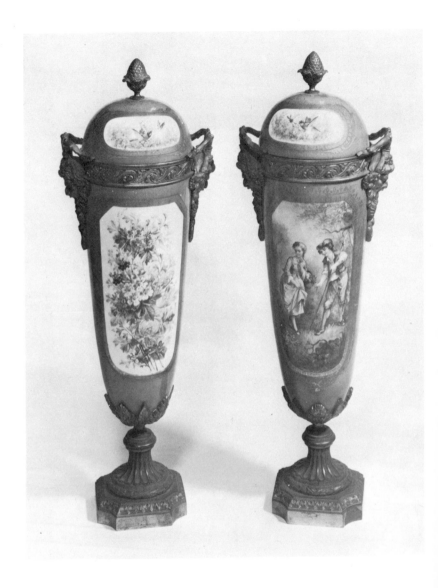

A pair of Sevres vases and covers, 18ins high. £310
(King & Chasemore, Pulborough)

A good Berlin plaque painted in subdued colours and showing a young girl in a long flowing dress, signed 'Wagner', impressed 'K.P.M.', 8½ x 5¾ins. £125

Pair of 19th century German vases decorated with country scenes. £230

German porcelain plaque painted with a female saint playing the organ, 12½ins wide. £280

17th century Italian majolica dish painted with the Rape of the Sabines. £725

Lilac and grey transfer printed plate with centre view of St. Petersburg, circa 1865, 10ins diam. £18

Italian majolica plate depicting the metamorphosis of Daphne by Arazio Fontana, circa 1540-50. £2,300

Berlin rectangular plaque painted with the 'Beggar Boys' after Murillo, 7¾ins wide. £180

A pair of Samson china jardinieres with gilt dog head handles, painted festoons and baskets of flowers, 7ins diam. £38

A fine, old Imperial German half-litre painted pottery beer-stein, 11¼ins high.

£52

18th century French
glazed teapot. £300

A Samson china circular
jardiniere, the blue ground
with gilt decoration and
reserves of Chinese scenes,
9ins diam. £20

A Marseilles faince two-
handled tureen and cover
painted in colours with
bouquets of flowers, 36cm
wide. £2,100

A fine pair of German Field
Artillery Reservists painted
half-litre beerstein, finely
painted with Prussian Royal
Arms. £44

Pair of 19th century French
pottery plates, decorated
with portrait medalions,
8ins diam. £25

19th century Mocha ware
spill vase, the beige ground
with dark brown and French
blue rings, circa 1840, 4¼ins
high. £18

A Berlin porcelain oval plaque
of a young nun, set in a gilt
frame, 9ins high. £48

A pair of large Italian St. Denis
grey ware vases decorated with
figures of girls and landscapes
in panels, 21ins high. £88

German matchholder of a
kitten in porcelain, with a
fluted green basket on
either side, circa 1890. £12

A pair of Continental porcelain twin-handled urns, decorated with enamelled floral sprays and figures in landscapes, 18ins high.   £95

(King & Chasemore, Pulborough)

FAIRINGS

The Last In Bed to Put
Out the Light. £8

A Difficult Problem. £15

Rip Van Winkle. £18

Shall We Sleep First
Or How. £22

Looking Down Upon
His Luck. £22

Three O' Clock In the
Morning. £24

Returning at One O' Clock
in the Morning. £25

The Flower Seller. £25

Twelve Months After
Marriage. £30

'Lor Three Legs I'll
Charge 2d. £30

Happy Father! £40

Tug Of War. £40

Five O' Clock Tea.   £40

That's Funny - Very Funny
- Very Very Funny.   £48

Hunting the Slipper.   £50

Lost.   £50

Good Templars.   £60

I Beg Your Pardon.   £68

How Quietly They
Repose.   £70

Slack.   £80

Go Away Mamma, I
Am Busy.   £85

Return From the Ball. £90

Don't Awake the
Baby.   £100

It's a Shame to Take the
Money.   £100

FAIRINGS

The Landlord in Love £110

A Long Pull and a Strong Pull. £120

Fine Hairs. £200

H'st My Dolls Sleep. £200

A Doubtful Case. £200

If You Please Sir. £200

English Neutrality 1870/71 Attending the Sick. £220

English Neutrality 1870/71. £220

Just in Time. £230

The Shoemaker In Love. £250

To Let. £300

Sir, Where's Your Gloves. £300

In Chancery. £300

Sedan. £320

English Neutrality 1870/71. £350

Every Vehicle Drawn. £400

Free and Independant Electors. £420

It's Only Mustache. £420

First Caresses. £450

Fair Play Boys. £450

80 Strokes of the Pulse In the Minute. £460

Let Us Speak of a Man As We Find Him. £620

Revu. £785

Don't You Like the Change. £920

171

CHINA
LIVERPOOL

A Liverpool flower brick, 6½ins wide. £126

Pair of Liverpool vases by William Reid, 11ins high, circa 1755. £780

Liverpool bowl by William Ball, circa 1760. £420

LOWESTOFT

Lowestoft Pap warmer, 10¼ins high, circa 1765. £350

Lowestoft blue and white vase, circa 1757-60. £620

Lowestoft blue and white coffee pot, circa 1757-60. £1,350

Lowestoft blue and white mug, circa 1765-68. £560

Lowestoft blue and white mug, circa 1757-60. £260

Lowestoft blue and white octagonal inkwell, circa 1762-65. £240

LUSTRE

Welsh lustre jug with blue ivy pattern on side with raised stags under a tree, circa 1835, 6½ins high. £28

Lustre mug in underglaze Flo blue with brick red flower design, circa 1830, 3ins high. £15

All over copper lustre jug, with raised ribbed border, 4ins high. £28

MASONS

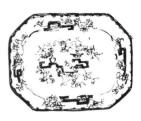

A Mason's ironstone china circular soup tureen and cover.   £15

A pair of Mason's ironstone octagonal covered vases, with Korean lion handles and Chinese style decoration, 15¼ins high.   £120

19th century Ironstone export platter, 1847.   £10

Part of a sixty-one piece Mason's ironstone 'Japan' pattern dinner service.   £300

Mason's ironstone mug.   £30

An ironstone vase and cover with pineapple finial. (A.F.), 37ins high.   £110

19th century Mason's ironstone blue and white toilet jug and basin.   £14

MEISSEN

Meissen ecuelle cover and stand.   £1,000

Meissen Kakiemon dish, 4½ins square.   £140

Rare Meissen pug dog tureen and cover, 7ins long, cross swords mark in blue.   £1,600

Early Meissen figure of a
Pagod in a pavilion, circa
1715, 6¾ins.   £26,000

Pair of Meissen jardinieres with
mask handles, decorated with
harbour scenes.   £140

An 18th century Meissen
porcelain snuffbox, the
top depicting the rape of
Silesia by Frederick the
Great, 3 1/8ins diam.
14,500gns

A pair of Meissen pagoda
figures by J.J. Kandler,
7¼ins high.   £1,450

German Meissen porcelain
snuffbox decorated to
commemorate the First
Silesian War by Johann Jacob
Wagner, with English gold
mount.   £15,225

A pair of 19th century Meissen
style porcelain pot pourri vases
with pierced domed covers,
painted with flowers and birds,
14¼ins high.   £185

Meissen Hausmaler milk jug.
£1,550

Set of seven Meissen parasol
handles each in the form of a
brightly coloured 'character'
head.   £190

An early Meissen porcelain
milk jug and cover with its
original silver gilt mounts.
by Elias Adam of Augsburg.
£1,000

A late Meissen figure of a semi-clad pretty young girl, stooping to throw a gilt ball, 14ins high. £130
(King & Chasemore, Pulborough)

Part of a Minton dessert service comprising twenty-two plates and five tazzas. £480

Minton game tureen, circa 1873. £50

Victorian Minton tile. £4.50

19th century Minton swan vase. £30

Pair of 19th century Minton jugs together with matching urn. £110

Three of a set of nine Minton ornithological plates, 9¾ins diam. £290

19th century porcelain bowl bearing a mark in Mangolian script 'Baragon Tumed', on the base. £80

A mid 16th century Turkish pottery polychrome deep dish, 11¾ins diam. £480

A Kornileffe Bros. ink stand pentray decorated with polychrome floral sprigs and gilding. £62

Early 20th century St. Cecilia studio pottery vase. £17

Pair of decorated pottery dishes by H. Schiltt. £240

Late 15th century Faenza alberello painted in colours with a portrait of a girl. £6,600

A medium blue and white copy of the Barberini vase, cracked, 11ins high. £60

A majolica plate, the central reserve showing a satyrical peeping tom watching two ladies having a bathe in a lagoon, 11¾ins diam. £27,000

A globular blue jug of Arabic origin, 9ins high. £3.50

A fine Victorian pot lid showing a swallow. £120

A pair of Continental grey ground Amphora shaped vases decorated with gilt and black circular motifs, 15ins high. £18

Porcelain ice-bucket from the Nymphenburg factory, 6½ins high. £500

A pair of Cantonese porcelain baluster shaped vases, decorated with panels of court scenes and dancers, Chinese, circa 1800, (handles restored), 25ins high.   £640

(King & Chasemore, Pulborough)

ORIENTAL

Two Chinese porcelain spill vases decorated in blue with figures and landscapes, 12ins high. £34

A chinese unglazed pottery figure standing in gathered robes and a dignitary's crown, 20½ins high. £48

A pair of 19th century Oriental hexagonal porcelain urns. £310

Tang H'si shallow dish, 15½ins diam. £260

A pair of blanc-de-chine porcelain liberation cups of the Ch'ien Lung period, 4¼ins high. £34

One of a pair of famille rose porcelain plates of the Ch'ien Lung period, 9ins diam. £180

Pair of enamelled Kakiemon tigers seated on rockwork, 25cm high, late 17th century. £8,190

A Japanese china baluster shaped vase decorated with a figure in famille verte colours, 18½ins high. £12

Pair of 19th century Oriental vases, 13ins high. £195

One of a pair of Ch'ien Lung export plates decorated with hunting scenes. £460

Large pair of 19th century multi-coloured Oriental vases, 24ins high. £350

One of a pair of famille rose porcelain plates of the Ch'ien Lung period, 9ins diam. £85

Early 19th century
Chinese sang de boeuf
vase in ovoid form.   £65

Two of a set of four famille rose plates.   £640

An 18th century famille
rose bottle vase.   £40

A 19th century Chinese
porcelain jardiniere with
blue and white prunus
flower decoration, 8ins
high.   £18

16th century Chinese porcelain
dish, decorated with a fish
design, 6¾ins diam.   28,000gns

Early 19th century Chinese
porcelain tea caddy with
English silver collar and lid,
hallmarked London, 1828,
maker W.B.   £140

A rare 14th century
underglaze red bowl.
£44,100

A blue and white Chinese
porcelain lidded jug. £50

A 19th century Chinese
porcelain jardiniere, 7ins
diam.   £25

One of a pair of blue and white
Chinese crackleware baluster
shaped vases, one decorated
with kylins, the other with
dragons, 10¼ins high.   £32

One of a pair of Chinese
glazed pottery horses with
cropped and bound tails,
two colour, with green
highlights.   £750

One of a pair of blue and white
prunus pattern baluster shaped
ginger jars and covers, with two
wooden stands.   £48

ORIENTAL

CHINA

19th century Japanese imari ovoid jar and cover, 7ins high.   £50

18th century Chinese export plate, the border of an escalloped ribbon, the centre a figure group containing Britannia.   £125

An exceptionally fine Chinese porcelain moon flask.   £165,757

19th century Chinese rectangular blue and white jardiniere, 13ins high.   £300

A fine Chinese blue and white cylindrical brush pot, on three simple bracket feet, circa 1650, 5¾ins high.   £420

One of a pair of Chinese stoneware fish tanks with dragons and scroll designs, 20ins diam., 20ins high.   £85

One of a pair of 19th century Japanese double-gourd vases decorated with horses in iron red and gilt, 15¼ins high. £230

A Japanese blue and white petal edged plate decorated with flowers, fence and birds, 12½ins diam.   £18

Early 19th century Chinese bottle in double gourd form.   £40

A large Japanese blue and white petal edged fruit bowl, 13¼ins diam. £28

A fine and rare Chinese porcelain Imperial dragon, standing on intricately carved wood stand surmounting carved base, 15ins x 8½ins wide.   £550

A Japanese dish with hexagonal lotus panelled edge, decorated with a pattern of leaves, 14½ins diam.   £48

CHINA
ORIENTAL

A rare blue and white porcelain stem cup and stand of the Hsuan Te period, 4ins high. £1,550

A 19th century copy of a Wan Li baluster vase decorated in underglaze blue £20

Baluster shaped porcelain vase decorated with famille rose enamels, Tao Kuang period, 7¼ins high. £18

A Japanese copy of a Yung Cheng bottle vase. £38

T'ang dynasty ceramic figure of a horse, the body covered in a finely crackled chestnut glaze, 24ins long. £25,000

A Kuang Tung ware white plate banded in pale blue with a polychrome foliage pattern, 14¾ins diam. £30

Chinese green glazed pottery dog of the Han dynasty, 13½ins long. £2,400

One of a pair of famille rose vases, 17½ins high. £220

Blue and white Nankin tankard with delicate geometric border around rim, the body decorated with a landscape scene, circa 1790, 4½ins high. £38

A superb Ch'ia Ch'ing fish bowl, 15½ins high. £2,100

A very rare late 18th century Nankin porcelain supper set, in blue and white, circa 1780. £125

A fourteenth century Mei P'ing of octagonal section, painted in blue with shaped panels of flowers. £231,000

One of a pair of Chinese, Ch'ien Lung period fish bowls painted in famille rose colours, 61cm diam. £2,500

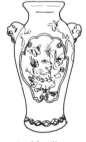

One of a pair of famille rose baluster vases, 14½ins high. £180

CANTON

Cantonese ceramic verandah seat, 1860, 19ins high. £200

A pair of Cantonese famille rose vases, 35ins high. £1,500

CHINA

A large Canton china baluster shaped vase, decorated with panels and figures and flowers, 23½ins high. £40

19th century·Canton vase, 24ins tall. £45

Pair of 19th century Cantonese vases, 26ins high. £160

19th century Canton dish, 12ins diam. £55

FAMILLE VERTE

A K'ang Hsi famille verte tea caddy, 6¼ins high. £155

Famille verte rectangular teapot and cover with simulated bamboo handle, (knob restored). £140

A famille verte tea caddy. £195

A small 19th century famille verte bowl. £10

Famille Verte porcelain teapot of the K'ang Hsi period. £295

A famille verte perfume casket of square section, on four cabriole feet, 5ins high, K'ang Hsi. £80

CHINA
CH'IEN LUNG

Pair of Ch'ien Lung period
Chinese bowls and covers in
spinach-green jade. £14,000

A Ch'ien Lung blue and white
vase. £70

A Ch'ien Lung famille
rose kendi, 6¾ins high.
£260

One of a pair of famille rose
porcelain plates of the Ch'ien
Lung period, 9ins diam. £85

A large blue and white Ch'ien
Lung plate decorated with
flowers and shrubs and rust and
gilt ducks, 15¼ins diam. £18

Ch'ien Lung blue and white
charger decorated with a
hunting scene, 17ins diam. £80

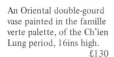

An Oriental double-gourd
vase painted in the famille
verte palette, of the Ch'ien
Lung period, 16ins high.
£130

A good pair of Ch'ien Lung
rose porcelain Ku of square
section, the central sections
with small landscape panels.
£250

A Chinese porcelain group
of the Ch'ien Lung period,
painted in famille rose
enamels. £1,400

A K'ang Hsi baluster vase with cut down neck decorated in the famille verte style, 11½ins high. £92

One of a pair of K'ang Hsi shaped enamel-sur-bisque dishes. £220

K'ang Hsi period blue and white vase, 8½ins high. £75

A K'ang Hsi shallow dish, decorated with floral design. £280

A large K'ang Hsi famille verte dish decorated with two figures beneath a tree, 15½ins diam. £35

A famille verte deep circular dish of the K'ang Hsi period, decorated with floral designs, 14½ins diam. £740

A fine Chinese rouleau vase, of the K'ang Hsi period, 17¾ins high. £680

A fine pair of K'ang Hsi famille verte porcelain bottles. £220

19th century Chinese vase, painted in the underglaze blue and green manner of the K'ang Hsi period, 17½ins high. £250

CHINA
IMARI

A pair of 19th century Japanese Imari baluster vases, 12½ins high. £85

A pair of 19th century Japanese Imari baluster vases, 12ins high. £80

An Imari circular box and lid decorated in underglaze blue with panels of rust and green chrysanthemums. £28

A 19th century Japanese Imari jardiniere, 13ins diam. £68

A 19th century Japanese imari dish, 11½ins diam. £52

Imari temple vase in multi-colour with cartouches of prunus blossoms and kiri flowers, signed Fukushina. £375

A 20th century Imari plate decorated with six panels of birds and flowers in polychrome, 12½ins diam. £18

SATSUMA

A pair of blue Satsuma baluster shaped vases decorated with panels containing poly-chrome figure scenes, 10½ins high. £14

Outstanding Japanese satsuma bowl with a gilt encrusted pictorial scene of the arrival of Chinese envoys, dated 1804. £500

A pair of Satsuma brown and green tapered cylindrical vases, 11ins high. £8.50

An Imari porcelain vase and cover, decorated with shaped floral panels, the cover surmounted by a Shishi, Japanese, early 19th century, 27½ins high. £480

(King & Chasemore, Pulborough)

CHINA
PARIS

Pair of Paris porcelain vases decorated with country scenes, 21ins high. £200

Pair of Paris vases with rich gilt necks, feet and scroll handles, 18¾ins high. £130

An attractive Paris porcelain plinth, finely painted with a woodland scene, 10ins diam. £28

Pair of Paris figures, 8ins high. £40

Paris vase by Francois Boucher. £300

POOLE

Poole pottery two-handled vase, circa 1924. £20

Poole pottery fish glazed in green with a black base, 17ins high. £50

Poole pottery unglazed jug, 8ins high, 1930. £20

Poole pottery vase with impressed mark, Carter Stabler Adams Ltd., England, 18ins high, 1927. £55

Poole pottery green glazed vase with sculptured handles in white, circa 1925. £40

Poole pottery vase by Truda Carter, circa 1927, 8ins high. £10

188

PLYMOUTH

A pair of Plymouth porcelain figures of a Toper and a Musician, 15cm high, circa 1770. £892.50

Two Plymouth figures of a gardener and his companion. £1,200

SALTGLAZE

Octagonal saltglaze plate. £235

An amusing saltglaze fish gin flask with impressed scales, fins and cork in opened mouth, 12ins long, circa 1820. £38

Gigantic and very heavily saltglazed stoneware ale pitcher, the handle formed from a greyhound, 10ins high, circa 1830. £48

SEVRES

Pair of Sevres pattern vases and covers, 11½ins high. £95

Pair of early 19th century Sevres vases. £1,950

One of a set of eleven Sevres plates, 9ins diam. £240

Sevres part dessert service of six pieces. £1,200

189

Pair of Sevres jardinieres decorated
with a continuous band of figures in
a garden, having ormolu mount, 8¾ins
high.   £220

Pair of Sevres pattern ormolu mounted
vases painted with the Birth of Jesus
and the Triumph of Ariadne, 34ins high.
                                        £1,550

Pair of 19th century ormolu
mounted Sevres decorated
vases, 29ins high.   £660

Sevres pattern cabaret set
richly decorated on a blue
ground, in a fitted leather
case.   £450

Pair of ormolu mounted
Sevres pattern vases and
covers, 25ins high. £600

A Sevres part dessert service painted with cupids, clouds and birds, on a bleu-de-roi ground with gilt
border.
                                                                        £1,200

A pair of Sevres covered vases with pierced
gilt ormolu galleries.   £700

Pair of Sevres pattern turquoise ground vases
and covers, 13ins high.   £250

Sevres ice cup decorated
with Angouleme springs.
£30

Sevres part cabaret service bearing the dateteller 1769. £520

One of a pair of Sevres covered
vases of compressed pear
shape, 7¾ins high, 1754. £220

A pair of Sevres style vases. £2,000

A pair of Sevres style vases,
decorated with domestic
scenes.   £780

Sevres pattern cabaret set painted with lovers in landscapes.   £210

An important pair of Sevres vases of urn shape
with gilt ormolu mask head handles, 25¼ins
high, 1764.   £940

Pair of Sevres oviform vases with gilt acorn finials,
15ins high, 1755.   £820

Above: An oval plaque decorated with a print after Sir David Wilkie, R.A., with the title "The Blind Fiddler" to the reverse, and the words "D. Wilkie Del" at the foot of the plaque.   £24

Below: An oval plaque decorated with a print after Sir Edwin Landseer, R.A., with the title "Highland Music" to the reverse, and the words "E. Landseer, R.A., Pinx" at the foot of the plaque. £30

(King & Chasemore, Pulborough)

STAFFORDSHIRE

CHINA

Equestrian figure of Marshal Arnaud. £200

Pair of figures depicting Uncle Tom and Aunt Chloe, 8¾ins high. £150

Equestrian figure of Abd-Ul-Medjid, Sultan ·of Turkey, 11ins high. £250

Staffordshire group of Giaffier and Zuleika, 12½ins high. £60

Rare figure of the champion greyhound Master M'Grath. £170

Figure of Jenny Lind as Alice in Meyerbeers opera, 13¾ins high. £260

A group of the Cushmen sisters as Romeo and Juliet, 10½ins high. £100

Pair of figures depicting Victoria and Albert, 11½ins high. £90

Rare figure of Omer Pasha on a black horse. £170

Equestrian figure of Omer Pasha. £170

Pair of figures of Uncle Tom and Eva, 8ins high. £70

A figure of a cricketer standing before a wicket, 9½ins high. £50

193

CHINA
STAFFORDSHIRE

Staffordshire group of gypsies under a grape bower, named 'Fortune Teller', circa 1860, 12ins high. £38

A rare Staffordshire group of three figures, named 'Turkey, England & France', depicting Abdul-Medjid, Queen Victoria and Napoleon III, circa 1854, 11¼ins high. £78

19th century Staffordshire pottery portrait named group of 'King and Queen of Sardinia', showing Queen Victoria and V. Emmanuel II, 13½ins high. £38

Staffordshire pottery watch stand, in the form of a castle, circa 1850, 10¼ins high. £38

A pair of Staffordshire figures of the 'Prince of Wales' and 'The Queen of England', 18ins and 17½ins respectively. £65

A fine unrecorded Staffordshire figure of Milton, resting on a pedestal and holding a book, 9ins high. £68

An unrecorded Staffordshire figure of William Shakespeare, 9ins high. £58

An amusing pair of rough chip coated poodles in Staffordshire pottery, circa 1850, 10½ins high. £58

19th century Staffordshire figure of a young girl holding a lamb, 9ins high, circa 1860. £18

A Staffordshire clock group of Napoleon I and Wellington, 9½ins high, circa 1847. £50

A very rare Staffordshire flat back orange cow, originally used as a dairy shop sign, circa 1845, 13ins high, 13½ins long. £68

A Staffordshire group of Miss Glover and Mrs. Vining as 'Yourawkee and Peter Wilkins', 7½ins high, circa 1840. £45

Staffordshire flat back group named "Prince and Princess", showing the Prince of Wales and Princess Alexandra of Denmark, 12ins high. £32

Staffordshire flat back group depicting a young man and woman with baskets of flowers, standing either side of a clock, circa 1860, 12½ins high. £28

A fine Staffordshire flat back group of a huntsman with a blunderbuss and orange spaniel, circa 1850, 13¼ins high. £28

A rare Staffordshire pottery castle, named 'Sebastopol', circa 1855. £38

Old Staffordshire group of a courting couple, circa 1855, 10ins high. £22

Staffordshire flat back Gothic castle, in pink buff, circa 1850, 9ins high. £19

A tall Staffordshire figure of an unidentified huntsman, with dead deer, 17¾ins high. £28

A pair of Staffordshire King Charles Spaniels, white with gilt spots, circa 1855, 10ins high. £35

Staffordshire figure named 'Warrior' with a seated soldier wearing chain mail and holding regimental flags, circa 1860, 14½ins high. £35

A Staffordshire clock group of Mrs. Siddons as Lady Macbeth and John Phillip Kemble as 'Hamlet', circa 1850, 8½ins high. £38

An early Staffordshire cow creamer decorated in tan and sepia, on an octagonal green base, 8ins long. £32

An unusual Staffordshire group of a man playing a fiddle and a girl playing a banjo, named 'Minstrels', circa 1870, 11ins high. £27

A Staffordshire vase group of a cow and calf, circa 1855, 11ins high.   £35

Staffordshire blue and white transfer meat platter, circa 1910, 19ins long. £25

Staffordshire group of unidentified theatrical figures, 14ins high. £38

A pair of Staffordshire opaque-white glass tea caddies, 14.2cm high.
£2,300

An early square based Staffordshire figure of 'Winter', circa 1795, 7ins high.   £38

A Staffordshire flat back figure of Louis Napoleon, 16¼ins high.   £39

Staffordshire Gothic Castle, on green and brown rocky base, originally used as a pastille burner, circa 1840, 6½ins high.   £45

An English Staffordshire pottery slipware dish by Samuel Malkin, circa 1712.   £8,400

A very rare Staffordshire toby jug in the form of a King Charles Spaniel, with blue scroll handle, circa 1850, 8ins high.   £34

A Staffordshire figure, "Lewis Nepolian". £70

A pair of Staffordshire King Charles Spaniels, coloured black and white with gilt collars, 12½ins high, circa 1850.   £48

A Staffordshire figure of "Lord Raglan". £170.

STAFFORDSHIRE

Staffordshire cow named 'Milk Sold Here'. £75

A Staffordshire zebra on base of green rocks, circa 1845, 9ins high. £38

Rare Staffordshire 'Jumbo'. £175

An attractive Staffordshire group of Siamese twins, 11½ins high, circa 1850. £48

Very large cup and saucer in Flo blue underglaze pottery, decorated with a figure on a bridge, Royal Staffordshire Pottery, Burslem, circa 1885. £26

Staffordshire figure of Christ, 16½ins high. £45

A well modelled Staffordshire figure of a sportsman with falcon and orange coloured setter, circa 1845, 15ins high. £48

A tulip girl Staffordshire slipware dish, by Ralph Toft, 16¾ins diam. £7,500

19th century Staffordshire pottery jug showing two hunting scenes, 6½ins high. £40

"Marshall Arnaud", a Staffordshire figure. £160

A rare pair of Staffordshire pugs, white with black markings, circa 1865, 10½ins high. £85

A Staffordshire figure, "The Sultan". £180

CHINA
SPODE

"Tower" two-handled covered centre bowl, marked Spode.   £39

A very rare marked Spode "Forest Landscape" dog's dish.   £45

A marked Spode comport, 'Long Elizas'.   £39

"Tiber" plate with pierced edge, marked Spode.   £21.50

"Gothic Castle", vegetable tureen, marked Spode. £25

Marked Spode cheese dish base, 'Driving a Bear from Sugar Canes',   £20

VIENNESE

19th century Viennese porcelain plaque signed F. Lezleh, 16ins diam.   £400

19th century Viennese porcelain plaque depicting King Neptune.   £460

19th century Viennese porcelain plaque signed F. Lezleh. £320

WEDGWOOD

Wedgwood dark yellow, black and white jasper vase and cover, 7½ins high.   £320

19th century Wedgwood blue and white teapot.   £25

Copy of the Portland vase by Josiah Wedgwood, circa 1790.   £18,000

19th century impressed upper 'case Wedgwood botanical plate, 9¼ins diam.   £12

A pair of Wedgwood black and basalt busts, 9¼ins high.   £360

An unusual Wedgwood punch-bowl, the interior painted in black and sepia enamels with various masonic emblems.   £480

A rare Wedgwood caneware bulb trough, 14½ins long.   £320

Wedgwood green and white jasper plaque, depicting classical figures.   £170

A marked Wedgwood ashet, 8ins long.   £10.50

19th century Wedgwood vase and stand.   £170

Teapot and stand in the Wedgwood style by James Dudson Brothers, circa 1900.   £20

A pair of 19th century Wedgwood white stoneware covered urns, mounted with girdles of dancing women.   £310

An unusual pair of Wedgwood black basalt vases, with Art Nouveau raised design of entwined ivy and fuchsias, circa 1900.   £58

CHINA
WORCESTER

A Royal Worcester vase and cover, the body painted by John Stinton, signed, 16½ins high, 1898.   £700

A pair of Royal Worcester vases decorated with peacocks in the desert, circa 1911.   £1,000

A fine first period Worcester blue and white bottle vase with knopped and flared trumpet neck, 11ins high.   £280

Worcester Barr part dessert service.   £720

A Chamberlain's Worcester part dessert service with apple green border and centres, painted with botanical flowers, comprising three shaped dishes, and three plates.   £155

Worcester blue-ground loving-cup with fruit decoration.   £190

A very fine Worcester butter tub, cover and stand, painted in the "Earl Manvers" pattern, circa 1770.   £3,200

First period Worcester coffee pot.   £420

A 19th century Worcester hexagonal vase and cover, 25ins high.   £75

A pair of Royal Worcester vases painted by Harry Davis, bearing the date mark for 1911. £1,400

Royal Worcester vase with a highland cattle scene on a blue ground, 20½ins high. £1,020

Worcester porcelain tea cup, coffee cup and saucer. £300

Worcester porcelain shell dish on three ball feet, 9ins long, circa 1895.   £25

A 19th century Worcester blue and white pickle dish.   £33

A Worcester sauceboat with workman's mark, imperfect. £50

A Worcester Flight Barr and Barr dessert service decorated in rouge de fer, red, blue and gilt with gadrooned border, comprising two small tureens and covers, one large comport, three oval dishes, four square dishes, three shell dishes and twenty one side plates. (36).   £340

Worcester pot pourri bowl
and cover.   £200

Worcester blue and white
tureen and cover, circa 1758.
£240

One of a set of six Worcester
sweetmeat dishes.   £300

Worcester blue and white bowl
depicting an Oriental scene,
circa 1758.   £750

Worcester blue and white vase,
22ins high, circa 1753.   £600

First period Worcester plate.
£120

One of a pair of Worcester
custard cups and covers, Davis
Flight period.   £80

One of a set of ten Worcester
dessert plates, each finely
painted by E. Salter.   £95

One of a pair of first period
Worcester bell shaped cups,
2½ins high.   £85

Worcester cup and saucer,
circa 1840.   £10

Royal Worcester soup
tureen, 1903.   £48

Dr. Wall period cup and
saucer.   £130

Royal Worcester Ewer. £525

(Henry Spencer & Sons, Retford)

An attractive 18th century miniature bracket clock by Williamson of London, 12ins high. £1,100

(King & Chasemore, Pulborough)

A 19th century Gothic-style rosewood bracket clock. £245

19th century bracket clock chiming on eight bells and with Westminster chimes. £520

Bracket clock with quarter chime on eight bells in an ebonised case with ormolu mounts. £835

A striking bracket clock in an ebonised case, of 18th century design with domed hood and brass handle and mounts, by R. Bryson & Sons, Edinburgh, 21 ins high, circa 1850. £140

A fine 19th century rosewood bracket clock with silent and chime on eight bells and Westminster, 32ins high. £390

George III bracket clock, by John Skinner, Exeter. £420

Mahogany bracket clock with silvered dial and lever escapement, circa 1830. £365

A large mahogany bracket clock, with musical chiming movement, and a silvered and chased dial, by James Hardy & Co., Aberdeen, circa 1850, 28ins high. £480

A very fine bracket clock by Daniel Quare. £16,000

BRACKET CLOCKS

An 18th century bracket clock by Williamson of London, with verge escapement, 12ins high. £1,100

Verge bracket clock, in ebonised case, with silvered brass dial, by Robert Ward, London. £595

Late Georgian bracket clock, hour striking on two bells with repeat mechanism, by John Bennett of London. £385

An Edwardian bracket clock with chime action. £190

18th century mahogany bracket clock with domed hood, brass acorn mount and brass inset spandrels, by James Cowan, Edinburgh. £580

An 18th century ebonised bracket clock, with silverised and chased arched brass dial, and strike and second movements, by John Fladgate, London, 18ins high. £420

Mahogany bracket clock with strike/silent regulation, centre sweep date hand, and engraved backplate and pendulum, by Phillip Gullock, Rochford, circa 1785. £775

A George III bracket clock, by John Skinner, Exon. £420

A late 18th century mahogany cased bracket clock by Thomas Simson. £450

Mahogany verge bracket clock with strike/silent regulation, date aperture and attractively engraved backplate, by Winch of Maidenhead. £745

Striking Regency mahogany bracket clock with silvered dial and brass stringing, by Runge. £310

A fine bracket clock, by John Moore & Sons, Clerkenwell. £150

A 19th century bracket clock, 25½ins high. £340

A large mahogany bracket clock with stepped domed hood, and silverised and chased brass dial, striking on eight bells, by James Hardy & Co., Aberdeen, circa 1850, 28ins high. £420

A walnut, quarter-repeating bracket timepiece, the case veneered in finely figured walnut, by Thomas Tompion, 12½ins high. £15,000

An 18th century mahogany bracket clock with domed top and brass carrying handle, by George F. Coldway, Strand, London, 19ins high. £500

A carved oak bracket clock with domed and canopy top, the silverised arched dial with musical striking movement, by Benson, London, 2ft high. £160

Ebonised two-train bracket clock, with shaped silvered brass dial, strike/silent regulation, by Walter Barry of London, circa 1790. £995

A mid 18th century musical bracket clock by John Smith of London, 21½ins high. £850

(King & Chasemore, Pulborough)

Gilt metal cased lever
movement carriage clock.
£240

Brass cased repeater
carriage clock with
lever movement. £240

Serpentine front brass
cased carriage clock
with lever movement.
£270

Miniature gilt cased alarm
carriage timepiece, 3ins
high. £180

Early 19th century repeater
carriage clock with alarm.
£700

Gilt metal and bevelled
glass cased carriage
timepiece, 4½ins high.
£100

Gilt metal cased repeating
carriage clock, 6ins high.
£230

Miniature carriage timepiece
contained in a gilt metal
case, 3ins high. £110

Gilt metal cased
repeating alarm carriage
clock, 5¼ins high. £180

CARRIAGE CLOCKS

A fine 19th century carriage timepiece, with original lever escapement.   £97

A small 19th century cased carriage clock.   £120

An early alarm carriage clock, with original cylinder escapement.   £147

A very fine Breguet brass-cased carriage clock with repeater and alarm movement, 5½ins high.   £5,000

A mid 19th century half hour striking repeating carriage clock with alarm, the white enamel dial and backplate inscribed Dent a Paris.   £375

Corinthian columned case grande-sonnerie carriage clock, 6½ins high.   £750

A brass carriage clock, striking the quarter hour, with a repeating movement.   £210

An oval cased hour and half-hour strike and repeat carriage clock, 6ins high.   £485

Mid 19th century English carriage clock with repeater and alarm, the dial with engine-turned surround, numbered 396 and with initials JS.   £240

Late 19th century timepiece with original cylinder escapement.   £78

19th century engraved carriage clock with a lever movement, push repeat, alarm and grande sonnerie, 6ins high.   £900

19th century brass carriage clock, with chased case and decorated dial.   £190

A fine French carriage clock.   £1,800

A fine quality French carriage clock, the movement contained in a gorge case inset with porcelain.   £1,800

Late 19th century timepiece alarm, with original lever escapement.   £136

Late 19th century French enamel brass carriage clock with pastoral scenes, on bracket feet.   £210

A French Champleve enamel brass carriage clock, with bevel glazed door, standing on bun feet, circa 1900.   £180

A late 19th century Champleve enamel carriage clock with white enamel dial within foliate border.   £215

CARRIAGE CLOCKS

A fine quarter striking and repeat carriage clock by Margaine, with subsiduary alarm. £445

A carriage clock with white enamel dial, in brass case, 3ins high. £66

A carriage clock with white enamelled dial by Parkins & Co., London, in brass case, 3½ins high. £48

A French carriage clock in brass case, 4½ins high. £55

A silver-cased grande-sonnerie carriage clock. £15,225

A fine grande sonnerie carriage clock with fretted and engraved mask to blue enamel dial. £775

A French carriage striking clock in brass and glazed case, 5ins high. £90

A French carriage clock in brass and glazed case, 4¼ ins high. £28

Miniature carriage clock by Margaine, timepiece only. £220

Strike and repeat carriage clock in fine quality brass case, with alarm and music box mechanism.   £1,250

A French carriage clock with white enamel dial, by J. Bennet, in engraved brass and glazed case, 5ins high.   £80

Superb grande sonnerie carriage clock by Drocourt, signed on dial and underneath.   £925

Cylindrical brass cased carriage clock with lever movement.   £280

A small grande-sonnerie carriage clock with masked dial and alarm, 4½ins high.   £740

An oval strike and repeat carriage clock.   £370

A French carriage striking clock, in brass case, 5ins high.   £125

A Breguet carriage clock.   £5,000

A miniature carriage clock in brass and glazed case, 2¾ins high.   £64

An English brass carriage clock by Dent of Cockspur Street, London, 8ins high. £620
(King & Chasemore, Pulborough)

A Louis XVI style gilt metal clock set, inset with china plaques, the clock 22ins high, the vases 18ins.   £260

Three-piece marble and ormolu clock set.   £380

19th century French ormolu clock set by Robin a Paris, 12ins high.   £260

Ormolu and cloisonne enamel French striking clock with matching ornaments, circa 1860.   £515

French Empire ormolu and blue porcelain garniture de Cheminee.   £170

A French brass garniture de cheminee of clock with two figures of Roman soldiers and a pair of double handled vases, the clock 13ins high, vases 8½ins high.   £170

A French champleve enamel and brass clock set, circa 1900, the clock 1ft 3½ins high, the urns 10ins high.
                £660

A white onyx, marble and ormolu French striking clock with matching sidepieces.
                £495

19th century French
marble and ormolu
mounted striking clock.
£295

A French Empire style gilt
metal clock set, the clock
17¼ins high, the two vases
12½ins high.   £340

A French bronze and porcelain
clock set, the dial and side
panels painted with figures by
H. Desprey, the clock 15ins high,
the two vases 10½ins high.   £120

Mid 19th century French
mantel garniture of ormolu
and porcelain.   £720

GRANDFATHER CLOCKS

A fine green lacquer longcase clock, with eight day movement, by Wm. Martin of Bristol, circa 1720, 78ins high. £825

A quarter chiming grandmother clock in walnut case. £475

A longcase clock by Obadiah Brandreth of Middlewich, in an oak case crossbanded in mahogany, 84ins high, circa 1770. £375

A mahogany grandmother clock with chased brass and silverised dial. £140

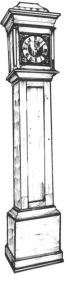

Stripped pine longcase clock, with single hand and brass dial, by Rick Felton, Bridnorth. £270

18th century mahogany longcase clock, with brass and silvered dial and brass weights. £385

A small Mahogany longcase clock converted to a regulator by Brockbank, Atkins and Moore, in 1891 £775

Green lacquer eight day clock by Thomas Bennet, London, with five pillar movement. £985

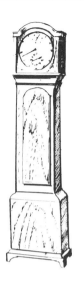

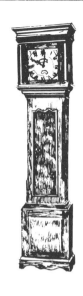

Early 19th century mahogany longcase regulator, signed on dial, S. Marks, Cowbridge.   £1,085

An oak longcase clock by Stevenson, Drayton, with brass face, 82ins high.
£325

Three train mahogany longcase clock with moon phases, quarter chiming on either four or eight bells.   £895

A fine 19th century longcase regulator, by Frodsham, with Graham dead beat escapement, the case re-veneered in walnut.
£1,175

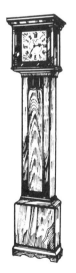

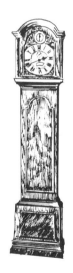

Mahogany grandmother clock with early 19th century weight-driven movement and later case.
£425

Early 19th century oak and mahogany longcase clock with eight day movement.   £200

Walnut longcase clock, the five pillar movement with strike/silent regulation by Wentworth, London, circa 1750.
£1,275

A superb early 18th century marquetry longcase clock, the movement of one month duration, by Robert Williamson of London. £4,100

GRANDFATHER CLOCKS

A fine longcase clock by Andrew Dunlop, in a lacquer case, circa 1720. £1,075

A continental longcase clock in carved oak case, decorated in the style of Teniers and having Westminster and Whittington chimes. £1,350

A fine early 18th century longcase clock, in a superb walnut marquetry case, by Robert Williamson, London. £4,100

A good quality mahogany longcase clock with a five-pillar movement, by James Smith, circa 1780. £750

A mid 18th century grandfather clock by Francis Dorrell in a 19th century carved oak case. £680

An unusual 19th century satinwood and marquetry domestic letterbox, with eight day movement, by Houghton & Gunn, Bond Street, 25ins high. £70

An early 18th century longcase clock with brass dial and red gilt lacquered case, by Thomas Gorsuch, Salop. £880

Early 18th century long-case clock with lacquered chinoiserie decoration, by Robert Sadler, London. £380

220

A longcase clock by George Etherington, with observation window in the door.
£1,050

Mahogany longcase clock by Bowen, London, the five pillar movement with strike/silent regulation, circa 1780.
£765

Longcase clock by Delander, with arched dial and eight day movement.
£875

A fine mahogany long-case clock with string inlay, brass finials and fittings, by W & C Nicolas of Birmingham, circa 1840, 89ins high.
£285

Longcase regulator by Pennlington and Batty, with Graham dead beat escapement, maintaining power.
£745

Mahogany longcase clock by Hilton-Wray of London, circa 1770.
£1,265

A fine quality mahogany longcase regulator of month duration, circa 1820.
£1,375

An early 19th century mahogany cased regu-lator clock, the move-ment inscribed 'F.T. Depree, Exeter', 6ft 9ins high.
£925

221

GRANDFATHER CLOCKS

Late Georgian country oak longcase clock, of eight day duration. £100

An oak longcase clock, signed Walker of Loughborough. £150

Longcase clock by Cowsin of Lincoln, with broken arch pediment. £440

An oak longcase clock, with painted arched dial by James Cameron, Selkirk. £110

18th century mahogany longcase clock by John Fletcher of Holbeck. £510

Early 18th century black lacquered, eight day longcase clock with brass dial, by Chas. Stordart. £600

Early 19th century longcase clock with shaped pediment and eight day movement. £100

Early 19th century oak thirty hour longcase clock, with striking birdcage movement, brass dial signed "Archer, Stow". £100

A grandfather clock with brass arched dial by Robert Sadler of London, in lacquered chinoiserie case. £380

An early 18th century longcase month clock by George Etherington, with a matt brass dial, in an ebonised case. £1,050

A small mahogany longcase clock with fine semi-regulator movement by Brock, Lewisham, 6ft 8ins high, circa 1830. £395

A fine mahogany longcase clock with eight day movement by John Ewer of London, circa 1760. £865

19th century mahogany longcase clock with eight day striking movement. £100

19th century mahogany longcase clock, with circular enamel dial, by Wm. Young, Dundee. £85

A magnificent musical longcase clock, by Hugh Lough, Penrith, dated 1775, with six-pillar, three-train movement, and a strike playing 14 tunes in all, 7ft 10ins high. £3,200

Fine mid 18th century oak-cased thirty-hour clock, by George Payne of Ludlow. £245

GRANDFATHER CLOCKS

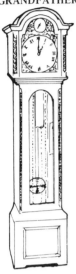

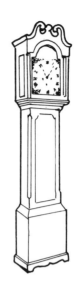

Edwardian longcase clock with brass and silverised dial, in a glazed oak case. £260

A fine floral marquetry longcase clock by D. Lestourgeon. £2,100

Longcase clock by James Menzies, Perth, circa 1820, in a finely figured mahogany case. £270

Floral marquetry longcase clock with 11ins square brass dial, circa 1705, £1,850

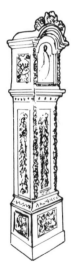

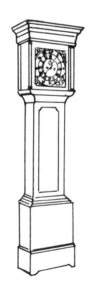

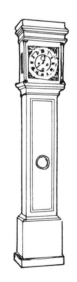

19th century elaborately carved oak grandfather clock with chased brass dial and chiming movement. £540

An oak cased longcase clock inscribed Grice. £155

A good walnut longcase clock by Windmills, London, circa 1710. £1,850

Walnut longcase clock by John Bevrg, London. £975

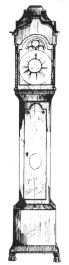

Late 18th century mahogany cased eight day grandfather clock with satinwood inlay. £270

A superb 18th century longcase clock with marquetry decoration to the case. £1,780

Early 18th century Dutch longcase clock by Nicholas Dornheck of Amsterdam. £1,200

Fine eight day clock by Richard Cramp of Canterbury, circa 1770. £825

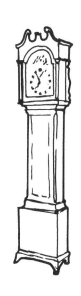

Walnut cased eight day clock by William Wright of Southwark, 7ft 2ins tall. £1,845

George III mahogany longcase clock, signed Thomas Mudge and William Dutton. £850

Dutch walnut marquetry inlaid longcase clock with bombe shaped base and domed hood surmounted with carved giltwood figures, by Van Meurs, Amsterdam. £2,600

Longcase clock by F. Bird, Bristol, 225cm high. £460

225

A 19th century mantel timepiece, the eight day movement signed Vulliamy, London, 13ins high. £580
(King & Chasemore, Pulborough)

A French mantel clock in tortoiseshell Louis XV shaped case with chased brass mounts, the enamel dial inscribed James Crichton & Co., 19ins high. £170

19th century mantel clock in carved mahogany case with domed cornice, 17ins high. £42

A mahogany inlaid mantel clock in lancet shaped case by Hamilton and Inches, Edinburgh, 12½ins high. £23

Louis XV style mantel clock with white enamel dial, the plated case surmounted by a figure of a child, on shell feet, 16½ins high. £140

19th century rosewood cased mantel clock with chain driven eight day striking movement, the backplate inscribed "Arnold Chas. Frodsham . . .". £700

19th century French porcelain mantel clock complete with giltwood stand. £160

Early 19th century eight day mantel clock with cloisonne decoration. £320

A mantel clock in black marble case with Ionic brass pillars and surmounted by a brass bust of Mercury, 18ins wide. £36

A mantel clock in brass case with Ionic pillars and domed top, on a giltwood stand, 16ins high. £125

227

MANTEL CLOCKS

A black and coloured marble mantel clock, with arched cornice and bronze mounts, 20ins high. £15

Late 19th century Dresden mantel clock, with cherub side figures and surmount, 12ins high. £110

Georgian spring clock with eight day fusee movement, the arched silvered dial inscribed W. Howse, London, 18½ins high. £600

Boulle mantel clock, with hour and half-hour strike, by Vincenti, Paris, circa 1860, 12ins high. £335

A Jacobean style carved oak mantel chiming clock, with bronze mounts, 20ins high. £8

An interesting French night clock in the form of a vase. £110

A mahogany inlaid lancet shaped mantel striking clock, on brass feet, 9½ins high. £34

An Edwardian mahogany mantel clock, by Elkington. £10

A brass and plate glass mantel clock, with white enamelled dial, by John Bennet, London, 15ins high. £100

An ebony, walnut and tortoise-shell cased mantel clock with brass and enamel dial, 11½ins high. £42

A French boulle and rosewood mantel clock, in rococo shaped case, with chased brass mounts and feet, by H. Marr, Paris, 17ins high. £150

A walnut clock by Charles Frodsham of London, circa 1830. £375

A timepiece in mahogany inlaid upright shaped case, 12ins high. £30

A mid 17th century Prussian rectangular gilt-metal table clock by Georg. Schultz. £8,400

A miniature carved oak longcase clock with chased brass and silvered dial, 1ft 8ins high. £90

A mantel clock with square brass and silvered dial, in oak case with carved domed hood, 25ins high. £55

A mahogany chiming mantel clock with silvered dial. £11

A walnut cased mantel clock with chiming movement and silvered dial. £22

229

MANTEL CLOCKS

19th century rouge marble mantel clock, mounted with two angelic metal figures, by Henri Marc of Paris. £100

A black coloured marble clock with bronze mounts, 20ins high. £8

Victorian ormolu mantel clock with calendar and lever movement, the dial inscribed by Thomas Agnew & Sons. £750

A 19th century carved and painted wood cuckoo clock. £16

A French gilt metal mantel clock with acorn festoons, trumpets and armour in relief, and surmounted by a figure, 18ins high. £38

A French chased and repousse brass mantel clock, with drop handles and china dial, by Duven, Marsailles, 13½ins high. £190

A burr walnut and brass inlaid mantel clock, with silverised dial, by George Makin & Sons, Manchester, 11½ins high. £500

A Victorian marble mantel clock in drum head, on shaped base with pillars, 18¾ins high. £26

A late 19th century mahogany inlaid mantel clock, 13ins high. £10

A late 19th century mahogany mantel timepiece, by Rattray, Dundee.   £12

French ormolu striking clock with cupid mount and musical motif, 12ins high, 12ins wide, 5ins deep.   £325

French mid 19th century boulle clock in excellent order, 17ins high.   £535

A gilt metal and china striking mantel clock, the painted dial with plaques, figures and flowers, 12½ins high.   £70

A 19th century marble clock, 32½ins high.
£230

19th century red boulle and ebonised French striking clock.   £275

19th century soft metal French mantel clock, with white enamel dial, signed Hry. Marc, Paris.
£34

An astronomical calendar clock in rouge case, by Lister & Son of Newcastle.
£250

A French style gilt metal mantel clock surmounted by a Roman figure and a horse, 18ins high.   £115

MANTEL CLOCKS

Victorian black marble
mantel clock.   £18

A small 19th century timepiece and barometer in brass
horseshoe pattern case, 6ins
wide.   £9

A watch timepiece
on wood stand. £5

Victorian ebonised
clock by Appleby,
Dorchester, 24ins high. £340

19th century Louis XV
style ormolu mantel clock.
                          £300

Victorian oak cased
cuckoo clock, 18ins
high.   £20

Four pillared clock surmounted
by an orrery by Raingo of
Paris, circa 1820.   £4,500

19th century boulle and
ormolu mounted French
striking clock, 10ins high.
                          £395

A 19th century Austrian 'pendule
d'officier', in an ormolu-mounted
engine turned case, supported on
Lion's paw feet, 5ins high.   £310

19th century French ormolu clock set with painted china dial, plaquettes and pillars, 17ins high. £310

Chariot timepiece by James McCabe. £360

A Victorian brass lancet-shaped mantel timepiece, 8ins high. £14

19th century cloisonne and glass sided mantel clock with a mercurial pendulum. £330

19th century spelter mantel clock on a white alabaster base. £22

Victorian, Chinese style brass mantel clock, 18ins high, with enamelled dial. £46

French striking mantel clock in blue cloisonne and polychrome enamel, 17ins high. £395

19th century French ormolu clock of Louis XV style, 8½ins high. £83

An unusual 19th century French brass mantel clock. £110

SKELETON CLOCKS

A fine skeleton timepiece, with five spoke wheels, skeletonised spring barrel and lever escapement.   £425

An attractive small, 19th century skeleton timepiece.   £245

Passing strike, brass framed skeleton clock, on an ebony base.   £185

A late 19th century brass 300 day clock under glass shade.   £10

Rare skeleton clock with twenty four hour dial.   £365

Small skeleton clock, with lyre shaped frame and five spoked wheels.   £215

LANTERN CLOCKS

Brass lantern clock with original Wing movement, 1670.   £800

An 18th century brass lantern clock, 12½ins high.   £340

A 17th century brass lantern clock by William Goodwin of Stowmarket.   £500

An 18th century Swedish cartel clock, signed G. Kjellstrome of Stockholm, 36ins high. £150
(King & Chasemore, Pulborough)

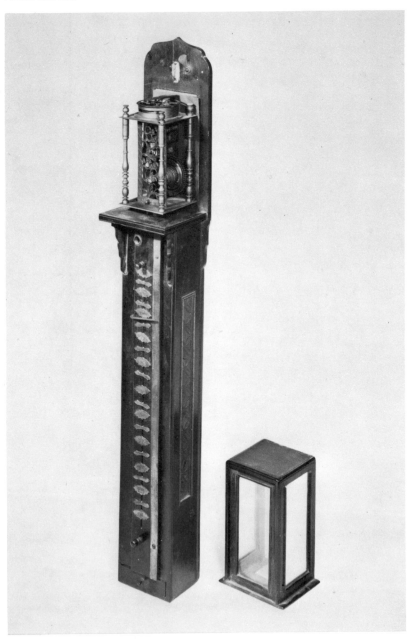

An unusual Japanese wall clock in an ebonised case, 20ins high.   £500
(King & Chasemore, Pulborough)

19th century French bracket clock, inlaid with tortoiseshell in the Boulle manner.　£870

An unusual musical picture clock depicting the Houses of Parliament, circa 1870.　£185

An American walnut wall clock with glazed door and demi pillars to sides.　£54

Victorian mahogany framed regulator wall clock.　£50

18th century Act of Parliament clock by James Wilson of Stamford.　£645

"Salt box" oak-cased wall clock, by William Anness of Cheapside, London, with finely engraved dial and anchor escapement.　£195

Victorian rosewood octagonal wall clock.　£30

Victorian circular wall clock by Jump, London.　£20

Act of Parliament clock.　£620

Louis XV ormolu cartel clock of scrolling foliate design, the case stamped Germain, 16ins high.　£500

A Victorian wall clock in brass case, mounted on a decorated ware wall plaque.　£25

Square wall clock by Charles Rennie Mackintosh, 15ins square.　£960

CLOISONNE

One of a pair of 19th century cloisonne vases. £80

Pair of Japanese bronze and enamelled vases, 7ins high. £45

A 19th century Japanese cloisonne enamel bulbous shape bottle vase, 13ins high. £95

Chinese bronze and cloisonne enamel double handled vase, 14½ins high. £40

Kin Luong cloisonne enamel circular deep dish, 17¾ins diam. £70

Gilt and enamelled double handled vase, 12ins high. £50

Pair of cloisonne enamel vases with green ground, 7ins high. £50

Pair of cloisonne enamel bottle shaped vases with blue ground, 11ins high. £32

Pair of bronze and enamelled barrel shaped vases with ring handles, 12ins high. £65

Chinese bronze circular bowl with inlaid cloisonne banding, 7ins diam. £18

Chinese brass and cloisonne enamel circular jardiniere, 12ins diam.　£48

A large pair of lidded cloisonne bowls of circular shape, the sides banded with cloud collars, 13¼ins diam.　£170

A pair of Chinese cloisonne enamel circular wall plaques of dragon designs within borders, 12ins diam.　£65

A pair of cloisonne enamel vases, 12½ins high.　£19

Mid 17th century Chinese cloisonne pear shaped vase, 20½ins high.　£500

Pair of 19th century cloisonne vases, 19ins high.　£32

A Japanese cloisonne enamel circular wall plaque, depicting a bird and tree.　£45

Pair of 18th century cloisonne enamel incense-burners modelled on standing quail, 5ins high.　£609

A pair of Chinese bronze and coloured enamel hexagonal vases with double ring handles, 11ins.　£60

239

A graduated set of six 18th century-style copper and brass skillets, 16ins to 24ins diam.   £120

(King & Chasemore, Pulborough)

A graduated set of antique copper and wrought iron saucepans, comprising six pans with lids and a matching steam cooker, 5ins to 12ins diameter.   £150

(King & Chasemore, Pulborough)

An old African brass amulet in the form of a mask, 4¼ins high. £20

Victorian copper saucepan complete with lid. £24

Late 18th century copper kettle. £18

A copper circular vase-shaped tea urn with brass handles and spout, 13½ins high. £26

19th century brass kettle with amber glass handle. £24

A copper four gallon measure. £48

Victorian brass cider pail. £15

A large oval copper salmon pan with brass loop handles. £22

18th century copper hot water jug. £15

An Oriental copper circular teapot. £10

An attractive polished steel fire grate, standing on two Adam style tapering fluted legs, with urns surmounting each one, circa 1790. £275

Victorian brass milk churn. £6

241

COPPER & BRASS

Brass and copper bowl on lion paw feet, 18ins diam. £45

Victorian copper jelly mould. £14

One of a pair of handsome Victorian doorstops of horses, circa 1860, 11ins long, 10ins high. £35

Queen Anne scone rack. £19

Pair of cart horse lames, circa 1850. £35

Cast iron horse weathervane, 39ins high, circa 1830. £165

Polished steel, bronze and brass water pump, in working order, circa 1800. £85

Copper frying pan, circa 1780. £38

Set of ten gun-metal standard capacity measures from bushel to quarter gill. £1,000

A steel kettle stand, with brass handles and cabriole legs. £15

19th century Indian brass jardiniere with mask handles. £8

Brass skillet by Jeffries and Price, circa 1710. £49

Small Victorian brass
preserving pan with folding
iron handle.   £6

19th century Butcher's
cleaver.   £18

Copper milkmaid's bucket
with swing over handle,
circa 1820.   £58

Wrought iron trivot,
circa 1740.   £35

An Indian copper and plated
vase-shaped coffee pot and
salver, and an Indian gilt metal
filigree box and cover.   £16

A large copper jardiniere,
20ins diam.   £75

A copper bed warming
pan with turned wood
handle.   £20

A set of three fire implements
with Adam style handles. £17

George II copper warming
pan engraved with floral
design.   £54

Victorian copper two-handled
urn, with brass tap and cover.
            £26

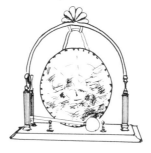

A Victorian brass table
gong on an oak base. £16

Bronze horizontal sundial
engraved T. Barrett, circa
1790.   £85

243

COPPER & BRASS

A solid cast brass standing horse plaque, stamped on back, 'Crowley & Co., Manchester', circa 1860, 9ins long, 7ins high. £12

George II steel footman with five 1ins flat slats across the top standing on cabriole ·front legs, circa 1740, 18½ins wide, 12ins deep, 13½ins high. £28

Cast brass sailing ships' watch bell, numbered 17 on top, with brass shackle and iron clapper, circa 1840, 10ins high. £35

Pair of 18th century andirons. £20

English spring badger trap in polished steel, in perfect working condition, circa 1760, 17¼ins long. £18

A brass and steel desk knife sharpener, with steel roller supports on pillars, circa 1825, 5½ins long, 4ins deep, 3½ins high. £25

A small cast iron chemist's mortar with two handles and four decorative bands, circa 1840, 3¼ins high. £12

Copper brewer's yeast vessel with loop handle and long pouring spout, circa 1890, 10ins high. £56

An unusual 19th century sieve enclosed in copper oval container, complete with carrying handles, circa 1850. £48

A metal weathervane of a flying griffon, the Roman capital letters in thick copper, circa 1810. £165

19th century brass head and shoulders profile of Oliver Cromwell, mounted on green baize and framed in octagonal mahogany stepped frame, circa 1850. £25

Queen Anne wrought iron gridiron with four feet to stand on embers, circa 1700, 9ins square. £28

Pair of brass horse hames.   £35

19th century Scottish alms dish in brass with circular motto in centre, circa 1850, 20ins diam.   £24

A polished copper shield of the 3rd Battn. Scots Guards, 10¾ins wide, 16ins high.   £28

A milkman's quart tin milk dipper with a curved brass handle to hang on the edge of the churn, circa 1850, 4ins high excluding handle.   £12

A pair of brass vases with mythological figures in relief, 5ins high.   £34

Brass sundial, with decoratively pierced gnomon, 9ins square.   £48

Brass spirit kettle, with glass handle, circa 1820.   £47

A small 19th century butcher's chopper in steel with turned oak handle, 13ins long.   £15

A copper jug with shaped iron handle, 4½ins high.   £9

Copper milkman's cream dipper, 22½ins long, 4ins cup.   £10

A pair of late 19th century copper busts of Moors, impressed Giesecke, 22ins high.   £390

A heavy polished steel Queen Anne trivet, circa 1710, 13ins high, 10ins diam.   £28

COPPER & BRASS

A large copper stock pot complete with lid, brass carrying handles and brass spigot, circa 1820, 12½ins high, 12ins diam.   £48

A sheet brass preserve pan with hand wrought iron loop handle, circa 1820, 12ins diam.   £22

A two-handled brass chemist's mortar, with filed band around centre and squared handles, circa 1820, 4¾ins high.   £10

An ornate cast brass watch stand of the Regency period, depicting greyhounds and eagles, circa 1810, 10ins high.   £35

A Victorian brass inkstand with two glass bottles. £22

A 19th century brass dolphin door stopper.   £25

One of an unusual set of three copper and brass, cone shaped spirit measures, circa 1850.   £178

A shaped brass casket with ringed lion carrying handles and standing on four claw and ball feet, circa 1750, 8ins wide, 3½ins deep, 4½ins high.   £48

A copper, Jersey pattern milk jug, 10ins high. £10

A copper one gallon spirit flagon with customs seal inside neck and large grip handle, circa 1820, 10ins high.   £45

A historical cast brass door stop of King George IV leaning on a pillar, 7½ins long, 8ins high.   £28

George III copper saucepan with wrought steel handle riveted to pan, 9ins diam.   £24

A heavy brass crown support for the classical tent style drapes of the domed tester bed, circa 1840, 9ins diam. , £45

A copper hot water can with finely executed hoops around the body, 14ins long, 9ins high. £18

George I brass mortar, with rimmed base and fillet bands around the body, circa 1720, 4ins high. £22

A 19th century Oriental brass vase, engraved with dragons, 12ins high. £18

19th century cast brass flat iron stand with pierced star motif and heavy peg legs, 9¾ins long. £9

A gigantic tole ware, copper and brass tea urn, originally used as a grocer's shop sign, circa 1850. £68

Sailing ship's watch bell, made of bell founders brass, complete with heavy clapper and hand rope, 9½ins diam., 13½ins high. £48

A fine brass preserve pan with swing over carrying handle, circa 1830, 9ins diam. £18

A polished copper stock pot, complete with brass tap and copper carrying handles, circa 1820, 13ins diam. £68

A George III brass globular tea urn, on four legs and ball feet. £38

An interesting one gallon measure from Woburn Abbey, 10ins high. £38

A very unusual shaped copper spirit jug with tinned interior, circa 1840, 8ins high. £20

A set of R.S.P.C.A. London Van Horse Parade merit badges, 1926 - 1939.   £77

(King & Chasemore, Pulborough)

Pair of 17th century brass candlesticks with barley-sugar twist stems and embossed cast brass bases, 10ins high. £125

A fine brass candlestick with four ejection holes in the sconce, circa 1685, 7½ins high. £68

Pair of 18th century brass candlesticks, 10ins high. £16

An exceptionally fine pair of French ormolu three branch candelabra with cut glass prism drops, 14ins high, circa 1830. £165

A French ormolu candelabra for three lights, on triangular shaped base, 19¾ins high. £70

Single French ormolu double branch wall light, circa 1880 £35

Pair of Victorian brass candlesticks on paw feet. £14

Pair of tall George II bell metal candlesticks with turned inside circular bases, 9¾ins high. £45

A pair of unusual wine cellar man's candlesticks with steel stems to the top, with brass sconces and drip pans, circa 1810, 9½ins high. £45

CANDLESTICKS

A pair of small George III brass taper candlesticks, 4ins high. £28

George I single brass candlestick, steeped cast brass with smooth underneath, circa 1725, 7ins high. £28

Pair of George III brass taper candlesticks, circa 1810, 4ins high. £27

A pair of 19th century brass candlesticks on octagonal bases, 12½ins high. £32

An important pair of 19th century brass candelabra, 1ft 8ins high. £146

A pair of brass candlesticks having square brass bases with diagonal corners and pusher ejectors in base, circa 1820, 8ins high. £18

A pair of 19th century brass candlesticks on circular bases, 9½ins high. £17

A rare example of a horse-coach internal spring loaded candleholder in brass, 6ins high. £24

A large pair of 17th century brass drip pan candlesticks, mounted on four claw feet, 6ins diam. £125

A pair of brass candlesticks, circa 1740.   £98

A single Queen Anne side pusher brass candlestick on an octagonal base, circa 1720, 6¾ins high.   £19

A pair of 17th century brass candlesticks with barley twist stems and embossed cast brass bases, 10ins high. £175

Pair of late 17th century William and Mary style brass candlesticks with drip pans in the centre of the baluster shaped stems, 8ins high.   £75

A pair of French ormolu candlesticks with figures of children on a shaped base, 8ins high.   £90

A fine pair of Adam style brass candlesticks, the fluted stem connecting to the stepped base with beading decoration, circa 1770, 10½ins high.   £45

An exceptionally fine pair of drip pan candlesticks, with cast brass baluster stems, and turned cast domed bases, 9ins high.   £95

19th century cast brass candle lamp with decorative scroll design below fluted column, on heavy hexagonal base, circa 1850, 21½ins high.   £38

Pair of early Victorian brass candlesticks to take glass storm shades, 10½ins high.   £48

DAGGERS

A scarce, Nazi R.A.D. man's dagger   £95

A good, Cossack silver mounted Kindjal, broad double edged blade 18½ ins.   £48

A good, old, large bowie knife, broad clipped-back blade 10 ins. £128

A 17th Century Italian Stiletto (stylet), triangular blade 5¼ ins. £70

A silver mounted South American gaucho knife, blade 8 ins.   £23

A good, silver mounted Bade Bade, recurving blade 7½ ins.   £32

A good, 17th Century European left hand dagger, possibly Italian, blade 8½ ins.   £75

A very fine, Victorian bowie type folding knife, clipped-back blade 5 ins.
£280

A fine, Indian dagger Kard, blade 7½ ins.   £78

A Japanese cloisonne dagger, straight multi fullered double edged blade 6 ins.   £38

A Nazi Luftwaffe officer's 2nd-pattern dagger, by S.M.F. Solingen.
£74

A large Bali Kris, straight watered blade 18½ ins.   £50

DOLLS

A composition shoulder-headed doll, with inset enamel eyes, cloth arms and wooden body, circa 1845, 15½ins.   85gns

A character child with brown flirting eyes and bent-limb baby's body, marked K * R, 17ins.   50gns

A wax-over-composition doll, the cloth body with kid arms, the fingers separated, wearing a blue silk jacket and striped skirt, 25ins high.   60gns

A china-headed doll with stuffed cloth body, the kid arms with separated fingers, 31ins.   190gns

A turned and carved wood baby house doll wearing 19th century printed cotton dress, circa 1760, 9ins.   260gns

A bisque shoulder-headed doll, the stuffed body with bisque arms, wearing original pink satin dress, marked S & H, 19ins.   140gns

A bisque-headed character-baby with sheepskin wig and composition baby's body, marked Simon and Halbig 116/A, 14ins.   55gns

A bisque-headed folie with fixed blue eyes, closed mouth, wearing sequins and silver lace streamers, 14ins.   55gns

A George II painted wood doll, the face partly repainted and fingers damaged, 22ins high.   £350

A carved and painted wooden doll, the face with painted blue eyes and stitched brows, the stuffed body with wooden arms, circa 1860, 31ins.   90gns

A bisque-headed child-doll with jointed composition body, marked Unis France 71 149 301, 23ins.   60gns

A brown bisque baby with sleeping eyes and closed mouth, on brown bent-limb baby's body, 13½ins, marked A.M. 341/3½K.   50gns

A bisque-headed child doll with jointed composition body, marked S.F.B.J. Paris 10, 23½ins.   55gns

A china-headed clockwork walking doll, gliding on three wheels in the base, 8½ins.   200gns

A bisque-headed child doll dressed in red, marked Dep 11, 25½ins.   45gns

A celluloid-headed child-doll with fixed brown eyes and jointed composition body, marked K & W W298/12 with a turtle mark, 26½ins.   35gns.

A wax-over-composition doll with Motchan-type florating hands and feet, 15ins.   25gns.

A metal-headed doll with moulded and painted hair, the stuffed body with wooden arms, marked Germany 5, 16ins.   25gns

DOLLS

A carved wooden boy-doll with painted hair and features, the body with wooden arms, 15½ins. 18gns

German bisque porcelain baby doll impressed A.M.   £58

Victorian bisque doll with fixed blue eyes, 14ins tall.   £75

A French bisque-headed doll dressed in pink and white.   £70

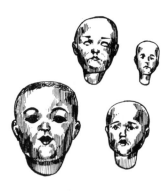

Four character dolls' and babies' heads.   420gns

An unusual late 19th century juggling clown automaton, 2ft 5ins high.   £320

A bisque-headed baby, marked AM351/3K, 12ins.   30gns

Wax headed doll, 21½ins tall, circa 1880.   £85

A bisque-headed character baby with composition baby's body, wearing sailor smock, 22ins, marked Heubach 342.9. 40gns

Coloured enamel scent bottle label named 'Eau De Cologne', decorated with pink and yellow flowers, on original brass chain. £9

White porcelain egg shaped box decorated with painted flowers. £8

An egg shaped Bilston box decorated with flowers. £130

Bilston box decorated with a picture of a lady. £60

French enamel box designed as a 'Billet Doux'. £180

Shoe shaped Bilston box, 3½ins long. £80

A miniature Bilston enamel egg, circa 1770. £65

Continental enamel snuff box in the firm of a tricorn hat. £85

Vienna enamel egg, hand painted with country scenes in the style of Wouvermans, 1 7/8ins diam. £165

Bilston etui decorated on one side with a huntsman. £60

A Karl Bank Viennese enamel and lapis lazuli ewer and stand, decorated in the cinquecento manner. £4,200

Bilston etui decorated on one side with a huntsman. £60

FLASKS

An embossed brass mounted copper bodied 3-way pistol flask.
£51

An unusual enamelled S. Eurasian brass priming flask of circular form.
£40

A scarce, copper bodied brass mounted 3-way pistol flask. £46

A 17th Century German triangular shaped musketeer's powder flask, 9¼ ins tall.
£100

A fine Persian shell powder flask.
£70

A scarce, cylindrical copper bodied brass mounted pistol flask.
£46

An embossed copper powder flask.
£36

An embossed copper powder flask.
£56

A scarce, embossed German silver powder flask.   £40

A copper powder flask, 'fluted', no hanging rings.   £15

A good, 17th Century German turned wooden priming flask, 3 ins diameter.   £55

A good quality, French copper powder flask, fitted with Boche Patent charger.
                £28

A good, 17th Century flattened horn powder flask, 12 ins, linear-engraved sides.
        £28

A good copper powder flask 'Dead Game' (R. 633. without hanging rings).   £35

A well made, late 17th Century Spanish belt powder horn, 9½ ins.
        £36

An embossed copper powder flask, 8½ ins.
        £32

An embossed copper powder flask, 8 ins.
        £56

An unusual leather shot flask, fitted with Boche Patent charger.
                £16

BEDS & CRADLES

William IV four-poster bed,
in medium coloured
mahogany, 7ft 10ins high,
6ft 9ins long, 5ft wide. £475

19th century Dutch floral
marquetry bed.   £600

A very fine late Tudor period
carved oak full tester bed. £4,000

Oak and marquetry Elizabethan
tester bed, 7ft high x 5ft 7ins
wide.   £3,200

Early 17th century hooded
oak baby's cradle.   £200

Late 18th century marquetry
bed with scroll ends.   £150

A Normandy carved oak cradle
with openwork end bobbin
panels, 3ft 4ins wide.   £85

A 19th century Indian
cradle.   £66

An early 17th century oak
hooded cradle.   £200

A fine quality walnut wall
cabinet with shelf above and
two glazed doors to cupboard,
30ins wide, 37ins high, circa
1840. £75

A fine set of pinewood kitchen
shelves, with two drawers in
the base, circa 1810. £58

A set of pine wood hanging
bookshelves, circa 1810,
6½ins wide, 28ins high. £56

An Edwardian revolving
bookcase, satinwood banded,
with mahogany inlay. £140

19th century rosewood dwarf
bookcase, with two end
cupboards and open shelves,
6ft 6ins wide. £90

A mahogany square revolving
bookcase. £44

An ebony open bookcase with
carved uprights of scroll design,
3ft wide, 3ft 2ins high. £40

A pair of 19th century French
dwarf bookcases, 49ins wide,
43½ins high. £160

A 19th century mahogany
and fretwork wall bracket
with bevelled mirror back,
21½ins wide. £20

261

BOOKCASES

George III mahogany breakfront bookcase, probably designed by Robert Adam. £7,600

19th century rosewood bookcase of unusual design, 47ins x 73ins. £70

George III mahogany breakfront bookcase with a central broken pediment, above a carved entablature, 3.80m wide. £7,600

A Georgian mahogany breakfront library bookcase with dentil cornice, the upper part fitted with adjustable shelves enclosed by glazed doors, 8ft 1½ins wide. £860

A mahogany inlaid breakfront cabinet bookcase with four glazed doors and three cupboards below, 6ft 10ins wide. £195

Georgian mahogany breakfront bookcase, with lattice glazed doors, 7ft 9ins high, 7ft 2ins wide. £2,600

A George III painted mahogany bookcase, 53ins wide. £580

A 19th century breakfront mahogany bookcase, 12ft. £860

A 19th century stained wood cabinet bookcase with brass trellis and flower rosette doors above, 4ft 9ins wide.

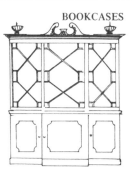

Chippendale period mahogany breakfront bookcase, 12ft 10ins wide. £1,260

A 19th century reproduction satinwood bookcase on splayed feet. £420

A 19th century reproduction mahogany breakfront bookcase, the upper section with astragal glazing. £940

Georgian mahogany breakfront bookcase, the top section with astragal glazing. £750

Fine quality 19th century mahogany breakfront bookcase, 12ft long. £1,475

George III mahogany breakfront bookcase with arched pediment. £1,250

George III mahogany breakfront bookcase. £330

George III mahogany secretaire bookcase with swan neck cresting, 7ft 4ins wide. £2,100

Edwardian satinwood and inlaid bookcase on splayed feet, 56ins wide. £320

BOOKCASES

Victorian mahogany breakfront bookcase with three glazed doors above, 5ft 2ins wide. £330

19th century mahogany dwarf breakfront bookcase, 6ft 6ins wide. £160

Victorian mahogany breakfront cabinet bookcase. £165

A Victorian walnut breakfront cabinet bookcase, with three glazed doors above and three pane panel doors below, 5ft 6ins wide. £480

George III mahogany library bookcase by Thomas Chippendale, 1764. £23,100

Oak cabinet bookcase. £125

Late 19th century carved mahogany secretaire cabinet bookcase, 4ft wide. £115

Sheraton satinwood breakfront cabinet, 7ft 1½ins. £12,000

Late 19th century mahogany bookcase in two parts, 5ft 4ins wide. £80

A 19th century Dutch colonial 'Block-Fronted' bureau, 3ft 1ins wide. £580
(King & Chasemore, Pulborough)

BUREAUX

A fine quality oak bureau with finely fitted interior, circa 1740, 3ft wide.   £545

Continental ebonised bureau, with ormolu escutcheons and handles, on ormolu encrusted cabriole legs, circa 1780. £285

17th century Dutch marquetry walnut bombe bureau, the shaped top inlaid with a vase.   £1,200

Georgian mahogany bureau, with original handles and oak drawer linings, 41ins wide, 21ins deep, 41½ins high, circa 1795.   £179

A fine Dutch marquetry bureau with cylinder top and three drawers below, on splayed feet with ormolu mounts, 45ins wide.   £1,600

George I walnut bureau. £400

Georgian mahogany bureau, 31ins wide.   £400

An 18th century walnut bureau, the fall flap with an unusual inlaid design depicting St. George and the dragon, 3ft wide.   £680

A Queen Anne walnut bureau, with sunburst, circa 1720, 36ins wide, 42ins high, 20ins deep.   £750

An inlaid mahogany bureau with satinwood banded borders and oval panel on folding over writing board, 2ft 6ins wide. £70

A 19th century yew wood kneehole bureau de dame, on cabriole legs. £195

A fine Dutch marquetry cylinder bombe fronted bureau, with nicely fitted interior. £1,600

A Georgian mahogany bureau of four long drawers, standing on bracket feet. £302

A late 18th century Dutch marquetry cylinder bureau, 37ins. £1,200

An Edwardian satinwood inlaid bureau, with rosewood banded borders, 2ft 6ins wide. £155

Early 18th century walnut bureau, with finely fitted interior, only 2ft 10ins wide. £1,600

A late 19th century Dutch bombe fronted, floral marquetry bureau, 4ft wide. £1,800

An early 18th century North German walnut bureau. £1,850

BUREAUX

Dutch marquetry bureau, 52ins. £2,300

An 18th century mahogany bureau with later marquetry decoration. £420

A George III walnut bureau with inlaid and crossbanded borders, on bracket feet, 2ft 3ins wide. £800

Georgian oak bureau, with a well and bracket feet, 32ins wide. 240gns

A small late 19th century mahogany and marquetry bureau a cylindre, 3ft 5ins high. £340

A small Dutch pine bombe bureau, with well. £285

A faded mahogany Hepplewhite bureau with crossbanded canted corners, inlaid in satinwood with boxwood stringing, standing on swept bracket feet, circa 1770. £680

A small stripped pine bureau on cabriole legs. £195

18th century inlaid walnut bureau on bracket feet. £1,900

A carved oak bureau with folding over writing board, three long and two short drawers below, 3ft 3½ins wide. £190

A fine Continental marquetry bureau on thick tapering legs with spade feet. £1,275

Mid 18th century mahogany bureau. £350

Late 19th century mahogany bureau on cabriole legs with ball and claw feet, 2ft 3ins wide. £62

A 19th century French rose-wood and parquetry bureau-de-dame on cabriole legs, the folding writing board with painted panel, signed Dumas, 2ft 4ins wide. £200

Georgian mahogany bureau with boxwood string inlay and bracket feet, 3ft 6ins wide. £300

Regency figured mahogany cylinder bureau. £1,000

18th century Dutch marquetry bureau, with finely fitted interior. £1,800

A French rosewood and marquetry inlaid bureau, on cabriole legs with chased brass mounts, 28ins wide. £140

BUREAUX

Small faded mahogany bureau with boxwood stringing, circa 1820, 2ft 10ins wide. £375

Louis XV style bureau de dame with parquetry decoration and ormolu mounts. £329

An 18th century Dutch walnut and marquetry inlaid bureau, with bombe front and sides, on cabriole legs. £1,700

Late 19th century American mahogany desk with a finely fitted interior. £430

Victorian French style mahogany desk on cabriole legs. £110

Miniature mahogany bureau, 8ins wide. £58

George III mahogany bureau with four drawers, 3ft 4ins wide. £180

19th century Oriental lacquered bureau on short cabriole legs. £70

Late 18th century mahogany bureau with serpentine shaped fitted interior, 41ins wide. £850

An Edwardian mahogany inlaid bureau with folding over writing board and three long drawers, 2ft 6ins wide.   £85

A mahogany cylinder fronted bureau with oval satinwood panel, on square tapered legs, 2ft 3ins wide.   £140

George III oak bureau in fine original condition with bracket feet and pierced brass handles, circa 1770, 39ins wide, 20ins deep, 43ins high.   £285

Small Georgian oak bureau with stepped interior, 36ins wide.   £400

18th century walnut bureau decorated with crossbanding and feather banding, 3ft wide.   £760

An Edwardian mahogany inlaid bureau with satinwood banded borders and four long drawers, on bracket feet, 2ft 6ins wide.   £95

Late 18th century bombe front Dutch marquetry bureau on paw feet. £1,800

Early 19th century French Empire style cylinder front bureau with brass decoration.   £450

18th century walnut bureau with crossbanding and feather banding, 3ft wide.   £760

An 18th century walnut bureau bookcase, 40½ins wide. £750
(King & Chasemore, Pulborough)

A Georgian mahogany bureau with bookcase above, enclosed by two panel doors, with dentilled cornice, 4ft wide. £380

German rococo walnut marquetry bureau-cabinet, 59½ins wide, 89¼ins high. £8,925

18th century walnut bureau bookcase with its original Vauxhall plate doors. £2,100

Early 18th century oak and elm bureau bookcase, 37ins wide. £820

18th century South German walnut bureau cabinet. £3,000

An 18th century Dutch marquetry bureau bookcase with bombe front and claw feet. £2,900

George III mahogany bureau bookcase with astragal glazed doors, 114cm wide. £360

Late 18th century mahogany bureau bookcase with astragal glazed doors and bracket feet, 37ins wide. £500

Early 18th century oak bureau cabinet with candle slides, 3ft 3ins wide. £330

BUREAU BOOKCASES

An inlaid mahogany bureau
bookcase.   £570

George II mahogany bureau
bookcase, with finely fitted
interior and standing on
bracket feet.   £480

Queen Anne walnut bureau
cabinet on bracket feet.
                £1,950

Late 19th century bureau-bookcase,
the upper part with two glazed
doors, the lower part with a folding
over writing board and four long
drawers, 2ft 6ins wide.   £100

A superb George I parcel-
gilt walnut bureau cabinet,
with carefully designed
architectural interior, 8ft
2ins high.   £16,000

An oak bureau bookcase, the
interior in need of restoration,
with original brass handles to
drawers, 36ins wide, 75ins
high, 20ins deep.   £185

18th century oak bureau
bookcase on bracket feet,
34ins wide.   £240

19th century mahogany
and inlaid bureau
bookcase, 38ins wide.
                £1,000

George III mahogany bureau
bookcase with astragal glazed
doors, 3ft 4ins wide.   £240

An 18th century oak bureau bookcase, the upper part with scroll domed cornice, 3ft wide. £480

An early 18th century walnut bureau bookcase. £2,600

Late 19th century mahogany bureau bookcase, on cabriole legs. £100

Edwardian mahogany bureau bookcase with delicate satinwood inlay, only 33ins wide. £490

A fine William and Mary double-domed walnut bureau bookcase, with nicely fitted interior. £4,500

A Queen Anne walnut bureau bookcase, with a double domed top, 3ft 4½ins wide, 7ft 2ins high. £2,500

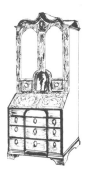

Early 18th century bureau cabinet with burr walnut veneer on oak, inset with bevelled mirror-glass. £5,040

An Edwardian mahogany bureau bookcase with astragal glazed upper section. £330

Georgian mahogany bureau bookcase with fine stepped interior, and shell inlay to fall with satinwood crossbanding, 97ins high, 45ins wide, 21ins deep. £775

CABINETS

Fine quality French cabinet in kingwood with painted porcelain plaque, and richly encrusted with ormolu. £695

An ivory and harewood inlaid side cabinet by Lamb, Manchester. £500

A small coromandel lacquer cabinet, 1ft 6ins. £325

An 18th century Oriental black lacquered cabinet on stand with gilt chinoiserie decoration, the interior fitted with numerous drawers and recesses, 3ft 2ins wide. £340

Mahogany kneehole cabinet of Chinese Chippendale design, 4ft 1ins. £1,100

A rare 17th century lacquer cabinet, with very fine architectural interior. £1,350

Edwardian mahogany cabinet with boxwood inlay, 5ft 2ins wide. £40

19th century porcelain mounted amboyna and ebony side cabinet. £420

A finely inlaid and mounted cabinet, circa 1860. £280

276

A 19th century boulle side cabinet, 35½ins.　£135

19th century French parquetry cabinet with a marble top.　£400

Black and gilt chinoiserie lacquer cabinet, 1ft 11ins.　£200

A Flemish oak travelling chest on stand, the multi-drawer interior enclosed by a pair of moulded panel doors, 2ft 7ins wide.　£250

Louis XV style marble-topped cabinet with parquetry decoration.　£325

18th century Dutch floral marquetry cabinet in two sections, 36ins wide, 67ins high.　£1,020

A fine early 18th century walnut chest on stand, comprising three short and three long drawers, the stand with turned legs and bun feet, 3ft 3ins wide.　£740

A Japanese stage cabinet with open shelves and sliding panel door cupboards, on elaborately carved dragon base.　£470

A Victorian papier mache cabinet by Jennens and Betteridge, opening to reveal six long graduated drawers.　£850

CABINETS

A pair of Chinese black lacquered cabinets, each with two panel doors decorated in coloured hardstones, lacquer and ivory with garden scenes, 2ft 10ins wide, 4ft 4ins high. £260

An unusual padoukwood cabinet with sunburst panels, 41ins wide, 19ins deep, 34½ins high, circa 1840. £165

A French ebony and boulle cabinet with panel door, canted corners and brass mounts, of Louis XIV design, 3ft 6ins high, 2ft wide. £170

Carved and lacquered cabinet on stand, the insides of the doors and the eight drawers similarly decorated with fruit, lion dogs, utensils and precious objects. £950

18th century Italian pietra-dure cabinet and stand. £1,900

A 17th century Dutch cabinet. £1,000

A fine quality Oriental hardwood and mother of pearl inlaid cabinet. £570

German walnut and marquetry bombe cabinet inlaid with ivory and mother of pearl figures to the doors, 86ins high, 56ins wide. £5,600

Very attractive English lacquer cabinet on stand, circa 1690, the door sides and interior drawers with raised incised lacquer, 71½ins x 39ins x 21ins. £1,250

A Continental oystershell walnut and coloured marquetry inlaid cabinet, on a walnut open bookcase stand with scroll end supports, 3ft 3ins wide, 5ft 10ins high.   £330

A reproduction satinwood cabinet.   £250

18th century Flemish padouk wood side cabinet decorated with knulling and brass fittings, 4ft 11½ins wide.   £210

18th century Italian cabinet on stand, inlaid with coloured and engraved ivory.   £2,300

Late 18th century red lacquer cabinet and stand, fitted with numerous drawers, 112cm wide.   £390

Profusely inlaid William and Mary cabinet on chest, on barley twist supports with shaped stretchers, 53ins wide.   £1,400

Early 19th century black lacquer cabinet on short cabriole legs, 3ft wide.   £280

Queen Anne period walnut cabinet, standing on bracket feet.   £800

An unusual Chippendale figured mahogany cabinet, 3ft 11ins.   £1,700

An antique Continental ebonised oak side cabinet, 39ins wide.   £380
(King & Chasemore, Pulborough)

An unusual mahogany rail canterbury, with drawer in the base, 1ft 5¾ins x 1ft 1ins.
£700

An attractive walnut canterbury with drawer, 20ins wide, circa 1850. £145

Early 19th century rosewood canterbury on finely turned legs.
£120

George III mahogany canterbury, 19ins.
£320

Victorian rosewood music canterbury with fretted partitions, 22ins wide. £100

Late Regency rosewood canterbury, with drawer at the back, circa 1830.
£175

Victorian figured walnut canterbury with galleried top.
£150

Regency lacquered canterbury with drawer in the base. £140

Victorian walnut canterbury, with a drawer at the base.
£75

A set of six 19th century mahogany dining chairs of Hepplewhite design.   £380
(King & Chasemore, Pulborough)

A set of six late Georgian mahogany dining chairs.   £180
(King & Chasemore, Pulborough)

One of a set of four rosewood dining chairs on octagonal legs.   £70

One of a set of ten Hepplewhite design mahogany dining chairs with shield backs, on square tapered legs.   £140

One of a set of six French style Victorian rosewood chairs. £310

One of a set of four mahogany dining chairs of Hepplewhite design with pierced splats, on square tapered legs. £40

One of a set of four Regency brass inlaid rosewood dining chairs.   £180

One of a set of six Chippendale mahogany dining chairs.   £600

One of a set of six late 18th century shield back mahogany dining chairs.   £300

One of a set of six rosewood dining chairs with Trafalgar seats, circa 1840.   £440

One of a set of six mahogany dining chairs with pierced splats and drop in seats.   £140

One of a set of six Chippendale carved mahogany dining chairs on cabriole legs with ball and claw feet. £400

One of a set of six walnut Queen Anne style dining chairs on cabriole legs, with cane backs.   £50

One of a set of six mahogany dining chairs with pierced splats, on square tapered legs.   £85

Set of six Victorian mahogany dining chairs, with carved top rails, on turned legs.   £100

Set of six Regency simulated rosewood dining chairs with sabre front legs and drop in seats.   £190

A papier mache and mother of pearl inlaid bedroom chair with cane seat.   £14

Set of eight George III mahogany dining chairs with carved and fluted spar backs, on square tapering legs.   £320

Victorian child's chair in ash.   £5

One of a set of four George I oak chairs.   £475

One of a set of six Regency mahogany dining chairs with sabre front legs, the centre rail inlaid in satinwood.   £575

An Edwardian Sheraton child's chair with boxwood stringing to each panel and struts.   £35

One of a set of eight mahogany dining chairs with pierced splats and drop in seats, on cabriole legs with claw and ball feet. (2 & 6)   £420

Edwardian Sheraton style chair of mahogany with boxwood stringing, 26½ins high.   £35

Set of four mahogany dining chairs on turned legs.   £38

A rare spindle back ashwood miniature chair with a rush seat, circa 1790, 17ins high.   £38

One of a pair of carved walnut seats of French design, on turned and fluted legs. £42

One of a pair of 19th century rosewood chairs, with cane seats and standing on turned legs. £32

One of a set of twelve mahogany dining chairs, with pierced splats and fluted top rails and uprights. £1,000

One of a set of eight Victorian mahogany dining chairs, on turned legs. £250

A tall red walnut chair, with cane seat, circa 1690. £140

One of a set of eight country chairs. £260

One of a set of six yew and elm wheel back kitchen chairs. 380gns

One of a set of six country chairs in elm, circa 1800. £198

One of a set of four Hepplewhite design mahogany dining chairs, on square tapering legs. £50

One of a pair of Regency mahogany dining chairs, the drop in seats in leather, on sabre legs. £18

One of a set of three Victorian walnut chairs, with carved and pierced splats, on cabriole legs. £44

An ebonised chair by Charles Rennie Mackintosh. £495

CHAIRS – DINING

One of a pair of late Victorian hall chairs.
£27

One of a set of six mahogany dining-chairs of early Chippendale design.
£540

One of a set of nine late Regency mahogany bar back chairs.
£395

A mahogany spinning chair, decorated with flowers.
£25

A set of four carved mahogany dining chairs on cabriole legs with claw and ball feet.
£120

One of a set of six mahogany dining chairs chairs with pierced splats, on square legs and stretchers.
£120

One of a pair of mahogany inlaid bedroom chairs, on square tapered legs.
£32

Set of six 19th century shield back dining chairs, on tapered legs with spade feet.
£130

One of a pair of Louis XVI style carved walnut chairs, on turned and fluted legs.
£60

One of a set of six early 18th century walnut and fruitwood dining chairs.
350gns

One of a set of eight mahogany side chairs, the front cabriole legs with original brass swivel castors.
£550

One of a pair of Georgian oak dining chairs. 40gns

One of a set of four
Regency mahogany
chairs, with rope
pattern spars to back.
£140

A set of four Regency
rosewood dining chairs,
with fluted top rails and
brass mounts to splats,
on sabre legs.   £150

One of a set of six
18th century elm
dining chairs.   £410

One of a set of six
Regency ebonised
dining chairs, with
brass mounts, on
sabre legs.   £360

One of a set of six
Victorian rosewood
chairs, on turned fluted
supports.   £200

One of a set of six
Regency style
mahogany chairs on
sabre legs.   £250

One of a set of nine
Regency rosewood
dining chairs on sabre
legs.   £920

One of a set of six
Victorian carved
walnut chairs. £240

Pair of fine quality
walnut chairs with
inlaid stringing to
the splat, circa
1690.   £475

One of a set of five
Regency mahogany
dining chairs on
finely turned legs.
£140

One of a set of six late
Regency dining chairs,
with turned legs. £490

Cast iron conservatory
chair, the three legs
entwined with ribbons
of iron, on leaf feet.
£58

287

CHAIRS – DINING

One of a set of eight early
19th century satinwood
chairs with gilt mounts.
£1,300

One of a set of seven elm
and ash farmhouse chairs,
including two armchairs.
320gns

One of a set of eight
Georgian style mahogany
dining chairs, (2 & 6).
£400

One of a set of eight
(2 & 6) 17th century
beech chairs, with cane
seats. £380

One of a set of six Regency
mahogany dining chairs, the
centre back rail with
satinwood fern and central
flower design. £575

One of a set of six early
Victorian figured
mahogany dining chairs.
£310

Early 17th century
Derbyshire chair.
£200

Set of eight 19th century
mahogany dining chairs,
on ball and claw feet.
£640

A set of six mahogany
dining chairs of the
Chippendale style, 39ins
high, circa 1850. £425

An early 19th century
Continental spinning
wheel chair, with bobbin
back splats. £45

One of a set of eight
mahogany chairs in the
Chippendale style, circa
1860. £365

A Harlequin set of six
17th century
Yorkshire chairs, with
arched and carved splats,
on bobbin turned legs.
£290

288

One of a set of six ebonised
Gothic side chairs, English,
circa 1830-40.   £90

George II elm wood
single chair, with rush
seat, circa 1740.   £28

One of a set of twelve
mahogany dining chairs
of late 18th century
design.   £1,320

One of a set of six mahogany
sabre-leg chairs with drop-
in seats, circa 1840.   £395

One of a pair of rush
seated children's chairs,
of polished beechwood,
circa 1835.   £52

One of a matched set
of seven Yorkshire oak
dining chairs.   £250

One of a set of six,
Empire style, mahogany
chairs, with upholstered
seats.   £280

One of a set of eight oak
chairs, with rush seats, on
pad feet and bulb stretcher,
circa 1860.   £195

A fine late 17th century
walnut chair.   £85

One of a set of six ebonised
side chairs with a caned
seat, turned legs and arched
splats in the arched back.
£90

One of a part set of
five provincial Queen
Anne walnut chairs.
£475

One of a set of six Sheraton
fruitwood dining chairs,
circa 1795.   £275

CHAIRS – DINING

One of a set of eleven, two arm two single, dining chairs in the Chippendale ladder back style.   £1,500

One of a set of four 18th century lacquered chairs.   £180

One of a set of four Victorian walnut spoon back dining chairs. £180

A handsome oak Yorkshire chair, circa 1650.   £140

One of a pair of walnut high back chairs, circa 1690.   £165

One of a set of six early 18th century elm ladderback chairs. £340

A walnut high backed chair, circa 1690.   £125

One of a set of eight Regency mahogany dining chairs. £440

One of a set of six 18th century Dutch floral marquetry chairs. £1,550

One of a set of three late 19th century dining chairs with pierced splats.   £38

One of a set of four 19th century reeded mahogany chairs on sabre legs. £110

One of a set of eight late 18th century Chippendale style chairs.   £440

A set of five 19th century walnut-framed dining chairs.   £85
(King & Chasemore, Pulborough)

A set of seven late 18th century French Provincial light oak dining chairs.   £290
(King & Chasemore, Pulborough)

Set of eight (6 & 2) oak Yorkshire wavy-line ladder-back chairs with rush seats, circa 1780. £585

Set of eight Regency mahogany dining chairs with lightly carved backs and rosewood panels inlaid with brass foliate scrolls. £2,400

Set of eight Regency mahogany dining chairs, with sabre legs. £850

Two of a set of eight Hepplewhite mahogany dining chairs. £500

Set of ten (8 & 2) Ormskirk ladderback chairs, circa 1820. £315

Set of twelve George III carved mahogany chairs. £5,200

Set of eight late 19th century mahogany dining chairs with shield backs.   £250

Two of a set of six Cromwellian chairs. £2,010

A good set of country Hepplewhite mahogany dining chairs.   £260

Set of ten Windsor Wheelback chairs, circa 1860.   £275

Set of eight (6 & 2) oak dining chairs of country Sheraton design, circa 1790. £395

A set of six George III mahogany dining chairs on tapered legs with spade feet.   £840

CHAIRS – DINING

Set of four William IV dining chairs, one carver, in mahogany, with bar backs. £130

Set of four, three single and one arm, 19th century mahogany chairs on square tapered legs. £70

Set of eight early 19th century mahogany dining chairs. £575

Two of a set of eight Hepplewhite style dining chairs. £260

Two of a set of ten reeded mahogany chairs, circa 1850. £495

Set of eight ladder back mahogany chairs in the Georgian style. £440

19th century set of twelve oak chairs with carved cresting rails and seat fronts. £475

A set of eight Georgian mahogany dining chairs on tapered legs with spade feet. £1,020

An interesting set of six (4 & 2) early 18th century oak and yew-wood chairs. £475

A set of eight (6 & 2) Hepplewhite style mahogany heart-back dining chairs with Prince of Wales plumes. £610

Set of ten mahogany chairs with vase shaped splats and cabriole legs with stretchers. £600

A set of six single and two carving Chippendale style faded mahogany ladderback dining chairs. £610

A set of twelve George lll dining chairs £4,000
(Henry Spencer & Sons)

A set of eight 19th century mahogany dining chairs of Chippendale design. £520
(King & Chasemore, Pulborough)

One of a pair of late 18th century Continental armchairs. £211

A carved oak corner chair with animal head terminals. £42

One of a set of six Regency ebonised dining chairs. £380

An oak arm chair with carved panel back and hardwood seat. £42

A set of early Victorian mahogany library steps which convert to a small arm elbow chair. £210

One of a set of five mahogany dining chairs with pierced splats. £150

One of a pair of Louis XV easy chairs. £282

Set of eight George III mahogany dining chairs with carved and fluted spar backs. £420

George III elm corner chair. £25

One of a pair of elbow
chairs with tapered legs.
£400

Windsor stick back arm
chair, made of ash with
elm seat, circa 1810. £38

One of a pair of
Charles I oak
armchairs. £1,700

One of a pair of mahogany
elbow chairs of French
Hepplewhite design. £2,100

A Victorian carved oak
high back arm chair, with
cane back and seat. £15

One of a set of twelve
Hepplewhite style chairs,
with shield backs. £1,600

A large oak arm chair
with high carved panel
back, on turned legs. £50

A Windsor armchair in
ash and beechwood,
circa 1820. £55

One of a set of five late
19th century oak dining
chairs, with pierced splats,
on square tapering legs.
£48

An ash and elm low back
Windsor armchair, with
pierced back splats, circa
1830. £52

One of a set of eight (2 & 6)
18th century elm and ash
chairs, with turned frames
and rush seats. £485

One of a pair of Menlesham
elbow chairs of fruitwood,
with figured elm seats and
boxwood stringing. £260

18th century primitive oak chair.   £75

A fine armchair, with tapestry seat, on carved cabriole legs.   £820

Yew and elm Windsor armchair, with saddle seat and crinoline stretcher.   75gns

One of a set of eight George III mahogany shield back armchairs with reeded and carved splats, on square tapering legs.   £5,400

James I oak armchair of good proportions.   £450

17th century oak wainscot chair.   £100

Late 17th century walnut armchair, with squab seat.   150gns

A late Victorian large mahogany open arm chair, the panel back with seat in damask.   £22

An elm and ash Windsor armchair, with pierced back splat and finely turned front arm supports, circa 1840.   £58

Late 17th century barley twist walnut arm chair.   £165

One of a set of six early 19th century mahogany frame elbow chairs, with caned seats and backs.   £1,400

19th century oak caquetoise.   40gns

A fine set of eight (6 & 2) Chippendale style mahogany chairs, circa 1860. £650

A child's Shetland rocking arm chair. £20

A set of seven mahogany dining chairs on cabriole legs with ball and claw feet. £190

One of a pair of carved mahogany arm chairs, with pierced splats, on cabriole legs. £42

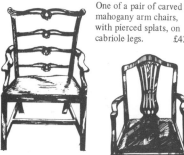

One of a valuable harlequin set of nine 18th century mahogany dining chairs. £1,800

A 19th century carved walnut open arm chair, on turnball legs and stretcher with foot rest, the shaped panel back carved with a coat of arms. £45

One of a set of six mahogany dining chairs, with pierced and carved ladder backs of Chippendale design. £180

Set of eight dining chairs of Georgian design, on square legs, (2 & 6). £250

A Victorian carved mahogany hall arm chair. £32

A set of four elm, Windsor arm chairs, on turned legs and stretchers, with loose cushions. £110

One of a set of eight oak dining chairs, with cane backs and seats, on spiral legs and stretchers. £180

An early 19th century child's Windsor style arm chair. £38

A Regency mahogany bar back arm chair, on sabre legs.   £35

An Edwardian mahogany inlaid circle back arm chair with sparred back and sides, on square tapered legs. £60

An oak arm chair, the high panel back carved with figures and scrolls.
£34

A Carolean oak arm chair with cane panel to back, on baluster legs and carved front stretcher.   £45

A Georgian elm arm chair with pierced splats, on square moulded legs.   £40

One of a pair of Queen Anne style ebonised arm chairs, on cabriole legs, painted with figures.   £50

One of a set of four Regency mahogany dining chairs on sabre front legs.   £100

A set of nine harlequin mahogany dining chairs, in the style of Chippendale.
£1,800

An ebonised chair designed by E.W. Godwin, circa 1870.
£200

One of a pair of carved walnut open arm chairs on spiral legs and stretchers, with carved giltwood surmounts.
£140

Late 19th century Windsor child's chair of ashwood with elm seat.   £35

Ash and beechwood Windsor armchair, circa 1795.   £54

301

CHAIRS — ELBOW

Chippendale period arm chair of faded mahogany, 21ins wide, circa 1780. £95

Early Victorian mahogany scroll arm chair which converts into library steps. £210.

18th century Indian ivory veneered chair of early Georgian style. £1,102

One of a set of four 19th century yew wood Windsor chairs. £310

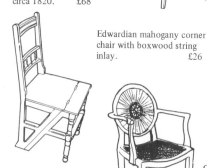

Lancashire fruitwood rocking chair with ashwood turnings, circa 1820. £68

One of a set of eight mahogany dining chairs on cabriole legs, the drop in seats covered in velvet, (2 & 6). £230

Georgian mahogany armchair with scroll arms, circa 1820. £115

Edwardian mahogany corner chair with boxwood string inlay. £26

19th century oak library chair steps. £16

One of a set of seven (1 & 6) early 19th century elm and ash wheelback chairs. £220

One of a set of eight 19th century Hepplewhite style mahogany dining chairs. £380

Chippendale period mahogany armchair, circa 1760. £150

One of a set of six Hepplewhite dining chairs in elmwood inlaid with mahogany, circa 1820. £325

A stained wood Windsor pattern arm chair. £26

Sheraton style mahogany carver on fine turned legs. £34

One of a set of eight 18th century Chippendale style dining chairs with ball and claw feet. £540

19th century walnut armchair on sabre legs. £28

An elegant chair by Charles Rennie Mackintosh, made for the owner of The Willow Tea Rooms, Glasgow. £9,200

19th century oak library steps with tooled leather seat and treads. £135

A fine George II oak corner armchair, circa 1750. £98

Armchair from a set of twelve George II mahogany dining chairs. £5,200

One of a set of eight Regency mahogany chairs with reeded sabre legs. £1,200

One of a pair of Dutch marquetry open arm chairs. £280

Victorian oak elbow chair with a cane back. £10

Late 19th century Windsor wheelback child's chair of ashwood with elm seat. £35

An unusual Edwardian child's high chair.   £30

An oak open arm chair, the high panel back with a carved Dutch panel of two men on horseback and coat of arms.
£80

A teak rocking arm chair, with cane back and seat. £38

An oak arm chair, the carved panel back with initials A.G. and dated 1696.   £48

A mahogany and ivory inlaid arm chair on cabriole legs. £31

A carved mahogany bergere arm chair on square tapering legs, with cane back and sides.
£12

A Windsor armchair in ash with beechwood seat in untouched condition, circa 1795.   £54

One of a pair of Regency library chairs.   £290

A small Orkney wing chair with hard wood seat.   £36

18th century oak corner chair, with turned cross stretchers and carved cabriole legs to the front.   £165

18th century oak child's chair. 260gns

A carved oak arm chair of Italian design on shaped supports.   £38

One of a set of eight oak dining chairs with leather backs and seats, on spiral legs and stretchers (2 & 6).   £135

A stained arm chair with hard seat.   £12

One of a set of eight chairs with cane backs, on spiral legs and stretchers, (6 & 2).   £160

A carved oak corner chair on turned legs, the splats carved and pierced with birds' heads.   £38

A primitive Welsh farmhouse spinning wheel chair of solid ashwood, circa 1760.   £48

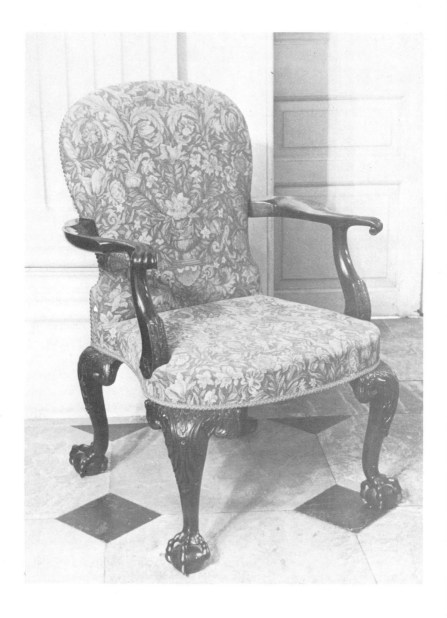

George II mahogany open armchair with shaped seat and back upholstered in floral machine tapestry. £430

(Henry Spencer & Sons, Retford)

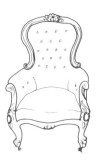

A 19th century lady's ebonised chair with upholstered panel back and seat.   £25

Victorian carved walnut easy chair with padded arms.   £150

One of a pair of Hepplewhite easy chairs on tapered mahogany legs and stretchers.   £44

Early 19th century wing chair on square legs with stretchers.   £140

One of a set of five, four and one, giltwood chairs.   £400

Early 19th century carved walnut armchair, 39ins high.   £145

Edwardian inlaid mahogany easy chair on short cabriole legs.   £60

Late 19th century lug easy chair on claw and ball feet.   £75

Edwardian inlaid mahogany easy chair on short tapered legs with spade feet.   £32

CHAIRS – EASY

A 19th century mahogany arm chair of Louis XV design, on fluted cabriole legs.   £75

A Regency scroll-back mahogany frame chair, upholstered in red and green brocade.   £95

A Victorian mahogany spoon back easy chair, with button back, standing on cabriole legs.   £100

George III oak armchair with panelled back, dated 1723.   £200

An Oriental carved and pierced circle back easy chair on scroll legs, the upholstered seat in rep.   £55

A well carved Victorian arm chair, circa 1860.   £155

A Victorian carved oak arm chair, the high panel back, arms and seat covered in velvet.   £44

A 19th century mahogany framed invalid's chair, with adjustable back and pull out foot rest.   £145

One of a pair of mid 19th century oak thrones with tall arched backs and the arms on arcaded supports.   £580

One of a set of six late 19th century mahogany open armchairs, on turned and fluted legs. £125

Victorian rosewood prieu dieu chair, with original buttoned coffee brown upholstery, circa 1845. £65

A Victorian mahogany arm easy chair, the back and seat covered in crimson rep. £34

One of a pair of Victorian rosewood chairs with spiral arms, legs and stretchers. £70

One of a set of four George II mahogany arm chairs, with cabriole legs and ball and claw feet. £9,000

An oak armchair in the William and Mary manner. £40

A rosewood circle back easy chair, on carved turned legs. £26

19th century lady's oak chair, on tapered legs. £10

A Victorian mahogany spoon back easy chair, on cabriole legs. £140

CHAIRS — EASY

A late 19th century mahogany framed rocking chair, upholstered in fawn moquette. £15

A Victorian waxed rosewood spoon back easy chair on turned legs. £100

A lady's Victorian walnut easy chair with upholstered panel back and seat, on turned legs. £44

Early Victorian rosewood button back grandfather chair, with original brass castors. £95

A lady's small easy chair, upholstered in green floral figured brocade, on turned legs. £40

A Venetian carved giltwood wing easy chair on cabriole legs. £110

A Victorian rosewood high back chair, with spiral pillars to the back, on cabriole legs. £55

A 19th century Venetian carved giltwood and painted chair, standing on carved cabriole legs. £125

A Continental walnut arm chair on square legs and stretchers. £10

Children's chair made from fourteen cow horns with velvet upholstered seat, 18ins high, 13ins wide, circa 1835.
£95

A pair of Victorian carved rosewood open arm easy chairs of scroll design on cabriole legs. £240

One of a suite of four fauteuils of Louis XV design. £1,000

A small carved mahogany wing easy chair on cabriole legs. £14

One of a pair of interesting, heavily carved Oriental hardwood armchairs. £330

A lady's spoon back easy chair, on rosewood scroll legs. £62

One of a pair of Italian walnut arm chairs.
£260

Early Victorian lady's chair. £74

A George II mahogany framed library chair.
£350

French Provincial walnut
framed arm chair.   £164

Early 19th century embossed
easy chair on fine mahogany
turned legs.   £190

A mahogany circle back arm
chair on cabriole legs.   . £9

One of a pair of 18th century
giltwood upholstered chairs.
                                       £352

One of a pair of small
upholstered easy chairs. £48

A high back upholstered arm
easy chair on turned legs with
club feet.   £11

One of a pair of Louis XVI
style giltwood fauteuils. £282

A Victorian papier mâche and
mother of pearl inlaid spoon
back arm chair, on cabriole legs.
                                       £52

Louis XVI Bergere chair on
fluted legs.   £152

One of a pair of Louis XVI style salon chairs with giltwood frames.   £235

Louis XVI style giltwood arm chair.´   £129

Louis XV walnut armchair on cabriole legs.   £176

A carved walnut arm chair of Louis XV design with high panel back, on square moulded legs.   £36

French empire style bergère chair.   £129

19th century wing easy chair on mahogany legs with fluted club feet.   £44

Louis XVI style bergère chair with carved giltwood frame.   £135

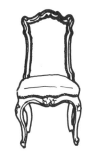

Louis XV style giltwood easy chair with carved cabriole legs.   £105

One of a pair of French walnut framed armchairs.   £235

CHAIRS – EASY

A rosewood high back chair, the upholstered back with spiral pillars, on turned legs. £60

Edwardian inlaid mahogany circle back arm chair on square tapered legs. £50

Victorian rosewood high basket easy chair on turned legs. £28

18th century upholstered easy chair on cabriole legs. £260

Late 19th century folding chair with carpet back and seat. £15

19th century carved and giltwood chair, the panel back and seat in floral brocade. £35

Fine quality William and Mary chair upholstered in gold velvet, circa 1690. £385

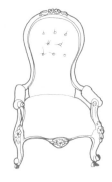

Victorian carved walnut gents' chair on cabriole legs with scroll feet. £170

Solid ebony prie-dieu chair with beautifully carved green silk padded back, circa 1900. £50

A fine George II mahogany open armchair with solid seat and cartouche shaped back panel. £580

(Henry Spencer & Sons, Retford)

CHESTS

18th century walnut chest of three drawers, standing on bracket feet, 2ft 9ins wide.   £70

A 19th century mahogany bow front chest of four long and two short drawers, 3ft 5ins wide.   £34

17th century oak block front chest of drawers, 40ins wide, 22ins deep, 37ins high.   £225

Early oak mule chest with panelled ends, circa 1700, 37ins wide, 24ins deep, 33ins high.   £145

Late 19th century mahogany inlaid, bow front chest of six drawers.   £60

A George III mahogany chest of drawers with brass drop handles, 33½ins.   £150

An attractive Queen Anne walnut chest of drawers on bracket feet.   £360

An Oriental red lacquered chest with two short and one long drawer, the fronts carved with gilt flowers and foliage, 2ft 8ins wide, 1ft 8ins high.   £201

An early 18th century veneered walnut chest of two short and two long drawers, on bracket feet, 41ins.   £205

An early 18th century walnut veneered chest of drawers, 2ft 8ins wide. £210

17th century oak chest with applied moulding to the front, 37ins wide. £210

A neat George III mahogany chest of three long and two short drawers, with fluted canted corners, on bracket feet, 2ft 10ins wide. £190

A fine 18th century walnut bachelor's chest. £2,900

A 19th century mahogany and walnut chest of four long drawers, on bracket feet, 2ft 4ins wide. £74

A William and Mary marquetry chest of drawers, circa 1695, 38ins wide, 37ins high, 22ins deep. £820

19th century Continental parquetry chest of three drawers, 34½ins. £340

18th century oak and walnut linen-press and chest, 31½ins wide. 180gns

Mahogany bow front chest of three drawers, circa 1820, 36½ins wide, 33ins high, 20½ins deep. £145

317

CHESTS

Queen Anne walnut chest of drawers on bun feet, 3ft wide. £365

An early 18th century walnut chest of drawers on bracket feet, 41½ins wide. £190

A fine and small Jacobean oak chest of drawers, on ball feet. £285

Early 18th century walnut chest with crossbanded drawers and slide, 2ft 8ins wide. £400

An 18th century Dutch walnut and floral marquetry chest. £1,350

Early 19th century mahogany chest of two short and three long drawers, 3ft 1ins wide. £55

A small George III mahogany chest of drawers, standing on bracket feet. £400

Queen Anne walnut chest, 39ins wide. £220

A fine oak chest of drawers, with deep moulded panels, circa 1685, 3ft 6ins wide, 2ft 1ins deep, 3ft 3ins high. £385

An early George III mahogany chest of four graduated drawers, with fitted brushing slide, 3ft wide. £200

Regency period camphorwood secretaire military chest. £360

A late 19th century mahogany chest of four long drawers, the front inlaid with husks and ribbons, standing on bracket feet, 31½ins wide. £72

A cross-banded, ebony-inlaid, bow-fronted chest of drawers, in mahogany, with original brass knobs, and oak drawer linings, 41ins wide, 21ins deep, 41½ins high, circa 1795. £179

18th century lowboy on later 19th century base, the drawers, back and sides also having been altered. £310

A Queen Anne walnut chest of drawers. £160

An oak-lined walnut chest of drawers with herringbone cross-banded top and drawer fronts, circa 1710, 34ins wide, 20ins deep, 33ins high. £395

Georgian mahogany chest of four graduated drawers and brushing slide. £300

George III oak secretaire chest. £100

319

CHESTS

Early chest of drawers with moulded drawer fronts, 39ins high, 43ins wide. £195

Late 18th century Dutch bombe front chest on heavy paw feet, 2ft 11ins wide. £200

19th century inlaid mahogany chest on bracket feet, 3ft 1ins wide. £80

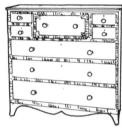

19th century military chest in two sections with sunken brass handles. £140

Small Georgian mahogany chest of nut brown colour, 85cm wide. £130

Regency mahogany chest of drawers, 46ins wide. £140

A William and Mary oyster veneered chest. £640

Empire style mahogany chest of three drawers with brass embellishments. £200

Small 18th century Portugese olive wood chest of three drawers on short carved legs, 24ins wide. £220

A George I walnut chest decorated with crossbanding and stringing, 3ft 4ins wide. £180
(King & Chasemore, Pulborough)

A 19th century American, mahogany highboy of Chippendale style, 3ft 3ins wide. £150

(King & Chasemore, Pulborough)

A George III mahogany tallboy, with brass loop handles and bracket feet, 3ft 6ins wide.   £230

A Georgian walnut veneered tallboy.   £860

A small mahogany bow front tallboy with seven drawers, 3ft 6ins high.   £40

Small walnut veneered chest on chest, circa 1740, 39ins wide.   £750

A fine Queen Anne walnut tallboy with deep cavetto frieze, and three short and six long drawers divided by brushing slide, 3ft 7ins wide.   £1,300

Early 19th century mahogany tallboy chest of eight long and two short drawers, 3ft 8ins wide.   £240

George III mahogany tallboy with original brass handles, 77ins high, 41½ins wide, 19½ins deep, circa 1740.   £340

Chippendale mahogany tallboy, 3ft 4ins.   £800

A 19th century mahogany serpentine front library tallboy chest of six long drawers and a brush board, on bracket feet.   £60

CHEST ON CHEST

A Victorian maplewood and simulated bamboo chest of six drawers, 35ins wide. £110

A Chippendale period mahogany tallboy, 47ins. £190

Georgian mahogany tallboy with brass loop handles. £140

18th century walnut tallboy chest with three long and two short drawers. £260

An 18th century walnut tallboy chest with six long and three short drawers, having brass drop handles and standing on bracket feet, 3ft 2ins wide, 5ft 9ins high. £150

19th century mahogany tallboy with five long and two short drawers, 3ft 2ins wide. £230

18th century Dutch marquetry tallboy chest, 59½ins high, 37ins wide, 18½ins deep. £625

A mahogany inlaid pedestal of eight drawers, 4ft 4ins high. £85

18th century mahogany tallboy with brass loop handles and bracket feet, 3ft 6ins wide. £210

A Queen Anne walnut tallboy in two sections, decorated with crossbanding and featherbanding, 3ft 7ins wide.   £640

(King & Chasemore, Pulborough)

CHEST ON STAND

A Georgian oak chest on stand, 3ft 3ins.   £230

Queen Anne oak chest-on-stand, with wavy stretchers, 41ins wide.
260gns

William and Mary walnut chest on stand, 3ft 2ins.   £900

Queen Anne walnut chest on stand.   £350

A mid 18th century black and gold lacquered chest on stand, decorated with oriental designs, 41ins wide.   £380

A Queen Anne walnut two-part chest on cabriole legs with unusual square cut feet, circa 1720, 69ins high, 42ins wide, 21ins deep. £680

18th century Dutch marquetry cabinet on chest, 6ft wide.
£2,900

William and Mary walnut chest on stand, with cabriole legs.   £320

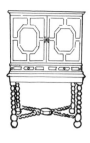

Italian pietra dura cabinet on spiral legs with cross stretchers.
£1,900

A William and Mary oak chest on a stand, 2ft 10ins wide. £300

(King & Chasemore, Pulborough)

An Empire period mahogany chiffonier, 2ft 8ins wide.   £220

(King & Chasemore, Pulborough)

Regency chiffonier in finely grained mahogany, 42ins wide, 47ins high. £268

Regency mahogany chiffonier, with brass grilles to the doors, 52½ins high, 36½ins wide, 16ins deep, circa 1825. £212

Rosewood chiffonier with pleated silks to the doors, circa 1835, 45ins wide. £265

A small stripped pine Regency bookcase. £125

Victorian inlaid walnut chiffonier with mirrored back and doors, 5ft wide. £180

George III mahogany dwarf bookcase. £200

A rosewood chiffonier of good quality and compact size, 39ins wide, 16ins deep, 48ins high, circa 1840. £135

Early 19th century rosewood chiffonier with brass grilles to the doors, 3ft 4ins wide. £345

An attractive rosewood chiffonier with grilled doors and ormolu mounts, 36ins wide, 16½ins deep, 52ins high. £215

329

CHINA CABINETS

French walnut display cabinet with brass decoration and a marble top, 30ins wide, circa 1830. £385

An Edwardian mahogany inlaid china cabinet with two glazed doors, on square tapered legs, 3ft wide. £75

Late 18th century marquetry cabinet on an oak base. £1,150

Edwardian inlaid mahogany display cabinet on short tapered legs with spade feet. £75

Edwardian inlaid mahogany kidney-shaped display table. £95

19th century ebonised display cabinet with ormolu decoration. £190

An Edwardian mahogany inlaid china cabinet with two leaded and glazed doors, on cabriole legs, 2ft 4ins wide. £100

19th century inlaid mahogany serpentine front display cabinet, 3ft wide. £200

Chippendale style mahogany china cabinet, circa 1870, 67ins high, 27ins wide. £165

19th century French display cabinet with decorative painted panels. £1,450

Late 18th century Dutch marquetry display cabinet. £1,400

Mid 19th century Vernis Martin vitrine. £975

Victorian walnut inlaid pier cabinet enclosed by a glazed door, 2ft 7ins wide. £68

19th century French ebonised and buhl display table, with glazed, hinged cover, 3ft wide. £140

Georgian mahogany display cabinet with adjustable shelves, 40ins wide, circa 1830. £175

Chinese Chippendale style mahogany display cabinet on stand, 2ft 6ins wide. £100

18th century Flemish display cabinet, finely carved overall. £800

An Edwardian mahogany inlaid breakfront china cabinet with glazed door, on square legs, 3ft wide. £95

CHINA CABINETS

19th century kingwood and marquetry vitrine, with glass door. £600

A 19th century mahogany display table, on cabriole legs, with chased ormolu mounts and feet, 27ins wide. £300

A giltwood wall display case, 2ft 2ins high. £20

An ebonised and gilt corner cabinet, the two cupboards with glazed doors and open shelves, 6ft 4ins high. £70

Georgian display cabinet in satinwood, 43ins. £820

A mid 19th century marquetry inlaid and ormolu mounted kingwood vitrine, 80ins high, 51ins wide, 21ins deep. £1,100

A very fine, small kingwood display cabinet. £2,200

An Edwardian mahogany inlaid china cabinet with shelves and three cupboards. £85

A late 19th century mahogany music cabinet with hasped mirror back, on cabriole legs, with undershelf, 22½ins wide. £32

An ebonised display cabinet, the frieze with five small china plaques, and having brass beaded borders, 2ft 9ins wide. £70

An Edwardian mahogany showcase, inlaid in various woods and painted bell flowers, 30 x 20ins. £190

Mid 19th century boulle side cabinet inlaid with brass scrollwork on red tortoiseshell ground. £325

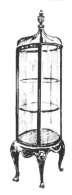

Dutch walnut and marquetry cabinet on chest, profusely inlaid with floral and bird marquetry, 3ft 1ins wide, 6ft 5ins high. £1,450

Edwardian inlaid mahogany display cabinet with bevelled mirror panels, 5ft wide. £210

A mahogany and glazed circular display cabinet with domed top, 2ft 4ins diam., 6ft 10ins high. £440

Late 18th century English gilt wood display cabinet. £525

18th century Dutch marquetry commode and display cabinet, 36ins wide, 77ins high. £1,350

A good Dutch marquetry display cabinet, with a bombe base and glazed upper section, 74ins wide. £3,000

Mid 19th century French kingwood vitrine mounted with ormolu and painted with panels in the style of Watteau.   £1,550

A mahogany inlaid bow front commode with hinged top and front of simulated drawers, 2ft 1ins wide. £38

Welsh child's potty chair, of fruitwood with a geometric loop design on the back, 24ins high, circa 1770. £38

An 18th century mahogany and marquetry inlaid basin stand, with double hinged top, cupboard and commode drawer below, 19½ins wide. £210

19th century mahogany inlaid commode with cupboard and drawers, 1ft 11ins wide. £26

Stripped pine commode with shaped apron. £55

Finely figured Sheraton mahogany night commode, with crossbanding between imitation drawer fronts, 25ins wide, 29ins high, 18ins deep. £95

One of a pair of stripped pine pot cupboards. £70

George III mahogany bedside cupboard with commode drawer, 21½ins wide. £45

Very small mahogany basin stand with drawer and cross stretchers, 12½ins square, 30ins high. £47

COMMODE CHESTS

Late 18th century commode chest with marquetry decoration. £825

An 18th century Italian walnut commode of four long drawers, with satinwood and marquetry inlaid panels, 4ft 9ins wide. £150

18th century Continental figured walnut commode of serpentine form, with brass handles and cross-banding, 42ins wide. £2,400

A French brass and red tortoiseshell inlaid commode, on bracket feet. £7,800

One of a pair of 18th century tulipwood and marquetry petit commodes, 1ft 10ins wide. £790

A semi-circular figured walnut commode. £1,000

Late 18th century satinwood commode of semi-circular shape, inset with oval painted metal plaques in the style of Angelica Kauffmann, 1.29m wide. £2,300

Exceptionally fine George III oak mule chest, with five dummy drawers and lift-up lid, and two drawers at the base. £360

A 19th century French kingwood and parquetry commode, of bombe shape. £950

Continental serpentine walnut commode, the three drawers with ornate ormolu handles, circa 1840.   £165

Chippendale figured mahogany serpentine front commode, 3ft 5ins wide.   £2,000

Hepplewhite period serpentine mahogany commode, banded with tulipwood.   £760

A fine Sheraton style satinwood commode, crossbanded in rosewood and painted with bouquets and classical scenes after Angelica Kauffman, 5ft 2ins.   £1,050

A French 19th century oval shaped mahogany commode of two drawers, the marble top with pierced brass gallery, 2ft wide.   £230

18th century English commode, 5ft 1ins wide.   £1,400

A late 18th century French Provincial serpentine-fronted walnut commode, 48½ins.   £270

Hepplewhite mahogany serpentine front commode.   £1,400

A Continental leather covered commode, with bow fronted centre and concave sides, the top and front with panels of painted flowers, 4ft 6ins wide, 3ft 1ins high.   £200

COMMODE CHESTS

Sheraton satinwood commode of semi-circular form, decorated with metal plaques painted by Angelica Kauffmann, R.A. £2,300

Early 19th century petit commode with painted panel and ormolu mounts. £517

Louis XV petit commode with marquetry decoration and a rose marble top. £705

Louis XVI style commode with ormolu decoration. £329

18th century half round rosewood and satinwood commode painted with classical and floral designs, 3ft wide. £400

One of a pair of 19th century Italian commode chests. £900

Small early 19th century marble topped commode with ormolu handles and escutcheons. £275

A rare French Provinvial oak commode of neo-classical design, circa 1789. £550

One of a pair of Danish, mid 18th century commodes, by Mathias Ortmann, 73.7cm wide. £12,000

Louis XV style kingwood and marquetry ormolu mounted serpentine commode with a pink veined marble top, 48ins wide. £380

17th century Dutch marquetry walnut bombe commode. £1,200

Hepplewhite period serpentine fronted mahogany commode with shaped apron. £760

Louis XV style ormolu mounted commode with parquetry decoration. £423

Louis XV style petit commode with a marble top and ormolu gallery. £200

Louis XVI style commode with a figured marble top and ormolu escutcheons. £200

George III satinwood commode in the style of Angelica Kauffman. £2,000

Late 18th century Dutch black and gold lacquered commode, 3ft 9½ins wide. £720

18th century North Italian commode of walnut, decorated in the rococo manner. £4,300

CORNER CUPBOARDS

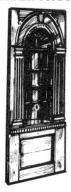

A stripped pine Georgian niche originally built into room recess. £250

An oak corner cupboard, enclosed by a glazed door, on stand with two shelves, 6ft 6ins high. £75

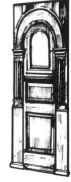

A Georgian stripped pine niche with fielded panel doors. £250

A mahogany corner cupboard with a panel door, 3ft 5ins high. £26

A Continental rosewood and walnut banded bow-fronted encoigneur on square tapered legs, and with marble top, 2ft 9ins high. £210

Victorian mahogany corner cupboard with glazed door. £40

Edwardian mahogany standing corner cupboard with satinwood inlay. £210

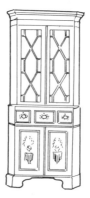

A mid 19th century satinwood and marquetry corner cabinet in two heights on bracket feet, 40ins wide, 86ins high. £300

A mahogany inlaid corner cupboard on a stained cupboard stand with a panel door. £75

A mahogany corner cupboard with a glazed door, on a stand with turned fluted legs, 3ft 1ins high. £40

Bow fronted mahogany standing corner cupboard, 33ins wide, 58ins high, circa 1840. £145

A mahogany inlaid and satinwood banded corner cupboard with glazed door, on square tapering legs, 5ft 4ins high. £130

A pine corner cabinet with panel door, 4ft 2ins high. £40

18th century oak corner cupboard with shaped and fielded door. £95

Late 18th century bow fronted oak corner cupboard with mahogany banding, 43ins high. £165

A satinwood inlaid corner cupboard with painted floral designs, on bracket feet, 6ft 7½ins high. £250

18th century barrel back pine cupboard, 42ins wide. £215

A mahogany and satined corner cupboard with glazed door above and panel door below, 6ft 3ins high. £90

341

CORNER CUPBOARDS

A mahogany corner cupboard with a glazed door.   £80

Oak display corner cupboard, inlaid with walnut, 44ins high, 33ins wide, circa 1760.   £125

A mahogany corner cupboard with glazed door, 3ft 7ins high.   £28

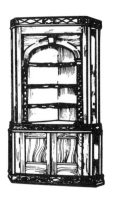

Free-standing, full length stripped pine corner cupboard of Chippendale style.   £325

Early 19th century pine corner cupboard with attractive mouldings, 72ins high.   £145

Georgian stripped pine full length bow corner cupboard.   £300

Georgian oak hanging corner cupboard, 30¼ins wide.   35gns

George III oak corner cupboard, the panel door crossbanded in fruitwood and with original dental cornice, brass handle and key escutcheon, circa 1770. £85

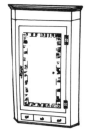

Late 18th century oak and mahogany banded corner cupboard with panel door, 3ft 9ins high.   £45

19th century mahogany corner cupboard with panelled door.   £28

A mahogany inlaid corner cupboard, with glazed door and swan neck pediment, 3ft 11ins high.   £70

Fruitwood hanging corner cupboard with glazed door, and satinwood inlaid dentil cornice, circa 1780, 42ins high, 27ins wide, 18ins deep.   £148

A small early 19th century pine standing corner cupboard.   £165

18th century pine corner cupboard with elaborate dentil frieze, 88ins high.   £220

Pine corner cupboard with glazed doors, circa 1800, 75ins high.   £195

George III oak corner cupboard the door panel crossbanded in fruitwood, with drawer in base, 45ins high, circa 1770.   £85

19th century ebonised bow front corner cupboard with two doors painted with George III and other figures, 3ft high.   £95

Victorian stripped pine corner cupboard with glazed doors.   £26

A 17th century oak tridarn, surmounted by gouged carved designs, 4ft 7ins wide.   £420
(King & Chasemore, Pulborough)

Tudor style oak court cupboard, 54ins wide. £190

17th century carved oak court cupboard. £400

Late 17th century inlayed court cupboard. £375

18th century oak court cupboard with fielded panels. £700

An early oak court cupboard enclosed by four moulded panel doors, 4ft 9ins wide. £400

A mid 17th century oak court cupboard on vase shaped feet. £380

A carved oak court cupboard of Elizabethan style, with a canopy top, 4ft 6ins wide. £125

18th century oak buffet, the doors inlaid with various woods. £525

A Dutch 18th century oak court cupboard with ebony inlay and mounts, 5ft 10ins high, 5ft 3ins wide. £1,900

A Victorian walnut credenza, decorated all-over with tulipwood crossbanding and satinwood stringing, the frieze and double doors each centred by blue and white, floral painted Sevres oval panels, 6ft wide.

King & Chasemore, Pulborough)

£760

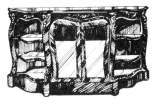

19th century boulle and ormolu-mounted credenza with serpentine front. £650

19th century ebonised credenza with satinwood inlay and marquetry designs, enclosed by a panel door and two glazed doors, 5ft wide. £150

A fine Victorian walnut credenza, with shaped ends and ormolu mounts. £950

A Victorian ebonised and gilt display cabinet with inset Wedgwood plaquettes, 6ft wide. £160

One of a pair of 19th century walnut credenzas, with Pietra Dura panels, 43ins. £1,000

A Victorian walnut inlaid credenza, the shaped ends with cupboards and glazed doors, decorated with brass mounts and borders, 6ft wide x 3ft 9ins high. £820

Late 19th century figured walnut credenza, with marquetry pillasters and ormolu caryatid mounts, 59ins. £460

19th century figured walnut credenza with marquetry pilasters and ormolu caryatid mounts, 59ins high. £470

A Victorian walnut credenza with satinwood marquetry designs and brass mounts and borders, 5ft wide. £290

CUPBOARDS

A Dutch carved oak dwarf cupboard with a panel door, on turned bulbous legs and stretchers, 3ft 6ins high, 1ft 10ins wide.   £48

Small oak spice cupboard with eight interior drawers, circa 1690.   £105

A 19th century carved oak dwarf cupboard, the panel door with thistle designs, 2ft 1ins wide.   £16

17th century oak cupboard in two parts, with original iron hinges and handles, 69ins high, 52ins wide, 18ins deep. £295

A rare carved and painted Elizabethan buffet in oak and fruitwood.   £2,900

Late 18th century padouk cupboard, 3ft 11ins wide, 1ft 5ins deep, 6ft 6ins high. £375

17th century French provincial corner cupboard, 6ft 2ins high, with carved decoration.   £500

17th century oak food cupboard, 50½ins wide.   500gns

A 17th century carved oak hall cupboard. £400

A 17th century oak hall cupboard with a single panelled door, 3ft 6ins wide. £170
(King & Chasemore, Pulborough)

DAVENPORTS

Walnut davenport, circa 1840.
£1,200

A Victorian walnut davenport
desk with stationery cupboard
and four drawers to side. £90

Victorian burr walnut davenport
with boxwood string inlay. £245

A late 19th century English
walnut davenport, 2ft 7ins
high. £240

A Burmese carved teak
davenport with panel back, on
bird and animal supports. £145

Early 19th century rosewood
davenport with a sliding top.
£315

A Victorian burr walnut
davenport desk, with four
drawers to the side. £210

19th century rosewood davenport, the side doors enclosing
four drawers. £145

Victorian burr walnut davenport
with pierced gallery. £280

350

Davenport in rosewood with baluster gallery and sphinx-carved supports.   £1,000

A late 19th century mahogany and satinwood inlaid davenport desk, with four drawers to side and four small drawers and mirror to back, 22ins wide. £135

Rosewood davenport with decorative brass inlay on drawers and sides.   £1,200

Victorian rosewood davenport with spiral pillar supports. £100

Regency rosewood davenport with sliding top.   £280

Victorian rosewood davenport with brass gallery, circa 1820, 21½ins wide, 22ins deep, 32½ins high.   £240

Regency rosewood davenport with sliding top.   £215

A Regency rosewood davenport desk, the interior with six small mahogany drawers, having original Vitruvian scroll brass gallery and flush brass handles.   £385

Figured mahogany davenport, with brass handles, gallery and castors.   £1,150

DRESSERS

Superb George III oak dresser, on cabriole legs, with tripod feet, the cross-banded drawers and spice cupboards with shell inlay, 78ins wide.　　£775

Late 18th century oak Welsh dresser, with three shelves, fitted drawers and plateau underneath.　　£400

A very small oak Welsh dresser with brass handles to the three drawers and original delft plate rack, 58ins wide, 14ins deep, 75ins high.　£690

A small 17th century oak dresser, the base with turned supports, 57ins wide.　£255

An oak Welsh dresser with four plate shelves and three drawer apron front, on turned legs and platformstretcher, 5ft 3ins wide.　· £540

Early 18th century Welsh oak dresser with Delft plate rack, the three drawers with original brass pull handles, 67ins wide, 16½ins deep, 73ins high.　　£685

Late 18th century oak dresser with cupboards and drawers to base, 5ft 4ins wide.　　£240

An 18th century oak dresser with pot board, 72ins wide.　£270

18th century oak dresser of good colour, 66ins x 18ins x 76ins.　　£595

19th century oak and elm dresser, with drawers and cupboards, 65ins.. £340

Oak dresser, circa 1760, 78ins high, 68½ins wide, 17ins deep. £580

An early 19th century country Welsh dresser of good colour. £325

18th century oak dresser with pot board and open shelves. £400

An 18th century oak Welsh dresser with triple delft rack to the top, the seven small drawers and two cupboards in the base having brass handles. £460

A well proportioned mid 18th century oak dresser of small size, 54½ins wide, 18ins deep, 75ins high. £765

An 18th century Irish pine-wood dresser, the base with three silhouette shaped front legs, the three drawers having brass handles, circa 1750. £235

A fine Queen Anne dresser. £600

An 18th century oak panelled Welsh dresser with three drawers and two lower cupboards. £310

DRESSERS

Large mid 18th century oak dresser with three reeded shelves over three drawers. £650

An 18th century oak kitchen dresser, 56½ins wide. £380

18th century stripped pine dresser, 59ins wide, 17ins deep. £155

A fine 18th century walnut dresser base on barley twist legs and stretchers. £375

Honey coloured 18th century oak dresser with spice drawers, 50ins wide. £385

An 18th century oak dresser with drawers in the frieze, on cabriole legs, 7ft 3ins wide. £210

Late Victorian oak dresser with carved cupboard doors, 4ft 8ins wide. £100

A very small oak Welsh dresser, circa 1740, with original brass handles, 58ins wide, 14ins deep, 75ins high. £690

A good 18th century oak dresser with panelled back. £360

An oak dresser base with good patina, circa 1760, 52ins long, 22ins deep, 35ins high. £365

An 18th century oak Welsh dresser with triple delft rack.
£460

An early stripped pine dresser base with rack added at a later date. £280

Jacobean oak dresser of three drawers, 6ft wide.
£420

An oak Welsh dresser with three drawers and plate rack above with two cupboards, on turned legs, 6ft 9ins wide. £210

A small Charles II period oak dresser with geometric mouldings on the two drawers. £850

18th century mellow oak dresser with three drawers and two cupboards, 65ins wide. £525

Charles I oak dresser with single plank top, 2ft 6ins high, 4ft 5ins wide. £1,000

Late 18th century oak and elm dresser. £340

A 17th century style oak dresser, 7ft 6ins wide. £520

(King & Chasemore, Pulborough)

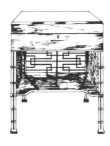

Late 19th century serpentine front mahogany kneehole dressing table, 4ft 3ins wide.
£95

Late 18th century Chinese Chippendale mahogany enclosed dressing table, 2ft.
£425

A walnut inlaid kneehole dressing table, of Queen Anne style, with a drawer and two cupboards, 3ft wide.
£70

A Louis XV Provincial walnut poudreuse, the frieze with two drawers and slide, 2ft 6½ins wide.
£480

Sheraton mahogany enclosed dressing table on tapered legs.
£190

Late 19th century inlaid mahogany kneehole dressing table, 3ft 6ins wide.
£55

An Officer's mahogany campaign chest, circa 1800.
£450

Louis XV style poudreuse with marquetry decoration.
£329

A mahogany kneehole dressing table with three drawers, on square tapered legs, 3ft wide.
£34

ESCRITOIRES

A late 19th century French parquetry serpentine secretaire a Abattant, 23ins. £550

French 19th century amboyna and mahogany secretaire, 2ft 5ins wide. £500

A 19th century escritoire in kingwood and marquetry. £580

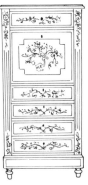

French Empire style inlaid escritoire with a rouge marble top. £470

Louis XVI escritoire of mahogany with gilt brass decoration. £325

Louis XVI style escritoire with marquetry decoration. £400

19th century Dutch walnut and coloured marquetry escritoire of Louis XVI design, the interior fitted with two drawers and shelves, 2ft 10½ins wide x 4ft 10ins high. £200

Victorian figured mahogany escritoire with fall front and five drawers, 3ft 3ins wide. £240

Dutch marquetry straight front secretaire, with a finely fitted interior, circa 1800, 39½ins. £800

A French 19th century amboyna and mahogany escritoire, decorated with floral marquetry designs, 2ft 5ins wide.   £500

(King & Chasemore, Pulborough)

A Queen Anne walnut escritoire decorated with crossbanding and featherbanding, 3ft 7ins wide. **£470**

(King & Chasemore, Pulborough)

Early 18th century oak lowboy, with pierced brass handles.   £160

18th century fruitwood lowboy with pad feet.   £100

An 18th century mahogany lowboy, 29ins.   £230

An 18th century oak lowboy, on cabriole legs, with two short and one long drawer.   £220

George I oak lowboy on square cut cabriole legs.   £230

A walnut lowboy, on cabriole legs with paw feet.   £210

A fine George I oak lowboy on square cut cabriole legs.   £230

18th century walnut kneehole writing table of Queen Anne design, on cabriole legs, 3ft 1ins wide.   £150

A small well-proportioned stripped pine lowboy in Georgian style.   £90

A Queen Anne oak lowboy on square cut cabriole legs.   £240

A George III mahogany lowboy on cabriole legs.   £285

A well proportioned oak lowboy, 30ins wide, 20½ins deep, 28ins high, circa 1730.   £445

PEDESTAL DESKS

Mahogany writing desk, 33ins.
£470

Camphorwood campaign desk
with ebony stringing, made in
China, circa 1830, 49ins wide.
£420

A small 18th century oak
kneehole desk.   £240

Mahogany Chippendale kneehole
desk, with a sliding tray and a
centre cupboard, 3ft 2ins x 1ft
8ins x 28ins high.   £850

An American port office desk,
with a finely fitted interior.
£440

Early Georgian walnut
kneehole desk, on bracket
feet.   £700

A fine mahogany cellaret
sideboard consisting of three
deepdrawers behind side
doors, centre cupboard and
centre drawer, 54ins long,
21ins deep, 36ins high.   £289

A Victorian mahogany partner's
desk, with drawers and cupboards
on reverse side, the leather inset
top with gilt tooling, 5ft x 3ft 10ins.
£585

A very small kneehole
desk, originally veneered
in walnut with oak
drawer linings, the feet
and handles not original.
£185

An 18th century English burr yew partners desk on paw feet.   £3,000

Queen Anne walnut kneehole desk, with one long and six small drawers, 3ft wide. £1,000

A nicely grained Queen Anne walnut kneehole desk, with pierced brass handles, 31½ins wide. £480

A Queen Anne walnut kneehole desk with double herringbone and crossbanding.   £1,000

A very attractive 19th century Oriental kneehole desk, with cupboard and drawers, 44ins wide, 28ins deep, 31ins high.   £365

A George III mahogany kneehole desk with crossbanded top and leather-lined slide, 3ft 3ins wide. £400

A George III mahogany kneehole writing desk, 33ins.   £460

Seddon-style carved oak and decorated kneehole desk, circa 1860.   £270

A very fine Queen Anne walnut desk, in need of restoration, 33ins wide.   £725

PEDESTAL DESKS

An 18th century English burr yew partner's desk on paw feet. £300

Late 19th century oak roll top desk. £85

Early 18th century walnut kneehole desk on bracket feet. £1,000

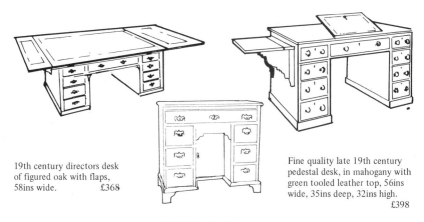

19th century directors desk of figured oak with flaps, 58ins wide. £368

Finely figured mahogany kneehole desk with slide, circa 1750, 38ins wide. £585

Fine quality late 19th century pedestal desk, in mahogany with green tooled leather top, 56ins wide, 35ins deep, 32ins high. £398

Late 19th century mahogany roll top desk of eight drawers. £200

A George III mahogany inlaid pedestal writing table with one long drawer in the frieze, 2ft 8½ins x 1ft 9½ins. £520

Late 19th century oak pedestal writing table of nine drawers, 4ft 3ins wide. £75

A George III mahogany kneehole writing desk with crossbanded top and leather-lined slide, 3ft 3ins wide. £400

(King & Chasemore, Pulborough)

An Architect's superb George III mahogany desk of fine patina, 122cm wide. £680

(Henry Spencer & Sons, Retford)

SCREENS

A small papier mache firescreen, painted with a bird in a landscape. £5

A most attractive mahogany-framed firescreen containing a glazed trumpet banner of the Household Cavalry, 38 x 26ins. £125

A Victorian walnut fan shaped firescreen, the panel embroidered with silk flowers. £18

Victorian scrap-work screen, each of the four panels having illustrations pasted on both sides of the leather base material, 6ft 2ins high. £80

Japanese ebonised and carved wood two leaf draught screen, 6ft 8ins high. £40

Late 19th century double-sided paper screen, each of the three folds with portrait and landscape ovals within carefully arranged foliate surrounds, 5ft 3ins high. £80

Victorian walnut framed firescreen with decorative woolwork picture. £26

A pair of Venetian carved gilt and white painted pole firescreen frames on pillar and tripod base with scroll feet. £60

19th century mahogany framed firescreen. £12

A Victorian mahogany fire-screen with needlework panel of Queen Victoria and Prince Albert on horseback. £50

A 19th century Chinese hard-wood table screen. £10

A Victorian brass two-fold firescreen. £21

A mahogany firescreen with a needlework panel of two girls and a dog in a landscape, 4ft high. £12

An attractive four-fold French giltwood screen, the panels painted in oils on canvas, circa 1840, 56ins high, 77ins long, fully extended. £285

A Victorian brass firescreen with crimson velvet and silk embroidered panel. £24

Victorian walnut framed pole-screen on cabriole legs. £22

Japanese six-panel wall screen, each panel of a different scene, signed Mitsuoko of the Tosa School. £162

A mahogany inlaid pole fire-screen of Hepplewhite design, the shield shaped panel embroidered with flowers. £18

SECRETAIRES

Louis XVI secretaire a abattant by Jean-Henry Reisener, of oak veneered with various woods.
£47,250

A George III mahogany secretaire chest, 39½ins.
£80

Late 18th century Italian marquetry secretaire. £1,650

A mahogany secretaire cabinet by William Vile, 2ft 4ins wide.
£29,000

Small mahogany secretaire chest, circa 1810, 33ins wide. £295

An ivory inlaid Portugese walnut secretaire cabinet, circa 1850, 2ft 8ins wide. £580

George III mahogany secretaire chest with satinwood interior and brass loop handles. £160

The travelling secretaire of Czar Paul I of Russia by David Roentgen, in mahogany with ormolu mounts. £11,437

An unusual George III mahogany writing desk, 38ins. £290

A fine late Georgian mahogany secretaire cabinet of rich patina, inlaid with boxwood lines, 112cm wide.
£700

(Henry Spencer & Sons, Retford)

SECRETAIRE BOOKCASES

George III mahogany secretaire cabinet with swan necked pediment. £700

A gentleman's mahogany wardrobe with secretaire drawer and two panel doors below, 4ft 4ins. £160

Late Georgian mahogany secretaire bookcase, with astragal glazed doors, 48ins wide. £275

Mahogany secretaire bookcase, with unusual glazing to the doors, the secretaire fitted with drawers and pigeon holes, 47ins wide, 22½ins deep, 97ins high, circa 1800. £650

Late 18th century Hepplewhite style secretaire bookcase, 7ft 10ins high, 4ft wide. £810

Hepplewhite mahogany secretaire bookcase with shaped apron and splay feet. £810

Late Georgian mahogany secretaire bookcase, 47½ins wide. £368

Early 18th century walnut secretaire cabinet. £400

A fine and rare Estate desk in satinwood and mahogany, with en grisaille painted panels enclosing beautifully fitted interior. £2,250

370

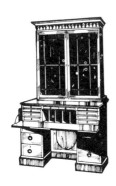

An Edwardian inlaid mahogany secretaire bookcase, standing on tapered legs with spade feet. £165

Georgian mahogany secretaire bookcase, the upper part enclosed by astragal glazed doors, 3ft 8ins wide. £500

Regency mahogany secretaire bookcase, 49ins wide, 83ins high. £550

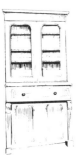

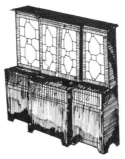

Victorian mahogany secretaire bookcase with glazed doors, 3ft 6ins wide. £110

George III mahogany breakfront secretaire bookcase with astragal glazed doors, 8ft 6ins wide. £1,500

An attractive secretaire bookcase in crossbanded faded mahogany, the cupboard with sliding trays and cellarette, 48ins wide, 23ins deep, 92ins high, circa 1840. £675

George III mahogany secretaire bookcase, 7ft 7½ins high, 4ft 1ins wide. £1,650

George III mahogany secretaire bookcase decorated with kingwood crossbanding, 3ft 6ins wide. £500

A 19th century stripped pine glazed secretaire bookcase. £295

A mid 18th century oak secretaire tallboy in two sections, 3ft 6ins wide. £200
(King & Chasemore, Pulborough)

Victorian mahogany settee on cabriole legs, 4ft 6ins wide. £130

Victorian carved mahogany framed, shaped back settee, 7ft wide. £170

A Victorian mahogany half back couch, on turned, fluted legs. £35

Louis XV style gilt and white settee, on cabriole legs. £176

19th century carved oak box hall settle, 6ft wide. £65

An early oak day bed, 66ins long, 22ins wide. £245

Victorian cast iron garden seat of fern leaf design. £40

Louis XVI style giltwood couch on fluted legs. £211

SETTEES & COUCHES

A mahogany inlaid arm settee, on square tapering legs, 4ft 6ins wide.   £42

Part of a late 19th century five-piece Burmese hardwood suite comprising settee, two open arm chairs, and two single chairs, all heavily carved and pierced with dragon designs.   £600

An attractive maple settee, circa 1830, 25ins x 76ins x 33ins high.   £230

An oak settle with carved panels, circa 1700, 43ins x 17ins x 41ins high.   £130

Swan neck Regency sofa on turned mahogany legs, 91ins wide.   £185

Small 19th century giltwood settee on turned and fluted legs, 4ft 3ins wide.   £80

A Moresque hardwood double seat, with tortoiseshell and mother of pearl inlay.   £250

Victorian walnut framed settee with open arms and cabriole legs, 5ft 6ins wide.   £275

A white painted Victorian scroll end settee. £85

Oak settle with crossbanded panels, 74ins x 25ins x 40ins high, circa 1760. £120

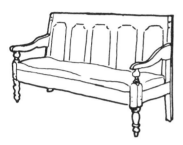

An oak settle with fielded panels, circa 1730, 75ins x 23ins x 40ins high. £120

French style carved and painted conversation settee, circa 1850. £575

A magnificently carved early 18th century oak settle. £145

Edwardian inlaid mahogany settee on cabriole legs. £100

Early Victorian walnut button-backed chaise longue with elaborately moulded frame and legs. £380

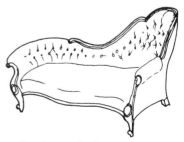

Victorian carved walnut spoon back settee on cabriole legs. £260

SETTEES & COUCHES

An oak arm settee with box seat, the high panel back and lower panel carved with scrolls, rosettes and a lion's head, 3ft 3ins wide.   £140

19th century carved oak settle with a cane back and lift up seat.   £100

An early Victorian walnut framed settee. £160

Late 19th century giltwood settee of small proportions.
£130

Queen Anne walnut settee, 6ft wide. £750

A richly carved and pierced Victorian chaise longue with shaped and studded back, supported on cabriole legs, 6ft 4ins long.   £360

A mahogany arm settee with matching square back easy chair, on square tapering legs.   £50

A French carved walnut chaise longue of Louis XV design, in three parts.   £350

Georgian oak panelled settle. £62

A carved oak hall settle, with carved lion mask arm terminals and box seat, 4ft wide. £75

A Victorian walnut-framed, double end settee. £270

A Georgian walnut frame three-seat settee, 5ft 3ins wide. £90

A small Louis XV design carved giltwood arm settee on cabriole legs. £130

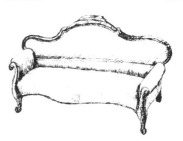

A Victorian mahogany shaped-back settee, standing on cabriole legs. £85

19th century mahogany circle back wing settee on cabriole legs, the frame carved with flowers and scrolls. £105

An Edwardian mahogany square back arm settee, with inlaid and satinwood banded borders and matching square back easy chair. £233

SIDEBOARDS

George III mahogany sweep front sideboard, on tapering legs with spade feet, 55½ins wide. £1,000

George III mahogany shaped front sideboard with boxwood string inlay, 3ft 11ins wide. £210

A late Georgian mahogany bowfronted sideboard with turned legs. £200

Mahogany bow fronted sideboard, circa 1795. £650

Regency mahogany sideboard, with fitted cellarette cupboard, circa 1815, 36½ins high, 21ins wide, 70ins long. £340

Mahogany breakfront pedestal sideboard, circa 1810, 48ins wide. £320

An Adam style mahogany sideboard, the fluted frieze with two drawers, 7ft 11ins wide. £150

Edwardian ebonised sideboard on cabriole legs. £20

Small Sheraton design mahogany bow fronted sideboard, 122cm wide. £160

Late Regency mahogany pedestal sideboard, 72 ins wide.   £60

George III mahogany inlaid, shaped front sideboard on tapered legs with spade feet, 6ft wide.   £220

A mahogany lunette shaped sideboard with three drawers and two cupboards, on carved cabriole legs, 4ft 8ins wide.   £75

Late 19th century serpentine fronted mahogany sideboard of Sheraton design, extensively decorated with satinwood crossbanding and stringing, 6ft wide.   £175

Sheraton period mahogany bowfronted sideboard with satinwood inlay, on square tapering legs with spade feet.   £1,100

A Georgian mahogany bow-front sideboard on turned tapering legs, 5ft 6½ins wide.   £300

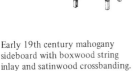

Early 19th century mahogany sideboard with boxwood string inlay and satinwood crossbanding.   £550

A mahogany inlaid sideboard on square tapered legs, 6ft 1ins wide.   £60

Small finely figured mahogany bow fronted sideboard, circa 1810, 42½ins wide.   £585

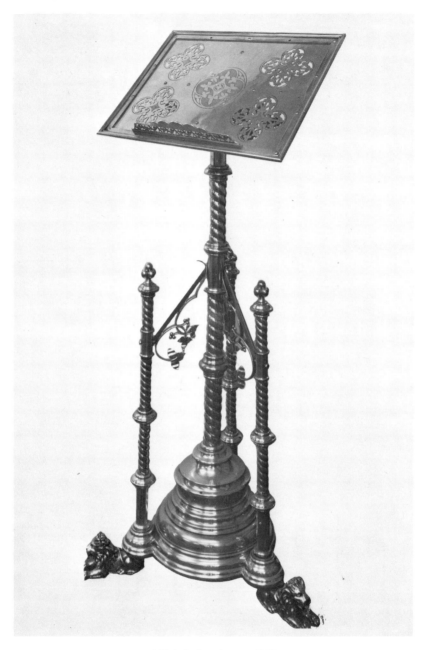

A Victorian brass lectern. £190
(King & Chasemore, Pulborough)

A Burmese carved teak circular jardiniere stand, the pedestal with carved figure of a bird, 2ft 9ins high. £32

Late Victorian French style octagonal plant stand with pierced brass gallery. £26

18th century mahogany basin stand, 2ft 8½ins high. £90

Single brass adjustable candlestick stand, the shaped lobed base covering iron weight, circa 1820, 9ins high. £28

19th century rosewood oblong plant table on turned legs, 18ins wide. £28

A lacquered folding magazine rack painted with flowers. £22

A Chinese carved hardwood jardiniere stand with inset marble top, 2ft 9ins high. £100

Unusual 18th century gentleman's wig stand in turned mahogany with walnut, 14ins high, circa 1790. £24

One of a pair of early Victorian mahogany circular lamp tables, on polygonal stems. £80

Chinese carved hardwood square jardiniere stand, 3ft 8ins high. £70

A rosewood inlaid easel. £55

381

STANDS

A heavy carved oak winged
animal stick stand, with
hinged cover, on circular
base. 2ft 7ins high.   £60

Hepplewhite design
towel horse. 2ft. £30

French mahogany circular
plant stand with pierced
brass gallery. 2ft 7ins high.
£35

Victorian spiral twist plant
pedestal. 54ins high.   £18

Victorian well carved wooden
bear hall stand. 89ins high.
£210

A brass and mahogany
shaving stand with
upright bevelled mirror.
£60

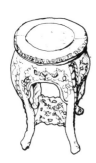

Circular Oriental carved
plant stand. 19ins high.
£42

A Victorian mahogany circular
stand for three decanters,
with cupboard below,
standing on three brass paw
feet. 30ins high.   £55

An ebonised jardiniere stand
with carved and pierced
birds and flowers. 18ins high.
£14

Mahogany urn table with tray top and small slide. circa 1760. 12ins high. £420

Chinese carved hardwood square jardiniere stand, 18ins high. £55

A stripped pine urn stand. £42

A late 19th century mahogany lamp stand. on pillar and claw base. 3ft 6ins high. £26

George III hat stand in mahogany, 72ins high. £135

One of a pair of Chippendale design mahogany torchères, 3ft 8ins high. £720

An attractive Welsh book-stand. shaped from a single piece of mahogany, with integral folding hinge. £35

William and Mary walnut candlestand with quarter veneered top and inlaid herringbone. £375

A Chinese carved teak circular jardiniere stand with undershelf, the top inset with marble, 1ft 11ins high. £30

STOOLS

An oak and elm stool, with shaped frieze and baluster turned legs.   £100

A rosewood inlaid music stool on cabriole legs, the hinged box seat covered in silk brocade.   £24

A late 19th century Chinese mother of pearl inlaid padoukwood stool, with marble-inset top. 1ft 2ins diam.   £165

Chippendale design stool on carved cabriole legs, 23½ins x 16½ins.   £140

A large Victorian carved serpentine shaped stool, on cabriole legs, 4ft 6ins long.   £120

One of a pair of Victorian circular footstools with beadwork tops.   £18

Carved pine stool of the Regency period with original needlework seat.   £60

A early oak stool of Gothic design.   £62

Queen Anne walnut stool. 1ft 10½ins x 1ft 4¼ins.   £400

Victorian rosewood adjustable piano stool.   £17

17th century oak joint stool. 18½ins wide.   220gns

A late 19th century giltwood cane seated duet stool.   £40

Pair of early 18th century
English stools, with walnut
cabriole legs. 56cm wide.
£2,200

An early oak stool, with
ringed and turned legs.
£180

19th century Ashanti
Chieftan's stool, carved
from a single piece of wood.
£38

A Victorian ebonised and
beadwork, circular footstool.
£10

A 19th century dressing
stool, on carved cabriole
legs and paw feet.   £55

Victorian circular foot
stool with woolwork
cover.   £14

19th century simulated
rosewood 'X' frame stool
with woolwork cover. £55

A window seat in the
Chippendale manner with
scrolled ends and gros-
point needlework. 4ft
long.   £420

Victorian oblong shaped
walnut dressing table stool
on cabriole legs, 20ins wide
£28

17th century oak
joint stool.   £110

A Queen Anne oak close
stool with simulated
drawers.   £125

An unusual 19th century
piano stool, the linen-covered
seat resting on four tubular
brass legs and central expanding
pole.   £48

STOOLS

An oblong dressing stool on carved mahogany cabriole legs with claw and ball feet.   £55

A mahogany inlaid oblong piano stool on square tapered legs.   £24

A rosewood circular stool on turned tapering legs.   £11

Late 19th century fender stool on cabriole legs with claw and ball feet. £24

Late 19th century ebonised stool on turned legs.   £15

Walnut and marquetry inlaid window seat with scroll arms, 2ft 6ins wide.   £46

Victorian cabriole leg dressing table stool, 1ft 10ins wide.   £34

Victorian fender stool with a beadwork top, 2ft 7ins wide. £30

A mahogany framed Bergere suite with cane back and sides, on carved cabriole legs, comprising a settee and two easy chairs. £290

Victorian walnut framed three piece suite on cabriole legs. £550

A Chesterfield suite upholstered in silk brocade, comprising knoll, three seater settee and two wing easy chairs. £95

Small 19th century three piece suite on short turned legs and brass castors. £110

SUITES

Part of a carved mahogany drawing room suite on cabriole legs, comprising an arm settee, two gentlemen's arm chairs, two lady's chairs and four single chairs. £300

A superb quality mid-Victorian period suite, comprising settee, grandfather chair, grandmother chair and two salon chairs, inlaid with ebony and amboyna wood. £695

Part of a suite of English satinwood seat furniture, comprising also a pair of armchairs and four side chairs, circa 1900. £780

Part of a set of twelve George II seat furniture. £3,800

A mahogany inlaid and satinwood banded drawing room suite with pierced trellis splats, on turned legs, comprising an arm settee, two arm chairs, and four single chairs.   £240

A carved mahogany drawing room suite, on cabriole legs, comprising an arm settee, two arm chairs and four single chairs.   £100

SUITES

Lounge suite in floral tapestry consisting of a settee and two easy chairs. £320

19th century inlaid mahogany drawing room suite comprising a couch, two easy chairs and six dining
chairs.   £550

Part of a superb eleven piece Louis XVI salon suite. £4,000

Edwardian inlaid mahogany three piece suite on short tapered legs with spade feet. £155

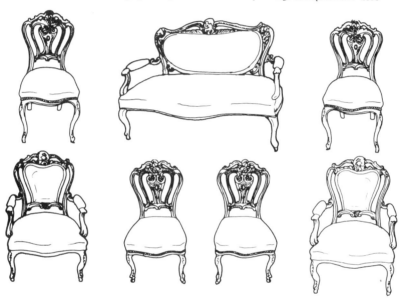

Victorian carved mahogany drawing room suite comprising a settee, two arm chairs and four single chairs.
£230

Three piece Victorian suite with scalloped crests and turned trumpet form front supports. £310

A William and Mary marquetry card table with shaped top, decorated all-over with floral and urn marquetry designs in various woods, 2ft 8ins wide.   £1,000

(King & Chasemore, Pulborough)

One of a pair of Regency rosewood card tables on platform bases.   £495

Victorian rosewood folding over top tea table on a central column and platform base.   £60

A Victorian rosewood folding over tea table on pillar and carved claw base, 3ft wide.   £130

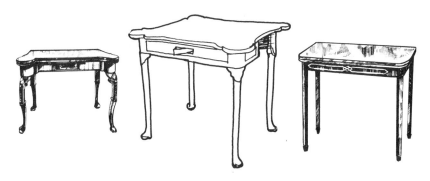

19th century Georgian style mahogany folding card table on square cut cabriole legs.   £180

Georgian mahogany card table with folding concertina action, 85cm wide.   £230

Mahogany inlaid folding over tea table of Sheraton design with satinwood banded borders, 3ft 3ins wide.   £100

A Victorian rosewood folding over tea table on pillar and claw support, with carved scroll feet, 3ft wide.   £115

Victorian burr walnut serpentine front card table with marquetry and ormolu decoration.   £475

George III mahogany folding card table on splay feet with brass toe castors. £170

CARD & TEA TABLES

A Victorian half circle fold over card table, on carved pillar and claw base, 3ft wide. £100

A Victorian walnut serpentine shaped, folding-over card table, on two carved end supports and stretcher, 3ft wide. £80

A Victorian rosewood folding over tea table, on centre pillar and block base, 3ft 1ins wide. £115

Inlaid boulle card table with baize-lined interior and ormolu mounts, 31ins high, 18½ins deep. £750

An 18th century parquetry games table, on slender cabriole legs. £300

A Chippendale style, mahogany folding-over card table, on carved square legs, with scroll designs, 2ft 9ins wide. £170

19th century mahogany folding over tea table, with rounded corners and turned legs. £32

A late 19th century mahogany oblong fold over card table, with drawer, on cabriole legs, 27ins wide. £24

A Sheraton style tea table. £165

Victorian inlaid amboyna-wood and ebonised games table with ormolu mounts, 29ins high, 24ins wide, 16ins deep.   £325

A very fine walnut card table by Thomas Johnson, 91·5cm wide.   £15,000

Dutch walnut and marquetry inlaid, oblong shaped fold-over card table with drawer, standing on square tapered legs, 2ft 9ins wide.   £260

Mahogany card table with inlaid stringing and cross-banding with both back legs opening to support flap, circa 1800, 36ins long, 18ins deep, 30ins high.   £185

A Regency mahogany tea table, rosewood crossbanded on centre support with four splayed feet, having brass terminals.   £180

Georgian period serpentine fronted card table with baize lining, 36ins wide, circa 1810.   £185

A Victorian walnut fold-over card table, on fluted end supports, 3ft wide.   £100

A William and Mary marquetry card table, with three drawers to the frieze, 32ins wide. £1,000

A fine quality Regency mahogany card table.   £280

A Hepplewhite period semi-circular fold-over top card table in mahogany with satinwood banding and hare-wood inlay, 2ft 11¾ins wide. £410

Victorian pollard oak fold over card table, 3ft wide. £80

Victorian rosewood inlaid envelope card table with drawer and undershelf. £145

Edwardian mahogany envelope card table with undershelf. £75

Regency rosewood fold over top card table, with satinwood bandings, 36ins wide. £430

Victorian inlaid burr walnut card table, on a stretcher base. £110

A George III mahogany card table on tapering legs with spade feet, 36ins. £140

Victorian mahogany and rosewood banded fold over tea table, 3ft 2ins wide. £90

A fine pair of Georgian faded mahogany half-moon card tables, inlaid with satinwood. £1,500

A Victorian walnut card table
with carved cabriole legs, 38ins.
£300

Victorian inlaid walnut
half round folding card
table, 3ft wide.   £150

A pair of Sheraton style
satinwood half-circle folding
over tables, with rosewood
crossbanded borders, 3ft
2ins diam.   £750

A fine quality mahogany tea
table on finely turned legs,
36ins wide, 29ins high, circa
1790.   £198

A Louis XV style, ebony and
tortoiseshell boulle, serpentine
shaped, folding over card table,
on cabriole legs, with chased
brass borders and mounts, 3ft
1ins wide.   £500

Mahogany Chippendale tea
table with oak-lined drawer,
32ins wide, 16ins deep, 19ins
high, circa 1765.   £248

Late 18th century Adam style
serpentine shaped fold over
card table on tapered legs with
block toes.   £205

Rare early 18th century
coaching games table.
£65

Georgian mahogany inlaid
half circle fold over card
table, 3ft wide.   £220

CONSOLE TABLES

Victorian console table in the manner of W. Cookès of Warwick, 4ft 6ins wide, 1ft 6ins deep, 3ft high. £175

A very finely carved console table, originally gilded. £240

Giltwood consol table with carved and pierced apron and bracket. £24

A carved giltwood serpentine shaped console table, on a scroll leg with pier mirror above in gilt frame, 2ft 10ins wide. £75

A French design carved giltwood console table of serpentine shape, with carved and pierced apron, on one scroll leg, with upright mirror above, 2ft 10ins wide. £95

SUTHERLAND TABLES

A small walnut Sutherland tea table with ebonised borders. £50

A rosewood inlaid oblong two-tier table with folding leaves and satinwood banded borders, 2ft wide. £55

Victorian mahogany Sutherland table on turned end supports, 3ft wide. £20

Victorian walnut oval shaped Sutherland table, 3ft 1ins wide. £82

A mahogany Sutherland tea table with two folding leaves, on turned supports, 3ft wide. £34

A small Victorian oval walnut Sutherland table, 22ins. £32

A superb George III mahogany drum library table of mellow colour and rich patina, 42ins diam.
£880
(Henry Spencer & Sons, Retford)

DINING TABLES

A Victorian walnut inlaid table on four carved centre pillars and scroll feet, 3ft 6ins wide. £70

A fine quality 18th century barrel-shaped mahogany breakfast table with cross-banded top. £800

Georgian mahogany snap top table on quadruple support, 3ft 4½ins diam. £90

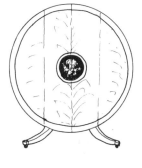

Late Regency satinwood, circular table, 53½ins diam. £360

A George III mahogany snap over table, with tray border on pillar, with bird cage and claws, 2ft 4ins diam. £115

An early 19th century breakfast table, the top inlaid with a bat's wing patera and chevron cross-banding. £900

Victorian walnut oval breakfast table on a quadruple base. £145

George III mahogany drum table on a quadruple base with brass cup castors. £500

A mahogany dining table on a rosewood and brass inlaid pillar and block base, 4ft wide. £110

Regency rosewood dining
table, on central pillar with
tripod base, 4ft diam.   £120.

A George III mahogany
supper table.   £485

A Regency burr elm drum
table with good patina. £610

French Empire style rose-
wood dining table with gilt
winged paw feet.   £720

Finely figured walnut loo
table on a quadruple base,
circa 1850.   £165

Early 19th century marquetry
loo table with a scrolled
quadruple base, 4ft 9ins diam.
   £620

A fine George III mahogany
drum library table, 42ins
diam.   £880

Early 19th century figured
mahogany breakfast table
with yew wood crossbanding
and reeded legs.   £600

Georgian faded mahogany
breakfast table, 4ft 7½ins
x 3ft 6ins.   £300

DINING TABLES

19th century mahogany oblong breakfast table on reeded legs with paw feet, 4ft 1ins wide.
£100

19th century mahogany circular dining table in two parts, on square tapering legs, 4ft 4ins diam.
£175

Late Georgian mahogany breakfast table, 128cm wide.
£150

Georgian mahogany circular tripod table, 36ins diam.
£32

Late 19th century mahogany oval telescope table with five loose leaves, full extent 11ft.
£230

Regency figured mahogany and brass inlaid circular table, 46ins diam.
£240

19th century Boulle circular drum table with heavy ormolu mounts
£860

Regency figured mahogany dining table on splay feet with a crossbanded top, 4ft diam.
£400

Victorian rosewood circular breakfront table on turned pillar and block, 4ft 4ins diam.
£140

18th century solid yew wood two-flap table, with elm frieze, 44ins x 57ins extended.   £85

A Georgian mahogany pembroke table with two 'D' shaped leaves and a drawer, on square tapering legs, 2ft 8ins wide.   £36

A large mahogany inlaid and crossbanded oval dining table with club feet, 5ft 1ins wide.   £400

19th century mahogany Pembroke table with two drop leaves, 3ft 9ins.   £105

Small 18th century oak gateleg table, 28¼ins wide.   95gns

A mahogany inlaid oval dining table with two drop leaves, on pillar and claw base.   £85

Mahogany supper table with cross banded top, circa 1820.   £230

George II oval drop leaf mahogany table on cabriole legs.   £325

Chippendale period mahogany breakfast table.   £310

GATELEG TABLES

Large mid 17th century walnut gateleg table, with barley twist supports, 41ins wide.   480gns

A fine walnut table with barley twist undercarriage, circa 1720, 44ins wide, 53ins long when open.   £325

A Charles II oak gateleg table, with bobbin legs, 4ft wide.   £200

An early Jacobean style oval gateleg table on turned legs, 4ft wide. £240

17th century oak gateleg table with Spanish feet, 54ins x 51ins.   £395

17th century walnut gateleg table.   £180

A Jacobean oak oval gateleg table with two drop leaves, on turned legs and stretchers, 4ft 2ins wide.   £180

A fine walnut gateleg table, circa 1700, 45ins wide when open, 27ins high.   £220

18th century oak gateleg table of good colour. £220

17th century oak gateleg table, the top opening to 3ft 6ins x 3ft.   £120

Early 18th century oak gateleg table, 43ins x 53ins extended.   £155

A well-figured oak gateleg table, in original condition, 44ins wide, circa 1750. £195

William IV rectangular rosewood centre table with two drawers, on turned and fluted pillars, 52ins wide. £130

George III Honduras mahogany dining room table extending to 10ft 3ins x 4ft 2ins. £875

Reproduction oak refectory table on bulbous end supports, 6ft long. £48

Late 17th century Flemish table, the legs formed as classically draped men and women, 3ft 5ins long. £5,200

A pseudo-Gothic oak table. 170gns

Late 19th century mahogany oval telescope dining table on turned legs, full extent 15ft 6ins. £135

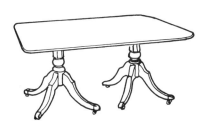

Georgian mahogany two pillar dining table with loose leaf. £480

A pine serpentine table in the French manner with ormolu mounts and centre drawer. £70

LARGE TABLES

Regency two-pillar dining table, seating twelve with extra leaf, circa 1815, 28½ins high, 51ins wide, 112ins long.   £800

A 17th century refectory table. £675

Welsh farmhouse oak refectory table, with two drawers having brass plate handles, circa 1730, 56ins long, 29½ins high, 26½ins wide.   £280

Early 19th century two-pillar dining table, of mahogany.   £800

Oak farmhouse table, 10ft long, circa 1800. £450

An early 19th century mahogany three pillar dining table, 145ins x 54ins. £620

A very rare cherry wood refectory table, 31½ins wide, 7½ft long, 29½ins wide. £460

17th century Flemish draw-leaf table. £900

An English oak refectory table, 8ft 6ins long, 2ft 8ins wide. £470

An exceptionally fine 19th century boulle centre table, in immaculate condition. £950

An early 19th century mahogany dining table, 7ft 7ins long fully extended. £325

Mid 19th century French walnut and kingwood marquetry centre table, 4ft 6ins x 2ft 5ins x 2ft 6ins high. £1,600

A fine 18th century elm refectory table, 7ft 6ins long. £295

Elizabethan oak draw-leaf table, with bulbous legs and ground level stretchers, 6ft long when closed, 11ft 2ins fully extended. £3,000

A 19th century French walnut and marquetry inlaid rosewood banded table, with 'D' shaped ends, 4ft 6ins long, 2ft 8ins deep. £740

An Italian walnut table, 2ft 8ins x 2ft. £400

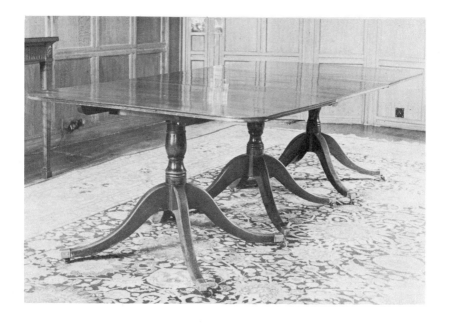

A Georgian triple pillar dining table.   £3,500
(Henry Spencer & Sons, Retford)

A Victorian walnut inlaid oval table, on pillar and claw base. £62

19th century mahogany teapoy, the interior fitted with four lidded compartments, 17ins wide. £85

Edwardian inlaid mahogany centre table, 28ins across. £15

Sheraton style satinwood oval occasional table inlaid with a shell motif, 1ft 9ins wide. £62

Small Spanish gaming table inlaid with ivory, tortoise-shell and rosewood, 25ins high. £175

A neat satinwood oval occasional table with painted Adam designs. £140

19th century Indian carved coffee table inlaid with ivory, 22ins diam. £18

A Victorian rosewood teapoy and work table with double hinged lids, the interior with three compartments and a glass jar, 16ins wide. £70

A rare Regency mahogany dining dumb waiter with mechanical action to convert into a side table. £80

OCCASIONAL TABLES

A 19th century mahogany tray top table on pillar and claw base, 1ft 11ins diam.
£30

Continental marquetry centre table in the late 17th century style, 47ins x 32½ins.   £350

A Burmese carved padoukwood table with shaped apron, on pillar and tripod base, 1ft 9ins diam.   £24

A rosewood and ivory inlaid folding over games table with four folding shelves, 2ft wide.   £84

A mahogany inlaid circular three tier cakestand.   £13

Louis XV harewood gueridon crossbanded in kingwood, with ormolu-mounted cabriole legs.   £300

A reproduction mahogany circular wine table, on pillar and claw, 27½ins high. £9

18th century Italian walnut table, decorated with plaques of pietra dura showing groups of houses and inlaid with tulipwood, 2ft 8ins square.
£2,000

A mahogany inlaid circular snap top table on pillar and claw base, 2ft 6ins diam.
£45

Georgian mahogany pedestal table, 1ft 10ins x 1ft 3¾ins. £150

A set of five late 19th century Japanese cinnamon lacquer tables, gilt-painted with dragons. £90

An unusual rosewood rent collector's table with ten brass slots for coins, on mahogany pedestal and base. £175

An Oriental octagonal table on folding stand carved and pierced with flowers, 21ins. £15

17th century Continental oak table. £440

A small serpentine shaped table with hairwood and marquetry border and centre motif, 1ft 8½ins wide. £32

A walnut library lectern with slanting covered top, standing on four scroll feet, circa 1830. £235

French walnut tip-up table with satinwood inlaid top and carved tripod base. £85

A fine George III mahogany architect's table. £400

OCCASIONAL TABLES

A fine silver table on central column with tripod base, 1ft 10¼ins. £350

A carved oak table, on turned legs and stretchers, carved "Anne Slingskye, 1679", 2ft 4ins wide. £40

Mahogany silver table of Chinese Chippendale design, 3ft x 1ft 11½ins. £375

A rare Georgian mahogany draughtsman's table, the top adjustable to several positions, circa 1810. £265

James I oak credence table with fold over top, the carved frieze inscribed SHL 1624. £380

A mahogany oblong table on pillar and claw base, 1ft 11ins wide. £19

Late 18th century oak cricket table, circa 1790, 27½ins high. £38

Nest of four lacquered tables, in good condition, circa 1840. £135

Oak cricket table with shaped frieze, and chamfered inside edges to legs, 27ins diam., 28¾ins high, circa 1770. £48

412

18th century oak tripod table, 27ins diam.   £27

19th century ebonised boulle centre table with fine inlaid brass parquetry design to the centre and sides, 29ins high, 63ins wide.   £750

One of a pair of black and gilt chinoiserie lacquer tables of Queen Anne design, 2ft 6½ins x 1ft 8ins.   £300

A walnut serpentine shaped oblong table with tray border, on square spindle cluster legs, 29½ins x 21½ins.
£125

A small, early 18th century walnut Spanish table, with drawer, 21ins high, 24ins long, 15ins deep.   £175

A nest of four lacquered tables decorated with Chinese landscapes in gold lacquer, 26ins wide.
£16

18th century oak and elm cricket table.   £52

A late 18th century mahogany architect's table with rising top.
£610

17th century walnut cricket table, 20½ins wide.   150gns

OCCASIONAL TABLES

Chippendale mahogany pedestal table with piecrust edge, 2ft diam. £180

A fine Dutch marquetry silver table, on cabriole legs. £1,000

Small 19th century walnut occasional table with clover leaf top. £74

19th century Chippendale style mahogany snap top table with piecrust edge. £90

19th century Pietra-Dura inlaid marble and ebonised table, 30ins wide. £495

Victorian papier mache occasional table with painted decoration. £75

19th century walnut oval shaped occasional table on shaped support. £38

19th century Louis XV style kingwood occasional table mounted with ormolu. £750

A circular garden table on three cast iron legs, 2ft diam. £28

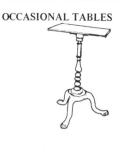

19th century mahogany
occasional table on a
tripod base.   £35

An Italian walnut table, the top
parquetry and marquetry inlaid,
on central pillar and tripod base,
2ft 8ins wide.   £80

Chippendale period mahogany
wine table with claw and
ball feet, 27ins high, circa 1780.
          £78

Victorian walnut occasional
table, with inset marble top,
19ins.   £50

An oak hall table with two drawers,
the frieze carved with birds' heads
and scrolls, on turned legs, 4ft wide.
          £85

An oak tripod wine table,
circa 1765, 14½ins diam.,
26½ins high.   £45

An Oriental damascind brass
circular coffee tray, on carved
wood folding stand.   £9

Late 18th century mahogany
architect's table.   £300

Victorian rosewood tray top
table, 16ins.   £55

A Regency mahogany occasional table.   £290
(King & Chasemore, Pulborough)

Mahogany library table, signed 'Gillow', with drop leaves and gold tooled leather top, 30ins high.   £225

Late 19th century English satinwood pembroke table, on tapered legs with spade feet, 2ft 5ins wide.   £300

A Hepplewhite period satinwood crossbanded and boxwood inlaid pembroke table, with serpentine shaped flaps, 3ft wide.   £195

Georgian mahogany and rosewood banded pembroke table on square tapered legs.   £85

18th century pembroke table in mahogany with rope decoration, 2ft 4½ins high, 3ft 2¾ins max. width.   £550

A Sheraton mahogany pembroke table with oval leaves.   £260

Mahogany pembroke table on reeded legs, circa 1800. £257

Sheraton oval pembroke table on tapered legs, 2ft 11ins x 1ft 4ins.   £850

19th century satinwood pembroke table, 32½ins wide.   £300

417

SIDE TABLES

A mid 17th century elm
side table.   £200

Late 18th century mahogany
bow front side table with a
crossbanded top, 33ins wide.
£115

A rare Georgian stripped pine
side table, the bracket not
original.   £95

18th century oak side table
on square legs.   £50

A William and Mary olivewood
side table, the oblong top
oyster veneered and with
pearwood geometric inlays,
37ins wide.   £470

Sheraton faded mahogany
bowfront side table, 3ft
3ins.   £400

Oak side table crossbanded
in mahogany and inlaid
with stars and box, on
cabriole legs, circa 1730.
£265

Stained walnut library
table, 3ft 7ins x 2ft
3¼ins.   £625

An attractive Charles II
oak side-table, 21ins wide,
34½ins long, 25½ins high.
£140

George I walnut side table, circa 1735. £340

18th century oak side table with single drawer. £135

Queen Anne fruitwood side table with single drawer and brass drop handles, circa 1710, 27ins high. £165

A small William and Mary oak side table, circa 1695. £285

Regency mahogany library table, inlaid with ebony, circa 1820, 29ins high, 27½ins wide, 42ins long. £170

Charles II oak side table with bobbin turned legs and stretchers. £225

Late 19th century mahogany side table on square tapered legs, 3ft wide. £32

18th century oak side table, with a carved frieze, 40ins wide. 65gns

George III mahogany side table on tapering legs with spade feet, 4ft 7½ins. £770

SIDE TABLES

One of a pair of English late 18th century tables attributed to John Linnell, in giltwood, with a marble top. £7,875

A Continental walnut inlaid oblong table with drawer, on turned legs and club feet, 3ft. 1ins wide. £75

William and Mary oak side table with turned stretchers, 29ins high, circa 1690. £295

George I gilt side table on cabriole leg supports, with a figured marble top. £375

A very elegant Queen Anne oak sidetable, on squared cabriole legs. £240

19th century consol table with marble top, 46ins wide, 41ins high. £165

A beautifully carved 19th century oak buffet with a green marble top, 60ins wide. £275

Victorian rosewood oblong table with drawer, 4ft 9ins long. £95

Mid Victorian walnut centre table with a parquetry top, 48ins wide. £40

A Regency mahogany sofa table extensively decorated with coromandel wood crossbanding 4ft 8ins fully extended. £320

A Regency rosewood sofa table, decorated with inlaid cut brass stringing, 3ft wide. £440
(King & Chasemore, Pulborough)

421

SOFA TABLES

A fine early Regency mahogany sofa table with brass cup castors. £660

Late Regency sofa table of mahogany, 37ins x 24ins with leaves down, circa 1830. £265

Sheraton mahogany sofa table, 4ft 10ins x 2ft 5¾ins. £2,400

An early 19th century mahogany sofa table with two folding leaves and two drawers, on turned end supports. £280

Sheraton period mahogany and rosewood banded sofa table, on splay feet with brass castors. £1,250

A George IV rosewood sofa table, on platform base with splay feet and brass castors, 44ins wide. £390

Georgian mahogany sofa table on splay feet. £530

George III mahogany sofa table with crossbanded top, circa 1800, 28ins high, 26ins wide, 51½ins open. £600

Regency period rosewood sofa table crossbanded in satinwood. £600

Late Regency rosewood sofa table, on a central pedestal with splay feet, 36ins x 26ins. £340

A Regency mahogany sofa table, decorated with coromandel wood crossbanding, 4ft 8ins fully extended. £320

Regency rosewood sofa table, on splay feet with claw castors, 58 x 25ins when open. £290

A fine George III mahogany sofa table, with original brass castors, 26ins wide, 35ins long. £675

A small mahogany inlaid sofa table with two folding leaves and a drawer, with satinwood borders and a shell motif on end supports, 2ft 4ins x 1ft 4ins. £175

A very fine early 19th century mahogany sofa table with crossbanded top, 38ins. £1,000

William IV mahogany sofa table, 39ins x 27ins. £200

A fine Georgian mahogany sofa table, the reeded legs with carved acanthus and brass castors, 5ft 3½ins long, 2ft 6ins wide. £460

A mahogany sofa table with two drawers, on end supports and stretcher, 5ft wide. £110

SOFA TABLES

Sheraton style satinwood inlaid sofa table with 'D' shaped leaves, 4ft 7ins wide overall.   £340

Early 19th century rosewood sofa table with crossbanded top and satinwood stringing.   £950

A rosewood sofa table, circa 1830.   £470

Late Regency mahogany sofa table on reeded legs.   £560

Rosewood and satinwood inlaid oblong sofa table with brass paw terminals, 5ft 2ins wide.   £300

19th century mahogany sofa table on a shaped platform base with paw feet.   £290

Regency rosewood sofa table on a central column with platform base. £175

Georgian mahogany sofa table with reeded legs.   £460

Regency mahogany sofa table with brass claw castors, 150cm wide when open.   £400

Small 18th century oak coffer. £145

A camphorwood chest with brass borders, 3ft 6ins wide. £45

Early 17th century oak coffer with a plank top. £125

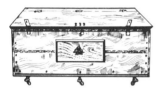

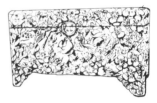

A teak hall chest with hinged cover, brass side handles, hinges and mounts, standing on paw feet, 4ft 6ins. £55

Korean finely engraved mounted chest, circa 1870. £270

A highly carved 19th century camphorwood chest. £235

Mid 18th century oak mule chest on bracket feet. £210

A small Jacobean oak hall chest with hinged lid. £70

Early 18th century mahogany hall chest with satinwood decoration. £185

An Oriental elm, iron-bound chest, circa 1830. £165

Korean brass-bound elm chest, circa 1870. £290

An 18th century teak hall chest, the front panels carved with rosettes, 3ft. £32

TRUNKS & COFFERS

19th century Dutch burr-elm veneered chest, on bracket feet, 48¾ins. £210

Early 18th century oak mule chest, carved with initials and date, 1708, the two drawers missing, 50ins wide. £36

Early 17th century Continental marriage chest painted with a courtly garden scene and dated 1605, with wrought iron bindings and two lockplates, 43ins x 20ins. £460

A small Henry VIII oak coffer with original lock plate. £600

17th century oak coffer, 54ins wide. £150

A fine English oak coffer with lunette carving on the top rail, arcaded panels and two side-runner drawers at the base, circa 1630, 56ins wide. £490

A fine quality 17th century oak coffer with a plain top, the four panel front finely carved with formalised flowers and plumes within arches. £260

A pine dough bin with finely carved mouldings. £95

A rare late 17th century yew tree coffer. £270

Early 18th century Dutch oak coffer, 38½ins wide. 90gns

Early 17th century oak coffer. £170

Spanish Matador's trunk, the pine frame covered with black leather, with ornate steel strappings and corners, 26ins high, 21ins deep, 34½ins wide. £39

Late 17th century oak coffer, with a finely carved front, 70ins wide. £160

An attractive oak chest with side-runner drawers, circa 1690, 34ins wide. £285

A fine Charles II oak coffer, the front with three carved panels, pegged joints to stiles, 44ins wide, 20½ins deep, 26½ins high, circa 1660. £195

An early 19th century lacquer chest, on cabriole legged stand. £385

An 18th century Portugese teak chest with hinged lid, brass double handles and embossed and engraved brass mounts, 3ft 3ins wide. £260

18th century oak mule chest with four dummy drawers at the top. £95

17th century oak coffer, with panelled front and sides, 57½ins wide. 190gns

A small, well carved, 17th century rectangular box, on trestle ends, 23½ins long. £180

An early 17th century coffer, in oak, with lozenge shaped walnut panels, 60ins long, 24ins deep, 29ins high. £345

Charles II oak coffer, with three carved panels to the front and panelled top, circa 1660, 44ins wide, 26½ins high, 20½ins deep. £195

A fine moulded front mule chest inlaid with bone and ivory. £525

A fine panelled oak mule chest with good patina, circa 1725, 50ins wide, 21½ins deep, 32ins high. £195

TRUNKS & COFFERS

Early 16th century Spanish carved walnut chest of good patina, 61ins wide. £475

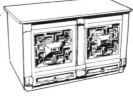

Victorian oak hall chest with geometric moulded front panel, 3ft 11ins wide. £40

17th century carved oak coffer, 57ins wide. £175

Louis XVI chest by G. Beneman, in ebony, ormolu and inlaid marbles, 4ft 5ins wide. £150,000

17th century oak coffer, 2ft 4½ins high, 3ft 11ins wide. £235

An old English panelled oak coffer, 56ins. £160

An unusual oak chest on cabriole legs, circa 1790, 41ins long, 21ins deep, 21ins high. £220

Chinese carved camphor-wood chest, 3ft 4ins wide. £45

18th century Portugese East Indian chest on stand in padouk wood, 36ins wide. £275

Charles II oak coffer with carved stiles and four-panelled lid, 44ins wide, 20ins deep, 24ins high, circa 1670. £195

An early oak vestry chest. £410

18th century sealskin travelling case decorated with brass studs. £55

Flemish elaborately carved
oak coffer dated 1599. £620

17th century iron treasure chest
with an elaborate locking system.
£300

19th century oak hall chest
with three carved panels to
the front, 4ft 7ins wide. £95

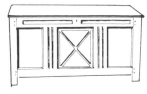

18th century oak coffer with
panelled front, 4ft 7ins wide.
£75

Late 17th century panelled
and carved oak coffer. £180

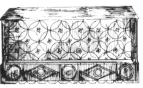

16th century walnut Spanish
chest carved with a geometric
design, 64ins wide. £385

Danish carved pine coffer
with traces of polychrome
decoration, circa 1700.
£295

Late 17th century panelled oak
coffer, 56½ins wide. £115

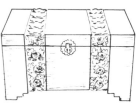

19th century Chinese carved
camphorwood hall chest, 2ft
4ins wide. £45

George III mahogany silver
chest with brass fittings. £135

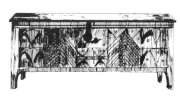

An early oak vestry
chest. £410

18th century oak mule chest,
with brass escutcheons and
handles on drawer, circa 1740.
£175

WARDROBES

Dutch walnut wardrobe, with bombe shaped drawers and short cabriole legs. £1,200

An 18th century oak press or court cupboard. £230

Stained oak wardrobe by Charles Rennie Mackintosh, circa 1890. £920

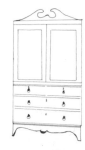

18th century oak press, dated 1721, with fielded panel doors. £255

Part of a fine four-piece bedroom suite. £170

Early 19th century Gentleman's mahogany wardrobe. £260

A mahogany breakfront wardrobe enclosed by four panel doors, inlaid and satinwood banded with oval designs, 6ft 6ins wide. £170

19th century mahogany gentleman's wardrobe with two short drawers, 4ft 3ins wide. £82

19th century heavily carved oak hall wardrobe on ball feet, 4ft 6ins wide. £380

Victorian carved oak hall wardrobe enclosed by two panel doors, 3ft 5ins wide.
£70

18th century mahogany linen press with finely figured and panelled doors.   £80

Early 18th century oak press, carved with 1713, and MH, 54ins wide.
650gns

A carved oak hall wardrobe with two panel doors and a drawer in the base, 4ft wide.   £55

19th century mahogany breakfront wardrobe with sliding trays and drawers to the centre, 7ft wide. £110

An extremely well proportioned pine press of Chippendale style with canted corners.   £270

A Victorian oak hall wardrobe, enclosed by two panel doors, the panels carved with figures of animals, 4ft 6ins wide. £55

Dutch marquetry wardrobe, in two sections, fitted with interior drawers and shelves, 71ins, circa 1740. £1,900

Victorian mahogany breakfront wardrobe with crossbanded borders, 6ft 8ins wide.   £120

WASHSTANDS

George III mahogany folding top washstand, 22ins wide. £45

Georgian mahogany corner washstand, 26½ins. £50

Late 19th century mahogany framed washstand with a tiled back. £20

Late 18th century washstand with folding top. £110

Late Victorian walnut washstand with a marble top. £14

Late Victorian pine washstand with a tiled back. £18

Victorian marble top washstand on a pine base. £18

Georgian mahogany washstand with folding top. £110

Victorian bleached walnut washstand with drawer in the centre. £15

A mahogany whatnot with cupboard containing inner pot-cupboard, 4ft 6ins high. £290

19th century three tier whatnot with inlaid decoration. £55

Victorian mahogany five tier corner whatnot. £55

Regency mahogany whatnot with cupboard and drawer, circa 1820, 63ins high, 19ins wide, 13ins deep. £215

Mahogany whatnot with four shelves and a drawer, on turned supports. £90

A Victorian walnut inlaid whatnot with four half circle shelves, on turned pillars, 4ft 9ins high. £58

Early 19th century rosewood and satinwood marquetry etagere, with ormolu mounts. £160

Attractive hanging or standing display shelves with turned oak supports, circa 1820. £68

A Victorian ebony and walnut banded oblong display table with glazed hinged covers and two undershelves, 1ft 5ins wide. £115

An Adam style mahogany wine cooler. £550
(Henry Spencer & Sons, Retford)

18th century mahogany and brass bound oval wine cooler, 2ft 3ins x 1ft 8ins.   £800

A fine wine cooler, in well figured mahogany, circa 1840, 24 x 20 x 19ins.
£165

Sheraton oval cellarette in faded mahogany with zinc liner, 2ft 2ins x 1ft 8¼ins.
£800

A Victorian oak hexagonal cellarette on six legs, 23ins high.   £20

An Adam brass-bound oval mahogany wine cooler, 2ft 2ins wide.   £6,600

Late 18th century mahogany wine cooler on stand.   £370

An English mahogany and brass-bound octagonal wine cooler with hinged lid.   £240

George III domed top mahogany wine cooler on square tapered legs.   £270

An English mahogany brass bound octagonal wine cooler, 21ins diam, 26ins high.   £240

WORKBOXES

Stripped pine sewing table with fitted interior and original ivory escutcheons and knobs. £115

18th century sofa games table with backgammon board, 2ft 6ins high, 2ft 4½ins wide. £1,450

A 19th century ebony work table with hinged top and rosewood banded panels, 1ft 10½ins wide. £50

A Victorian oval shaped work table, with hinged lid, on turned end supports and claw feet, 24½ins wide. £85

A mahogany work table with hinged top, on pillar and fluted claw, with brass paw terminals. £65

A mahogany and rosewood octagonal work table with hinged top, 16¾ins wide. £32

An early 19th century mahogany work table. £130

A Victorian rosewood serpentine shaped games table with folding over top inlaid with backgammon and chess boards, 21½ins wide. £160

A reproduction satinwood work table on tapered legs with spade feet. £240

A Victorian games/work table, 27ins wide, on turned supports. £110

19th century mahogany work table, the hinged box top with panel of red and gold lacquer, 1ft 9ins wide. £40

Mid 19th century Chinese export lacquer work table, the fitted interior with a basket below, 2ft 1¼ins wide. £210

A Victorian papier mache, mother of pearl inlaid and painted octagonal shaped work table, on shaped tripod feet. £95

Georgian rosewood sewing table with two drawers and sewing compartment, the base with brass toe castors, circa 1820. £385

A fine satinwood worktable, circa 1790, 2ft 5¾ins high, 1ft 6ins wide. £650

Mid 19th century French floral marquetry worktable. £350

A Victorian rosewood octagonal table with hinged lid, on pillar and claw base. £44

Victorian papier mache workbox decorated with mother of pearl. £210

WORKBOXES

A mahogany work table with parquetry worked top, circa 1830, 27ins x 19ins.   £185

Regency period parquetry work table with elaborate toes and castors.   £265

Victorian burr walnut work and games table on a stretcher base.   £160

Victorian games table in mahogany on a central column with platform base.   £40

Faded rosewood work table with sewing compartments, circa 1830.   £385

Regency mahogany games table complete with playing pieces.   £340

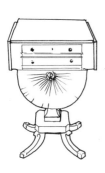

Victorian rosewood work table with two drawers and well.   £145

19th century marquetry work table with ormolu embellishments, 20ins wide.   £275

Victorian mahogany work table with drawer and well, on central column with shaped base.   £85

A satinwood bonheur de jour, by Waring & Gillow, extensively decorated with kingwood crossbanding and inlaid with ribbons and laurel garlands, 1ft 3ins wide. £230

(King & Chasemore, Pulborough)

WRITING TABLES

Hepplewhite style mahogany writing table, circa 1770, 37½ins wide. £375

A lady's Sheraton mahogany inlaid writing table, on turned, fluted legs and cross stretchers, 1ft 10½ins wide. £55

A fine Regency rosewood writing desk, with brass beading and edging, 42ins wide. £1,800

19th century inlaid boulle bonheur-de-jour, inlaid with red tortoiseshell, and with ormolu mounts. £435

A fine Regency rosewood writing desk embellished with brass beading, 3ft 6ins wide. £1,800

A reproduction satinwood bonheur-de-jour. £250

Louis XV kingwood and purple heart writing table with black tooled leather top, bordered with a band of moulded ormolu. £820

A late Victorian writing desk. £280

Mid 19th century French kingwood bureau-plat, richly decorated with ormolu mounts, 6ft long. £1,400

Kingwood bureau plat of
Louis XV design, 4ft 9ins
x 2ft 5½ins.　　　£1,300

Louis XV period bureau plat
and cartonnier, by Jean-
Francois Dubut, 1.28m long.
　　　　　£55,000

Mid 19th century walnut
kidney-shaped writing table.
　　　　　£280

Late 19th century satinwood
bonheur de jour with painted
decoration.　　　£600

19th century satinwood
Carlton House writing desk,
on square tapered legs. £440

Regency lady's mahogany
bonheur de jour, 32ins wide,
on finely turned legs. £200

Victorian mahogany writing
table on turned and tapered
legs.　　　　£18

19th century rosewood sheveret,
with drawer action opening a
shutter front stationery case,
2ft 4½ins wide.　　£200

A mahogany writing table
with two drawers, on lyre
end supports, 3ft wide. £80

WRITING TABLES

Regency rosewood writing desk decorated overall with brass beading and edging, 3ft 6ins wide.   £1,800

Late 17th century oak writing table, the three drawers to the frieze crossbanded with walnut, 2ft wide.   £175

19th century mahogany oblong kneehole writing table on square tapered legs, 3ft 7ins wide.   £60

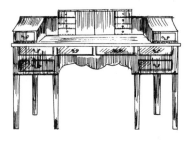

19th century satinwood Carlton House table on square tapering legs with spade feet.   £995

Gillows-made marquetry inlaid kneehole writing desk, probably late 19th century, 4ft wide.   £900

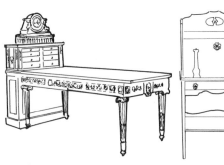

Louis XVI ormolu-mounted ebony bureau plat and cartonnier, the cartonnier surmounted by a clock signed by Robin Paris.   £240,000

Edwardian mahogany fall front secretaire, 23ins wide.   £35

Late 19th century mahogany kneehole desk on cabriole legs with claw and ball feet.   £190

442

A satinwood bonheur-de-jour, the panels painted with floral bouquets. £240

(King & Chasemore, Pulborough)

A fine Galle glass table lamp, signed, circa 1900, 14ins high. £530
(King & Chasemore, Pulborough)

A mid 19th century Bristol clear glass jug. £45

Tiffany Lava/Cypriote glass vase, in pale yellow, 1900. £1,600

Mid 19th century Bristol clear glass jug. £45

St. Louis fuchsia weight, 3¼ins diam. £640

Set of four barrel shaped blue spirit decanters with gilt labels, circa 1790. £250

Tiffany peacock lily-pad vase, 1900. £220

A deep-coloured marbled glass beaker by Freidrich Egermann, 4¼ins high. £1,795

Mid 19th century Bristol clear glass wine cooler with characteristic prismatic cutting round the neck. £40

Tiffany feathered vase, richly feathered in green, gold and peacock, iridescent shades, 1900. £700

A pair of small Bristol blue coloured sauce bottles with lozenge stoppers, 6ins high. £50

A rare Jack-in-the-pulpit Tiffany peacock iridescent glass vase, 1900. £3,600

GLASS

An Orrefors glass vase, by Vicke Lindstrand, circa 1930, 3½ins high. £210

A fine Faience dog by Emille Galle, 12½ins high. 300gns

A finely engraved and cut glass jug, 12ins high. circa 1850. £45

A good heavy art deco glass vase, by Andre Thuret, 1930. £420

A Lalique oyster shell pattern ceiling bowl, 9½ins diam. £25

Very decorative Bohemian glass vase with overlay white on cranberry background, on 5ins circular base, circa 1845. £12

One of a pair of 1845 opaline overlay pink vases, with gold arabesques and polychrome floral decorations, 11ins high. £85

Faience cat, by Emille Galle, 13ins high. 350gns

A Ravenscroft syllabub jug, gilt on sloping shoulders with the label 'Honey Syllabub'. £2,500

An amber flash beaker with gilt lower half by Mohn Jnr., 4¾ins high. £1,995

A Bristol opaque white decanter and stopper. 800gns

Glass beaker with enamelled band of flowers by Mohn Jnr., 4½ins high. £2,520

Glass candlestick with a rare stem comprising different varieties of knops, 7¼ins high. £440

A cranberry coloured murano type jam dish in an epns holder with spoon. £12

A full size Georgian glass decanter. £28

A green glass jug with waisted cylindrical body and folded rim, 7½ins high. £3

A large glass sphere with internal colourful transfers on a white ground, 12ins diam. £22

A baluster shaped glass claret jug etched with stylised acanthus leaves and foliage banding, 12ins high. £52

A fine example of an English sealed wine bottle, the seal showing a comet with five trailing rays, indicating the comet year 1811, 12¾ins high. £58

Late 19th century glass ewer mounted in silver-gilt, 16ins high. £170

A tapered cylindrical glass claret jug with bulbous base and a Victorian silver mounted lid and handle, 12ins high. £65

An iridescent glass honey-pot. £130

A gilded blue glass tulip design wine cooler signed by Isaac and Lazarus. £250

An early 18th century glass beaker with gilt decoration. £100

447

GLASS

An attractive pair of iridescent carnival glass vases, circa 1890, 10½ins high. £12

A Georgian cut glass punch bowl and domed cover, on cut stem and square base, 17ins high. £67

Pair of blue and gilt glass goblets on laticinio stems, 11½ins high. £40

Angular pate-de-cristal vase by Gabriel Argy Rouseau, cast in emerald green marbled glass, 1925. £400

A leaf shaped cranberry coloured lustred carnival glass dish, 8ins diam. £6

Argy-Rousseau pate-de-verre vase, 12¼ins high. £2,500

George Woodhall cameo glass vase, 12ins high, with kingfisher blue ground. £8,925

A handsome pair of glass candelabra each for five lights with four branches, slice cut, the bell shaped candleholders with wax pans and amber cut glass pear shaped drops, 23½ins high. £175

One of a fine pair of French mid 19th century Cristalleries de St. Louis vases with 'crown' paperweight bases, 25.7cm high. £2,300

A fine, early Victorian, frosted glass and silver Pompein jug.   £250
(King & Chasemore, Pulborough)

A pair of 19th century red glass goblets, profusely gilded, 12¼ ins high.   £160
(King & Chasemore, Pulborough)

A large globular purple chemists bottle with stopper and gilt and black "Syr. Phos. C." label, 14ins high. £30

A clear Victorian cylindrical twist bodied vase with flared neck. £3

19th century green glass decanter. £28.50

A Victorian four-colour oviform vase. £1,650

An attractive Victorian vaseline glass vase with opaque frilly edges on top and bottom rims, circa 1860, 6ins high. £14

Rock crystal engraved decanter, probably by Joseph Keller, 10½ins high, circa 1885. £48

A rare 17th century diamond-point engraved ewer. £380

A pair of custard cups with cranberry coloured bowls and clear handles, stems and bases. £10

A milk glass tapered cylindrical vase with enamelled roses, 13ins high. £3.50

A beer mug of bottle glass with white enamel splatter and a fine early handle. £35

A large apothecary's jar, made of crude bottle glass with enamel splatter. £40

Mid 18th century engraved glass tankard. £300

451

DECANTERS

One of a pair of bulbous decanters with diamond cutting and double ringed neck, circa 1820.   £110

One of a pair of ship's decanters with flute cutting and bulls eye stoppers, circa 1810.   £250

One of a pair of quart-sized decanters with bands of diamond and step cutting, circa 1820.   £110

Quart-sized decanter with a central bank of diamond shaped cutting, circa 1810.   £50

One of a pair of Georgian pint size glass decanters.   £72

Ship's decanter with flute cutting and double ringed neck, circa 1810.   £150

Rounded base decanter engraved with floral festoons, with a snake coiled round the neck, circa 1840.   £45

Shouldered mallet shaped decanter, engraved 'Port', circa 1770.   £200

Bottle-sized glass decanter.   £35

One of a pair of decanters with broad bands of flute and diamond cutting, circa 1810.   £120

One of a set of four decanters with bands of diamond flute and step cutting, circa 1810.   £200

Quart-sized, wheel engraved decanter with thistles and roses and triple plain ringed neck, circa 1790.   £100

Left: An 18th century Fiat glass with air twist stem. £160
Right: A small bell shaped goblet engraved and monogrammed H.A., 5ins high. £125

(King & Chasemore, Pulborough)

WINE GLASSES

An opaque twist wine glass with floral decoration to the bowl.   £40

An English baluster goblet, with inscription, circa 1762.   180gns

Facet stemmed wine glass.   £25

18th century wine glass.   £58

A wheel-engraved Silesian goblet, made at Warmbrunn, circa 1760.   £950

One of a pair of 1851 Great Exhibition goblets, both wheel engraved with scenes of Windsor Castle, 5¼ins high.   £130

An opaque twist ale glass.   £38

A clear Georgian rummer.   £11

18th century wine glass, 8 1/8 ins high.   £175

18th century wine glass.   £90

A wine glass with half moulded funnel bowl, on a multi-spiral and gauze opaque twist stem.   £25

An airtwist ale glass, 7½ins high.   £68

18th century wine glass, the moulded bowl with engraved border, 5¾ins high. £24

A Georgian rummer glass. £9

18th century wine glass, 3 7/8ins high. £65

An opaque twist wine glass. £34

An English privateer glass inscribed "Success to Oliver Cromwell. Paul Flyn, Commander." £1,100

A wine glass, the waisted ogee bowl spirally moulded to half height, supported on an opaque corkscrew stem, 6ins high. £21

An opaque twist stem wine glass, circa 1760. £36

Multiple series air twist wine glass, circa 1760. £35

18th century wine glass. £145

18th century ale glass with folded foot and trumpet shaped bowl etched with hops and barley design, circa 1790, 10ins high. £35

18th century wine glass. £100

Stipple wine glass with decoration in the style of David Wolff, 7½ins high. £1,150

SCENT BOTTLES

Dutch glass scent
bottle.   £350

A small early 18th century
glass scent bottle.   £75

A large early 18th century
gilded glass scent bottle.
£15r0

Double ended red glass
scent bottle with
engraved plated top. £8

Scent bottle by G & W,
Birmingham, 1899. £20

Double ended blue glass
scent bottle with silver
gilt mounts.   £16

Scent bottle by Deakin and
Francis, Birmingham 1888.
£40

Two amber ground cameo
bottles, made by Thomas
Webb, or Stevens & Williams.
£780

Early 18th century glass scent
bottle decorated with a
garden scene.   £150

A deep green jade bottle of rectangular form, 2½ins high.   130gns

Well-hollowed jadeite snuff-bottle, the opaque green stone veined with darker striations.   £1,050

A carved hornbill bottle depicting a maiden among peony branches.   900gns

A rare portrait snuff bottle by Tzu I–tzu, the reverse side bearing an inscription.   £1,200

Chinese ivory panelled table snuff bottle encased in a turquoise studded metal frame.   £80

A very rare interior-painted glass snuff-bottle of flattened upright form, signed T'ing Yu-Keng, dated 'Winter month, 1904'.   £1,800

An opaque turquoise snuff bottle, the white and black double overlays carved in high relief, 2½ins high.   280gns

Chinese cloisonne snuff bottle embellished with dragons and carp, of the Ch'ien Lung period.   £85

Chinese cloisonne snuff bottle, of the Ch'ien Lung period, decorated with a dragon and phoenix.   £70

Disc-shaped opaque white bottle, brilliantly enamelled in colours in the Ku Yueh Hsuan style, 2¼ins high.   400gns

An interior painted snuff bottle.   £1,700

A Ch'ien Lung Peking enamel snuff-bottle painted in famille rose colours.   £1,050

HELMETS

An officer's shako 1869-pattern of the 61st Regiment of Foot. £70

An officer's lance cap of The 16th (Queen's) Lancers. £370

A good Cabasset, circa 1600, formed in piece. £50

A good, Victorian Albert-pattern white metal helmet of The Glasgow Yeomanry. £290

An officer's Albert-pattern Life Guards helmet. £160

A very rare officer's gilt helmet of the King's Dragoon Guards. £450

An officer's forage cap of The 1st V.B. Royal Fusiliers. £54

A rare Imperial Russian Gendermerie black felt helmet. £155

An interesting Guatamalan military officer's kepi. £15

An officer's bell-top shako of The 9th (Norfolk) Regiment of Foot. £390

A good, late 16th Century German Morion, formed in one piece. £135

An officer's Albert shako of The 21st (or 2nd West York) Militia. £135

An officer's Busby of the 13th Hussars. £175

A French 19th Century Cavalry helmet. £65

A good, Indo-Persian 'Demon Mask' Kula Khud. £130

A post 1902 trooper's helmet of the 2nd County of London Imperial Yeomanry. £140

An officer's post Crimea shako of the 47th Regiment of Foot. £40

A Victorian officer's black cloth spiked helmet of The 1st Middlesex R.V.C. (Victorias). £75

HELMETS

An unusual Japanese helmet bowl, Kabuto of 'Peach Stone' form.
£65

A post World War I German leather Fireman's helmet.
£32

A Polish officer's helmet Zischagge, circa 1640.
£280

A good early Victorian officer's helmet of the Worcestershire Yeomanry.
£290

A good, mid-17th Century Cromwellian lobster-tail helmet of siege weight. £70

A scarce, Prussian Dragoon officer's Picklehaube.
£120

A 17th Century Burgonet of rather crude construction.
£95

An other rank's Busby of the 14th Hussars.
£50

An English close helmet, circa 1560-70.
£600

An officer's 1869-pattern shako of The 17th (Leics.) Regiment of Foot. £105

A good, late 16th Century Italian Cabasset. £210

A Victorian officer's cap of The Seaforth Highlanders. £68

A Breman police shako. £85

An other rank's lance cap of The 12th Prince of Wales Lancers. £95

A 19th Century Swedish Cavalry leather helmet of Grecian form. £80

Prussian artillery non commissioned officer's Picklehaube of The 46th Field Artillery Regiment. £135

A late 16th Century Burgonet. £165

A Victorian officer's blue cloth helmet of the Ist V.B. The Yorkshire Regiment. £56

Pair of gold opera glasses, the body encrusted with diamonds. £3,900

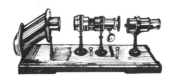

A very rare mid 19th century laboratory bench microscope, of lacquered brass and bronze, by Newton & Co, Fleet Street. £250

Georgian ivory spy glass, circa 1800. £34

A set of brass parcel scales on an oak base, with six brass weights. £35

Large 19th century circular brass and polished steel weighing scales. £28

A chemists' balance by Griffin and Tatlock in oak and glazed case, and a set of metric weights. £17

Late 19th century English brass binocular microscope, in original case, 20ins high. £220

A brass microscope with eyepiece and six objectives, in a mahogany case. £40

A late 19th century microscope, by W.W. Scott, in case. £25

Late 18th century ebony and brass octant with ivory scale, with green baize lined mahogany case. £110

A brass astronomical telescope on folding tripod table stand, barrel engraved Troughton & Simms, London, with mahogany box. £195

A fine sextant by Lilley & Son, London, with platinum scale and rosewood handle, circa 1860. £165

A thermometer in a folding ivory case. £30

19th century cast brass sextant, in original mahogany case, by Simpson & Roberts, Liverpool, circa 1840. £125

A fine late 18th century ship's captain's octant, of ebony and brass with ivory scales, by I. Steele & Son, Liverpool, complete with original oak carrying case. £185

An important microscope by John Marshall of London, 1715. £2,600

Very small 18th century polished steelyard sach scales, stamped P. Beach. 33.m 13½ins long. £18

An 18th century steelyard with lead wight, circa 1760, 16½ins long. £24

A very fine 19th century sextant, by Lilley & Son, London, with platinum scale, and rosewood sighting handle, in original mahogany box. £165

Mid 19th century brass binocular microscope by Hugh Powell of London, 18½ins high. £340

Compound monocular microscope of solid polished brass, engraved 'John Martin', on base, circa 1850. £95

A very fine Ship's Captain's octant, made of ebony and brass with ivory scales, by I. Steele & Son, Liverpool, circa 1790. £185

An 18th century brass Georgian type reflecting telescope by James Short of London, 24¼ins long. £500

Early 19th century brass sextant by Carry of London, 8½ins radius. £85

INSTRUMENTS

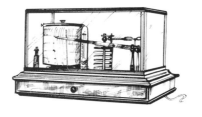

A barograph by Whyte Thomson & Co., Glasgow, in a mahogany and glazed case.   £68

Brass pantograph by Trouton and Simms, 1826.   £95

19th century astronomical telescope by H. Hughes and Sons, London.   £165

Naval officer's brass telescope with tooled leather cover, circa 1810.   £65

Joiner's level by J. Buist, 1850.   £9

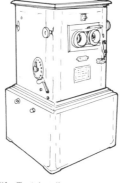

Oak-based postal scales with nickle plain pans, and brass circular weights, circa 1895.   £10

"Le Taxiphote", stereoscopic viewer by Jules Richard of Paris, circa 1922.   £40

A brass microscope with eye-piece and two objectives by R. & J. Beck Ltd., London, in a mahogany case.   £13

A Donaldson's celestial globe, dated 1830, engraved by W. & A. K. Johnston, the stand with ebony turned legs and stretchers, 11½ins high.   £72

Small telescope with stand, circa 1850.   £85

Polished steelyard sach scales, complete with pear shaped weight, circa 1790, 25ins long.   £22

A rare polished iron coffee bean roaster, circa 1760.
£58

A Johnston's 12inch celestial globe, dated 1860, on four ebonised legs and stretchers. £75

Brass and mahogany jockey scales with hide seat, circa 1850. £265

A saw-type pot hanger of polished steel, circa 1690, 26ins long. £24

Surveyor's level in pinewood box, circa 1840, 14ins long.
£75

Mahogany cased surveyor's magnetic compass and sights, by 'W.C. Cox of Devonport'.
£185

A small pair of late 18th century celestial and terrestial globes by J & W Cary, dated 1791, 3ins diam. £500

Victorian set of scales with three weights. £14

Victorian ships' compass in brass binnacle, 11ins high. £35

A very fine Nova-Brunsviga calculating machine in perfect working order. £150

A fine brass and steel Spring balance sack scales weighing to 100lbs., 9½ins brass dial, circa 1860. £28

Painted metal stamp. £3.50

A superb 19th century brass Armillary Sphere with engraved rings and standing on four turned cast brass legs and engraved base, 13ins high, 10ins diam. £975

Thomason's Patent continuous double action corkscrew with ivory handle and brush. £28

A 19th century brass ship's binnacle with circular viewing glass, 10ins high. £28

A mahogany brass-banded military Surgeon's Instrument set, circa 1840, the instruments are ebony handled and in mint condition, by J & W Wood, Manchester. £245

A superb example of a William and Mary period wrought iron meat spit jack, with original cast iron driving weight and wheel governor, 12ins high, circa 1690. £275

George III wall hanging thermometer by Lione & Co., Hatten Garden, London, circa 1820, 18ins long. £95

An oak barograph by Lennie. £36

Polished steel engineers' inside and outside calipers with curved flat arms, circa 1860. £10

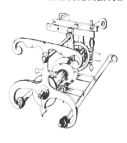

Mahogany cased metronome with brass plaque 'Metronome Maelzel Paris, France', circa 1870, 9ins high.   £18

A pottery handled brass beer pull by Loftus of London, circa 1860, 17ins high.   £28

Rare steel Spitjack, circa 1700.   £245

A British Ericsson telephone, in a walnut wall cabinet.   £35

An interesting farmhouse cheese press, with wrought iron frame, 20ins high, circa 1800.   £48

A rare miner's beam engine counter, with 3ins central dial divided from 0-100, and five smaller dials, by John Straton, Devizes, dated 1819.   £250

19th century Norwegian ship's telegraph by a/s Hynnes Maskin in Forretning, Trondheim, 43ins high.   £95

A fine brass-banded teak ship's wheel standing on a circular brass-banded teak column, 19ins high.   £95

A rare 18th century Waywiser with 23ins diam. steel wheel, the handles of turned mahogany, by Benjamin Cole (Senior).
                    £360

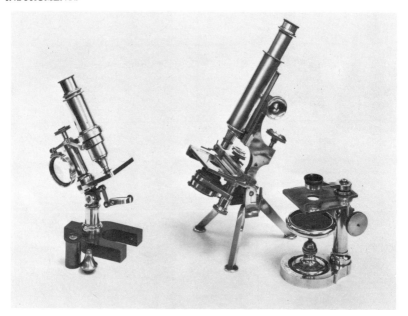

Left: A mid 19th century French brass microscope, signed E. Hartnack and A. Prazmouski, Paris, in a fitted mahogany case, 10ins high.   £38

Centre: A Victorian brass microscope, signed C. Baker, London. £32

Right: A mid 19th century French brass dissecting/aquatic microscope, signed Nachet Et Fils, Paris, 5¾ins high.   £25

(King & Chasemore, Pulborough)

Left: A 19th century marine chronometer by Wm. Bond & Son, of Boston, 4½ins diam. £400

Right: A 19th century marine chronometer, by John Bruce & Sons, 4¾ins diam. £240

(King & Chasemore, Pulborough)

Wrought iron andirons, circa 1710, 16ins high. £38

A pair of polished steel firedogs of the Art Nouveau period, design by Ernest Gimson and made by Alfred Bucknell, circa 1910. £700

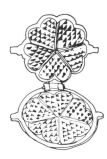

  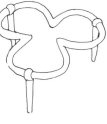

Victorian waffle iron £9

19th century Irish iron horse shoe trivet. £8

An improved Albion Printing Press by W & J Figgins, London, No. 1187, 1874. £150

Victorian box iron. £8

A fine Imperial Russian iron group of a mounted Cossack bidding farewell to his sweetheart, 16½ins high. £90

Late 19th century wrought iron half circle fender, 2ft 4ins wide. £8

An early iron and brass flat iron. £16

IRON & STEEL

A very rare Queen Anne period hand wrought eel spear, 23ins long. £45

Cast iron wall plaque of an eagle, 18ins wide, 10ins high. £35

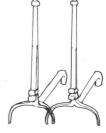

An exceptionally fine pair of hand wrought fire dogs of Elizabeth I period, with spit hooks, 29ins high, circa 1570. £225

19th century iron griddle pan with brass handle. £10

16th century polished cast iron cauldron, with swing handle, 11ins diam. £58

A rare polished steel Larkspit, 30½ins high, circa 1750. £45

A polished steel steak fork with turned screw type handle, circa 1840, 24ins long. £8

A 16th century cast iron cooking cauldron, with original hand wrought swing handle, standing on three feet, 13ins high, 9¼ins diam. £58

Cook's cast iron hot water kettle, of two gallon capacity, with wrought iron swing handle. £28

Cast iron miniature fire-grate surmounted by a lion, with brass fire bars, circa 1820, 13½ins wide, 12ins high. £34

A cast iron owl figure money box, 7½ins high. £14

A polished cast iron tobacco jar with bronze acorn finial, circa 1820, 7½ins high. £35

Victorian cast iron door stop of a horse, on a stepped base, 11¼ins long, 10ins high. £18

Very fine three gallon hot water kettle made of cast iron, 18ins high, circa 1840. £35

Old steel, tin smith's ladle, with finger grip wooden handle and brass ferrule, 16ins long. £6

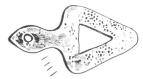

19th century sheet steel flat iron with triangular pierced motif, 8½ins long. £5

Victorian polished steel cooking pot. £8

Adjustable Queen Anne wrought iron rush light and candle stand, circa 1700. £125

A pair of heavy cast iron door stops of zebras, circa 1820, 10½ins long, 8ins high. £45

19th century iron hob kettle and pot hook. £24

Cast iron cooking pot with hollow handle and medallion on front, circa 1840. £12

A pair of cast iron fire rests with winged lion head fronts and brass mounts. £15

IVORY

A Japanese sectional ivory carving of a fisherman, 3ins high. £50

A Chinese carved ivory group of a man with two monkeys, 9¼ins high. £90

A Japanese carving of a banana and mouse in ivory. £110

One of a pair of Bali carved ivory heads of females, 6¼ins high. £10

A late 19th century Japanese group of terrapins, 4¾ins. £160

Two small French carved ivory figures of cavalrymen, 4¼ins high. £55

An Oriental ivory carving of a temple shrine, 6½ins high. £40

19th century French carved ivory domed casket, with copper gilt handles and lock. £1,100

Carved ivory group of a man with two children, 5¼ins, high. £64

An ivory figure of a basket seller carrying his wares, 9ins high. £215

19th century German tusk carved with hunting scenes. £1,300

French ivory figure of Napoleon, 12ins high. £280

19th century stained ivory articulated crayfish, 14½ins long. £340

A Japanese ivory carving of a banana, circa 1900. £48

Ivory nude on green marble base, 1862. £780

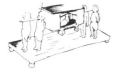

A Bali carved ivory tusk with head of a man, 9ins high. £8

A pair of 19th century German carved ivory ewers, carved in relief. £2,300

A Japanese ivory carving of a peasant, 9½ins high. £165

19th century Oriental ivory group, 4½ins long. £17.50

An ivory dog's whistle in the form of a dog's face. £35

A very well executed Japanese ivory carving of a bunch of fruit. £240

19th century German ivory figure of King Arthur, from tomb of Kaiser Maximilian at Innsbruck. £820

A 19th century ivory Youth and Maid in medieval costume. £1,650

A Chinese carved ivory group of a man with monkey and cockerel, 10¼ins high. £110

IVORY

Oriental ivory group of two acrobats, 6¾ins high.   £55

A Japanese oval wall panel, with applied ivory and mother of pearl, 18½ins.   £13

An old Native carved ivory figure of a kneeling man in elaborate head-gear, 11½ins high.   £68

A very rare and interesting Imperial German Army regimental 'Casino' ivory hammer of the 74th Infantry Regiment.   £46

European carved ivory classical female figures depicting Summer and Autumn, 8¾ins high.   £230

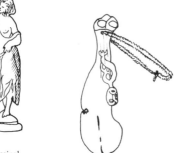

A Maori bone club carved in high relief with grotesque figures, 38cm long.   £820

Set of six mid 19th century ivory and boxwood musicians and dancers, the tallest 8ins high.   £400

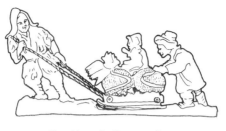

Carved ivory family group of a man pulling a sledge, 10¾ins long. £320

Japanese ivory of a woman supporting a child on her left shoulder, 8¾ins high. £100

Oriental ivory figure of a man with a beard, 9¼ins high. £50

A Maori axe handle of bone with Tiki-like carving, 25.5cm long. £150

A pair of finely carved French 19th century ivory statuettes, depicting Cupid and Psyche, raised on circular ebonised bases, 1ft 8ins high. £620

European ivory figure of a young woman carrying a parasol, 9½ins high. £150

Oriental ivory figure of an old man carrying a child, 9¾ins high. £90

An enormous pair of elephant tusks, 6ft high. £850

Oriental ivory of a man with a gourd standing on a rock, 9ins high. £46

IVORY

French prisoner of war bone model of a Spinning Jenny, 6ins high. £150

Japanese black lacquered panel with applied carved ivory. £45

A Japanese carved ivory model of a pagoda shrine, 13½ins high. £52

A carved ivory group of three figures, 7ins high, on carved wood stand. £32

Japanese carved wood and ivory figure of a man and demon on wood stand, 8ins high. £55

The Savernare Horn, of eleventh century ivory with early 14th century mounts, bearing the arms of the Earls of May. £210,000

Ivory figure of a woman musician wearing an embroidered gown, 9½ins high. £65

Japanese black lacquered wall panel with applied ivory and mother of pearl. £35

A 19th century coconut containing an ivory shrine to Kuan Yin. £40

Jade medallion carved and pierced with basket of flowers, 2¼ins diam.   £22

Large pole celadon jade carving of Kuan-Yin, 14ins high.   £1,207

Jade medallion carved and pierced with two fish.   £34

Jade medallion, carved and pierced with baskets of flowers and fruit, 2¾ins wide.   £30

One of a pair of early 19th century Chinese circular plaques with fine jade figures and flowering trees in high relief.   £200

One of a pair of jade circular bangles, 3¼ins diam.   £46

Jade medallion carved and pierced with birds, 2ins wide.   £22

A beautiful jade mottled pony.   £5,460

Green jade boulder on a gilt metal stand, depicting figures in a mountainous landscape, K'ang Hsi period, 30.5cm high.   £8,190

JEWELLERY

A Scottish Victorian silver and agate shield. £25

Small 19th century silver cross in the form of two wooden boughs. £25

Victorian pendant of pavé set turquoises on 15 carat gold. £550

Late 18th century flat-cut garnet witch's heart, set in gold. £40

A pair of diamond and emerald, ruby and enamel set drop hoop earrings. £640

An early 19th century flat cut garnet brooch with pendant drop, foiled and closed-back in gold. £45

A pair of mid 19th century white paste drop earrings, set in silver. £50

An unusual Victorian mourning bracelet of woven hair with silver serpent clasp. £40

A yellow sapphire and scrolled gold stick pin. £38

French gold pendant of the mid 16th century, 1 5/8ins wide. £3,200

A Scottish silver and agate round boss brooch. £29

A Scottish silver and agate brooch of the Victorian period set with three cairngorms. £38

Late 17th century gold and faceted crystal heart pendant with plated hair under the crystal. £45

A Victorian gold bangle set with diamonds and pearls. £650

An enamelled gold pendant, possibly English, circa 1600, 3¼ins high. £6,500

One of a small pair of black enamel earrings completed by seed pearls. £45

A gold and garnet brooch with leaf decoration. £265

18 carat gold double sided locket set with four small diamonds. £50

A gold and half-pearl hair brooch. £250

Pair of pink foiled crystal and paste drop earrings, circa 1690. £85

Small Victorian cross of turquoises set in an intricate 18 carat gold frame. £25

A Victorian diamond and emerald festoon necklace. £520

19th century paste wheatsheaf, set in silver, open-backed, circa 1830. £35

Pink foiled crystal and paste necklace, set in gold, circa 1830. £175

White paste and crystal Irish Crowned harp, in silver, circa 1830. £110

French paste button brooch in silver, circa 1810. £65

Victorian snake pattern gold bracelet, with diamond and emerald central boss. £400

18 carat gold locket intricately engraved with leaves and flowers. £55

JEWELLERY

Victorian agate brooch. £150

Platinum cross-over ring set with two diamonds. £410

Early 19th century pendant' in the form of a cross. £220

A Scottish vinaigrette in the shape of a powder horn with silver mounts. £50

Victorian gold, enamel and half pearl brooch and earrings. £465

A diamond and pearl brooch set in gold, in the form of a bee. £55

Victorian oval moss agate pendant. £175

Gilt bracelet extensively embossed with marine emblems, flowering branches and exotic birds. £32

A 19th century Pique ornamental tortoiseshell cross. £20

A gold and cornelian seal. £85

Victorian agate arrow and shield brooch. £45

A diamond star brooch. £500

An oval mother of pearl brooch painted with a harbour scene. £24

Victorian half pearl, diamond and enamel bangle. £500

Victorian sapphire and diamond bangle. £1,200

Victorian green and white paste memorial ring, pave-set in gold, engraved on the reverse 'In Memory of W.W.. 1862. £39

9ct. gold bar brooch mounted with a spider. £30

19th century pearl and ruby cluster ring, set in gold with carved gold shoulders, circa 1840. £35

Georgian gold and turquoise bow and pendant drop brooch. £275

A diamond spray brooch. £1,000

Early 19th century striped agate necklet. £340

A ruby and diamond pendant. £290

A diamond brooch. £880

Victorian diamond bangle. £1,450

A metal-framed, hexagonal shaped lampshade, inset with six lithophanes. £55

A bronze-framed model of a church, the sides inset with lithophane panels of church and country scenes.   £55

(King & Chasemore, Pulborough)

A Lucas gas lamp. £10

One of a pair of fine copper pub lamps, with original green glass, 32ins high, circa 1850. £210

An adjustable brass desk oil lamp with white shade. £26

A brass Corinthian fluted pillar oil lamp on square base. £26

A rare tinned sheet iron double crusie or Betty lamp, with pierced flower discs, circa 1850, 12ins high. £16

A tall brass oil lamp with fluted font and base, etched globe. £24

Spelter figure lamp, 28½ins high. £30

A ship's copper navigation oil lamp. £15

Lacemaker's lamp. £75

A ship's brass column globe oil lamp. £16

LAMPS

Victorian style hanging oil lamp. £28

An Art Deco table lamp and shade by Daum, of pink tinted opaque glass having reeded, slightly bulbous stem, 20ins high. £220

A tall brass oil lamp with twin reservoirs and frosted globes. £37

An 18th century brass table crusie lamp, with solid cast brass circular base, 18½ins high. £35

Brass hall lantern with four leaded stained glass panels, circa 1860, 22ins high. £45

A 19th century gilt brass hall lantern, of octagonal form, decorated with hooves and ram's heads. £250

One of a pair of brass carriage lamps with eagle surmounts. £25

Brightly polished brass motor car side lamp, 11ins high. £18

A brass oil lamp on circular base, with opaque glass shade. £20

A brass adjustable desk oil lamp and white shade. £21

One of a pair of old horse coach lamps in black painted tin, with cut bevelled glass panels, circa 1850.   £58

A rare 19th century cast iron wick lamp with detachable screw off lid and swing carrying handle, 11ins high.   £34

A large 19th century china oil lamp, decorated with flowers on blue ground, 2ft high.   £38

A brass circular oil lamp with crimson glass shade, 23ins high.   £46

A brass oil lamp on circular base with glass shade.   £25

A very handsome Victorian oil lamp made in bronze and Paris porcelain, circa 1860.   £78

An elegant three spout brass crusie table lamp, circa 1790, 18ins high.   £28

One of a pair of high domed and pierced brass hall lamps with single suspension handle, 11ins high, circa 1840.   £67

CHANDELIERS

Victorian wall brass candle sconce, 11ins wide.   £6

A bronze chandelier with six scroll branches, fitted for electric light.   £80

Attractive five branch brass chandelier, circa 1850.   £98

A 19th century brass and glass chandelier with eight scrolled arms, 39ins long.   £165

One of a pair of 19th century cut glass chandeliers.   £820

A glass chandelier with eight fluted scroll branches.   £210

19th century brass and porcelain electric chandelier of French design, 2ft 6ins high.   £240

Victorian brass hanging pendant lamp.   £12

19th century plated chandelier, 5ft deep.   £410

A 19th century walnut carved and fluted pillar electric floor lamp and silk shade. £58

A mahogany electric standard lamp on a circular base. £10

An Indian engraved brass oil floor lamp with shade. £32

Victorian mahogany spiral pillar electric floor lamp on carved claw feet. £45

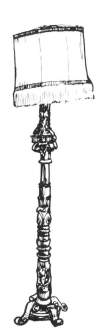

19th century Italian carved walnut floor lamp. £55

A Victorian brass electric floor lamp, with fluted and chased pillar, on circular base with feet. £80

A carved gilt standard electric lamp with fluted column. £22

A Victorian brass, electric floor lamp, with ball chain festoons, on a circular base, with paw feet. £75

Lead set of Snow White and Seven Dwarfs by Britain's, 1938.   £35

Britain's model lead figure.   £2

A good old English lead tobacco
jar, 8ins high, 4¼ins diam.   £20

18th century lead tobacco
jar of octagonal shape with
scroll decorative bands
around the top and bottom
rims of the base, 5¼ins high,
5ins long.   £28

Mid 19th century lead
figure of Mercury, 46ins
high.   £185

Lead garden urn, 2ft 5ins
high.   £100

Britain's Somerset Light Infantry, 1905.   £9

Head of girl in marble, by
William McMillan, R.A.,
17½ins high. £100

An elegant pair of lathe turned
marble vases of dove grey
colour with alternate bands of
variegated Venetian red and
cream marble, 9ins high, circa
1820. £85

18th century Bath stone
sundial pedestal, with fluted
column and turned top on
square base, with 14ins
square brass sundial. £145

A large mid 19th century
marble figure of the muse
Polyhymnia, 6ft 6ins high.
£500

A white marble statuette of a
classical lady holding an urn
and drapery, 2ft high. £55

A 19th century Italian carved
marble standing nude female
figure, 5ft 4ins high. £142

Victorian marble vase, 15ins
high. £18

A white alabaster statuary
group of the Lovers, on an
oblong shaped base, 2ft 7ins
wide. £78

A white marble bust of a
philosopher by Orazio
Marinali, 22ins high. £440

MINIATURE FURNITURE

A miniature commode chest, the false drawers with brass handles, 23¾ins long, 17ins deep, 18½ins high, circa 1750. £58

A miniature Welsh dresser, arm chair and single chair. £32

Miniature continental commode, circa 1760, 17ins wide. £485

A miniature rosewood pedestal sideboard, of Regency design. £36

A miniature mahogany circular breakfast table, in pillar and block. £16

A miniature walnut oblong table of William and Mary design, 13ins long. £24

A miniature Sheraton style satinwood bureau bookcase, 4ft high. £380

A miniature 19th century Dutch walnut commode. £110

A miniature early 19th century Dutch walnut and marquetry display cabinet, 4ft 5ins high. £510

A miniature mahogany wardrobe enclosed by two doors, with carved beaded borders, 16ins high, 13ins wide. £28

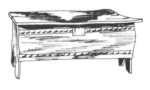

A miniature 17th century oak kist. £85

Mid 19th century Japanese miniature cabinet, mounted with metal and porcelain decoration, 12ins high. £38

Victorian overmantel mirror in carved and gilt frame, 4ft 9ins. high.   £48

One of a pair of upright scroll shaped wall mirrors in carved gilt frames, the bases with three candle branches, 2ft 9ins high.   £50

Victorian giltwood overmantel mirror, 5ft high overall.   £23

19th century wall mirror in carved gilt frame, 2ft 10ins tall.   £35

One of a pair of Chippendale style overmantels.   £600

An oval bevelled wall mirror in gilt fluted frame with ribbon cresting, 3ft high.   £35

19th century bevelled wall mirror in mahogany frame, 3ft 3ins high.   £28

19th century oval wall mirror in Italian carved gilt frame with four scroll candle sconces, 4ft 6ins high.   £48

19th century upright wall mirror in shaped mahogany and gilt frame, 2ft 10ins high.   £38

MIRRORS

A 19th century rosewood inlaid dressing mirror with box base, 2ft wide.   £85

A Hepplewhite mahogany serpentine front box toilet mirror, 16¼ins wide.   £150

A Regency mahogany toilet mirror, 31ins high.   £42

A mahogany inlaid dressing mirror on shaped box base with three drawers, 2ft wide.   £36

An early 18th century walnut and marquetry toilet mirror on bureau base   £220.

A small mahogany inlaid oval dressing mirror, 15½ins high.   £28

Chippendale period carved and giltwood mirror, 49ins x 27ins.   £820

One of a pair of Chippendale style overmantel mirrors, circa 1760.   £600

A George I period giltwood and gesso wall mirror.   £400

A mahogany dressing glass on box base with three drawers, 1ft 10ins wide. £18

Georgian mahogany toilet mirror, 19ins wide, 26ins high. £62

Early 19th century Sheraton mahogany toilet mirror, the oval frame with satinwood stringing and brass handles at either side, 13ins high. £48

A walnut upright dressing glass, the base with three drawers, 16ins wide. £35

A George III gentleman's shaving mirror on a stand, with fine rosewood and satinwood stringing, circa 1790. £68

A 19th century tortoiseshell mounted, upright dressing glass, 16¾ins high. £23

Adam period giltwood and walnut pier mirror. £190

Chippendale wall mirror, 6ft 9½ins x 4ft 3ins. £1,500

A George I giltwood and gesso wall mirror, 44ins x 23ins. £400

MIRRORS

A small walnut inlaid dressing glass with turned spindle supports and stretcher, 12¼ins high. £20

18th century giltwood mirror with superb deep carving. £365

William IV dressing glass with bevelled plate. £36

A George II walnut and gilt gesso mirror. £1,000

Regency convex mirror in gilt ball pattern frame, 3ft 6ins high. £55

An upright wall mirror in ebonised and carved gilt frame, with three candle branches at base, 2ft 9ins high. £42

A carved gilt wall bracket with three shelves and mirror to back, 3ft 6ins high. £36

A 19th century mahogany cheval mirror on fluted pillar supports. £58

A reproduction yew wood and carved gilt framed upright wall mirror, the cresting with a gilt bird, 3ft high. £40

Walnut veneered toilet mirror with drawers in the base, circa 1725.   £295

19th century Continental carved walnut mirror, 26ins x 24ins.   £75

Early 19th century serpentine front toilet mirror.   £45

Victorian upright wall mirror, 2ft 5ins high. £15

One of a pair of George II giltwood girandoles plates 34 x 14ins.   £1,417

19th century bevelled wall mirror with side plates in embossed brass, 23ins high.   £24

A walnut framed cheval mirror with turned pillar supports.   £38

One of a pair of pier glasses in the Chippendale manner. £2,500

19th century walnut framed cheval mirror, 53ins high.   £42

MISCELLANEOUS

Late 19th century handbag with mother of pearl flowers and gilt clasp. £15

A fine silver-mounted horn jug and two beakers with glass bases, by Edward Barnard & Sons. £200

A tortoiseshell and ivory mounted purse and peacock feather fan. £16

An 18th century cut steel key, 5¼ins long. £70

Two large early iron keys. £7

A small 18th century cut steel key, 4ins long. £40

Victorian shellwork composition under a glass dome. £38

Tachibana Gyokuzan and Suzuki Tokoku inro. £7,800

A composition formed of eight stuffed birds and grasses, on stand under glass dome, 22ins high. £22

An elephant's foot converted into a cigar and cigarette casket. £40

An ivory and painted fan in gilt and glazed case. £20

One of a collection of fifty black and white glass lantern slides by C.T. Milligan and fourteen positives by T. H. McAllister, circa 1860. £525

A Scrimshaw cow horn beaker, incised with a picture of four horses pulling a mail coach, circa 1820. £37

An elephant foot and brass jardiniere, with ring handles. £25

17th century key, the head with geometric motif, 4½ins long. £28

Ammonite, the fossilised shell of large size, 1ft 2ins wide. £22

An 18th century cut steel key with a comb end, 5½ins long. £80

17th century steel key with geometric motif, 5½ins long. £42

Victorian dyed ostrich feather fan. £10

A hippopotamus foot jardiniere. £12

A bloodstained handkerchief reputed to have been the property of Charles I and removed from his person immediately after his execution. £367.50

A carved and pierced soapstone vase on soapstone stand, decorated with a figure, birds and foliage, 15ins high. £20

17th century stumpwork picture. £380

A Chinese carved soapstone figure of Kuan Yin, on a carved wood base, 14½ins high. £24

MISCELLANEOUS

One of a pair of attractive triple branch gilt and gesso candle wall lights with detachable gilt shaped back wall plates, circa 1835, 14ins high. £165

A 19th century painted plaster figure of a negro boy, life-size. £330

Stuffed animal's head. £5

A fine commemorative silver-mounted horn beaker. £75

A Continental steel, circular shield, with repousse figures and beaded borders, 22½ins diam. £32

A Blackfoot type skin shirt, with porcupine quill designs. £1,087

A fine American pre-revolutionary gun powder horn, engraved with drawings. £260

An 18th century leather dog collar. £20

Very fine late Georgian painted fan with decoration to the ivory sticks, with Chinese scene on reverse. £75

Handsome 19th century pine fire surround, of classical design, with applied gesso floral swags to centre panel, 59ins long, 54½ins high, 9ins wide. £185

Japanese suit of armour, bearing the badge of the Daimyo of Kokura. £12,600

English oak door of Norman Gothic shape, 4ft 5ins wide, 7ft 2½ins high. £110

Turned beechwood tray 'Lazy Susan' with revolving top, and supported by a birdseye maple and ebony stand with shallow carving, circa 1860.   £38

Leopard skin rug. £40

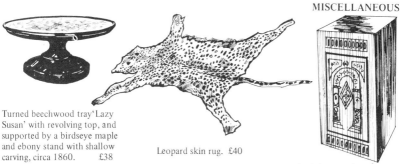

A miniature oak court cupboard, used as a posting box.   £20

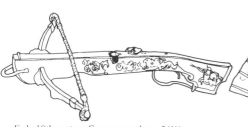

Early 18th century German crossbow, 26¼ins long.   £2,625

Ivory and sequinned fan, circa 1930. £10

MODELS

Scale model Bentley, 14ins long. £682.50

Bassett-Lowke coal-fired, 1½ins scale model of a Burrell single-cylinder general purpose traction engine, 23ins long, circa 1958. £650

19th century model of an English cottage made from oak.   £35

A carved and pierced fretwork model of the frontpiece of Westminster Cathedral, in wood and glazed case, 3ft 6ins high.   £18

Victorian model of a stationary steam engine.   £55

MODEL SHIPS

Model English galleon made of wood, with cloth sails, circa 1870.   £16

A model of a three masted sailing ship, in a mahogany and glazed case.   £45

Late 19th century model of an American clipper ship, "Sovereign of the Seas", 3ft 4ins long, 2ft 2ins high.   £190

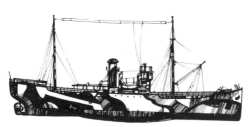

A Dockyard model of R.F.A. Celerol, "Dazzle-camouflaged", World War 1 style.   £1,400

19th century French bone model galleon, 14ins wide.   £480

A fine 19th century seaman's ship model.   £49

Two models of three masted sailing ships, and three other boats, in a glazed display case.   £60

A French prisoner-of-war bone model of a galleon, 14ins long.   £480

Atlantic type 4-4-2 steam locomotive and tender by H. Bell, circa 1930. £350

Steam model of a four coupled tank engine, 3½ins gauge. £420

Brass 0-6-0 railway spirit fired engine, circa 1920. £185

A gauge model of a Midland Railway compound 4-4-0 locomotive and tender, with a fully-brazed riveted super-heated copper boiler, 5ft long. £630

A tin train-set with track circuit, four rolling stock, two level crossings, a station and buffers. £14

A 5-inch gauge model of the Class T9 locomotive and eight-wheeled tender, built by B. Mount in 1967. £1,417

A 5-inch gauge model of the Adams 4-4-0 locomotive and tender No. 563 built by H. W. Webb, Stoke D'Abernon, about 5ft long. £1,050

A gauge 1, 0-4-4 model, solidly built steam engine of the North Eastern Falls. £60

MUSICAL BOXES & POLYPHONES

Edison Home Phonograph, Model A. No. H124524 in green oak case, 1ft 6ins long, circa 1901-04. £150

A very rare 19th century disc organette. £200

An Edison phonograph with a particularly fine brass horn. £240

A German "Zuleger and Mayenburg symphonion" with 22 discs, circa 1880. £580

An Edison Bell standard phonograph with loud speaker. £46

A mid 19th century miniature chamber barrel organ. £350

A radiogram in mahogany serpentine fronted cabinet. £34

A fine German mahogany cabinet polyphon on stand and 20 discs, 2ft 2ins wide, 6ft 4ins high. £520

19th century ten-air barrel organ by Keith Prowse & Co., London. £840

H.M.V. 'Lumiere' gramophone in turned oak case, 1ft 4½ins x 1ft 11ins, 1924-25.   £210

A Swiss musical box with ten airs in rosewood inlaid and ebonised case, 22ins.   £290

A Beltona square gramophone with chromium plated horn.   £70

A rare Gavioli marquetry table barrel organ, 2ft 2ins wide, circa 1870.   £620

Edison Home Phonograph complete with horn and cylinders.   £200

Late 19th century Swiss three cylinder musical box on stand, 3ft 5ins wide.   £240

German walnut marquetry symphonion on stand and 47 discs, circa 1880, 1ft 10ins wide, 2ft 10ins high.   £360

A beautifully inlaid street barrel organ, with a playing rank of piccolo pipes to the front. £1,500

Victorian " Penny in the slot" polyphone.   £400

MUSICAL BOXES & POLYPHONES

E.M. Ginn Expert Semior
'Oversize' gramophone. £22

19th century musical box
playing eight airs , Paris 1878.
£95

Victorian polyphone with eight
ten inch records. £160

19th century Swiss musical box
in a burr walnut case crossbanded
with ebony, 3ft 11ins wide. £900

19th century automaton
musical doll. £260

19th century French musical
box in burr yew wood and
ebonised case, 24ins wide.
£500

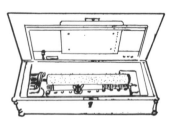

Edison standard phonograph,
circa 1907. £60

Unusual Harp-Mandolin-
Picole cylinder musical
box, 17ins wide, by
Bremond and Greiner.
£425

Thomas Edison phonograph,
together with nineteen cylinders.
£94

A 19th century French gilt metal cage containing three brightly-coloured musical birds, 21ins high. £190
(King & Chasemore, Pulborough)

MUSICAL INSTRUMENTS

Victorian banjo 'The Broadcaster'.   £32

French accordian with mother of pearl keys, 7ins wide when closed.   £42

Early 19th century harp by Sebastian Svard, 5ft 6ins high.   £400

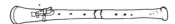

18th century tenor oboe by Thomas Cahusal.   £1,150

A fine boxwood thirteen key cabinet, by Buffet, Crampion & Co., Paris.   £75

Simple system ebony piccolo with alternative flageolet mouthpiece, 11½ins long.   £25

Keyed bugle by Clementi & Co., 18ins long, circa 1820.   £55

Silver mounted violin bow by W.E. Hill and Sons.   £126

A copper coaching horn with brass centre band and mouth piece, by Harris & Nixon, circa 1840, 41½ins long.   £38

Mid 19th century French guitar, 17¾ins long. £95

Pianino by Chappel and Co., mahogany case inlaid with ebony stringing, 22½ins wide, circa 1830.   £250

Italian composite Chitarrone labelled Michele Atton, 1610, 79½ins long.   £294

18th century Military side drum by Robert Horne, 12ins diam. £15

Violin by Antonio Stradivari, Cremona, in the Amateur style, circa 1670-75, 14ins long. £6,500

Small sidedrum signed Thomas Emblin, 1776 with two pipes. £126

Eleven keyed rosewood flute by Henry Hill, 28¼ins long. £120

One keyed boxwood flute by William Milhouse, 21¼ins long, circa 1790. £210

Twelve keyed copper Ophicleide with crook and mouthpiece, circa 1840. £75

A Victorian brass bugle. £12

Copper and brass coaching horn, circa 1870, 4½ins diam. £28

A silver plated nickle hunting horn, with elegant solid silver shield, hallmarked for Birmingham, 9ins long. £28

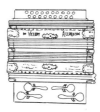

Mandoline labelled Stridente Fabrica Di Mandolini, Via Antonio, Napoli, 24ins long. £23

'The Viceroy', accordian complete with case. £14

A cello and bow in canvas case. £50

MUSICAL INSTRUMENTS

A good quality herald's silver-plated trumpet with slide valve, by H. Potter of London. £36

Silver mounted violin bow by W.E. Hill & Sons. £126

Italian tenor viol de Gamba by Giavanni Pietro Guarneri, Mantua, 1689, body 18ins. £3,150

Banjo with vellum head having forty tensioners and ivory turning pegs, 37ins long. £36

Chitarra Battente signed on the head Andreas Ott, Prague, 37ins long. £3,675

Italian guitar labelled Giuseppe Sciale, Via Del Cordo, Nig, Roma, 1838, 17½ins long. £42

Guitar labelled Louis Panormo, London, 17½ins long. £55

18th century Italian guitar, 36ins long. £3,675

A large Georgian military drum with wooden frame, 20½ins diam. £110

German Gebunden clavichord by George Friedrich Schmahl, Ulm, 1807, 54ins wide. £2,310

An early 19th century military tambour, with all-brass shell. £58

Gold mounted violin bow by W.E. Hill.
£200

A good quality herald's silver-plated
trumpet, by H. Potter, London. £40

18th century French
guitar, 37ins long.
£2,940

Grecian double action harp,
signed on the neck Erard's
Patent Harp, 66½ins high.
£273

Milanese Mandora, signed
Antonio Stradivari
Cremona, circa 1700,
20ins long.   £200

Lute labelled Joachim
Tielke, Hamburg, 1748,
40¾ins long.   £115

Early banjo, vellum head
with six brass tensioners,
35¾ins long.   £30

18th century Italian
guitar, 36ins long.
£1,890

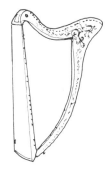

A rare Georgian copper kettle
drum of the Honourable East
India Company, 19ins diam:,
19ins high.   £50

Irish 'Royal Portable' harp,
signed J. Egan, Dublin, 35ins
high.   £273

A fine early 19th century
military tambour, having
all-brass shell with cords to
brass securing rim holding
skin.   £62

NETSUKE

A netsuke of carved ivory, in the shape of a man with corn on the cob. £15

Netsuke depicting four rats eating an egg. £72

Netsuke of three seated men. £40

Netsuke of a masked carver. £46

Netsuke of a priest and attendant. £48

Hotei with woman and children. £68

Three figures under a carp's tail. £44

A carved ivory netsuke in the form of a grotesque animal. £17

A carved ivory netsuke of a horse. £19

19th century netsuke representing content-ment. £85

Netsuke of reclining man. £38

Wood netsuke of a badger, signed Minko. £140

Netsuke depicting a rat on a lake. £58

A carved ivory netsuke of a man. £17

Netsuke of a woodcutter. £38

Netsuke of a man with a drum. £30

Pewter cube-form inkstand, the base inscribed "Coutts Banking House, 1790". £170

19th century French double-litre measure by Bunel a Villedieu-le-Poeles, 10¾ins high. 160gns

A Britannia metal oval biscuit box. £16

18th century pewter Clocken-kenne, made in Zurich. £450

18th century pewter mounted pottery tankard. £102

A pewter tappit hen with London touch mark, 10ins. £20

A pewter baptismal bowl, etched with flowers. £24

Pair of pewter candlesticks, 9ins high, circa 1820. £58

Pewter wine funnel with goblet shaped body and copper hanging ring to rim, 6½ins high. £28

Charles II silver Peg tankard, York 1672. £2,000

Art Nouveau pewter sugar bowl. £8

Victorian pewter coffee pot. £14

511

PEWTER

Cylindrical pewter tankard stamped on rim 'T. J. Birch, Pint'.   £18

George III pewter wine funnel, circa 1820, 5ins high, 3¾ins diam.   £15

19th century lidded pewter tankard with glass bottom and open arched thumb-piece to double domed lid, 7½ins high.   £45

18th century Continental measure, 10½ins high.   80gns

18th century pewter charger by Christopher Cillarius.   £78

18th century Continental measure of Normandy type, 8¼ins high.   45gns

Early 19th century German tankard inscribed M. Heydanin, 1808, the body engraved with three oval panels, 9½ins high, by Friedrich Ferdinand Braune, Kamenz.   170gns

A miniature polished pewter firegrate with Royal coat of arms, circa 1820, 11ins wide, 15ins high.   £38

A very fine pewter pint measure in the form of a spouted tankard, with fish tail handle, by Edwards, Clerkenwell Road, circa 1840, 5ins high.   £28

Early 19th century Scottish quart tankard, by J. McGlashan & Co., Glasgow.   30gns

18th century charger with moulded rim, 14ins diam.   28gns

A heavy pint pewter ale tankard, with the touch mark of C. Bentley, circa 1840, 5ins high.   £28

A half-pint, glass bottomed pewter tankard, with the touch mark of Townsend and Compton, circa 1810. £18

Pewter hot water dish with swing handles and small rectangular hinged cover in top to add hot water, by Thomas Alderson, 8ins diam. £32

Late 19th century German measure inscribed 'M' and dated 1891, by Joseph Schiller, 12¼ins high. 95gns

19th century French litre measure, by Humbert Leclerc a Lisle, 8½ins high. 60gns

Deep German pewter plate with single touch mark of angel holding scales and crown above, 9ins diam. £28

19th century French demi-litre measure, by Oudard Rudot, 6¾ins high. 48gns

An unusual German tapered beaker with rococo decoration in relief all around body, 5ins high. £18

A cast pewter plaque of a trotting horse, circa 1830, 11¼ins long, 8ins high. £18

19th century French litre measure, 9ins high, stamped D.A. et Cie. 45gns

Early 19th century quart tankard, by Joseph Morgan, Bristol, 6½ins high. 45gns

19th century plate with waved border, 9¼ins diam. 28gns

One of a set of five measures of tappit-hen type, 8½ins high. 120gns

PEWTER

A Victorian Britannia metal coffee pot. £12

18th century Continental plate, with moulded rim, 11¼ins diam. 25gns

A large pewter tappit hen. £40

A French pewter circular alms dish, the border etched "J. Gruson Roi, 1865", 12½ins diam. £20

One of a pair of half pint tulip-shaped pewter tankards, by Joseph Morgan of Bristol, and with Customs and Excise mark for Carlisle, 3½ins high. £25

A circular pewter alms dish, 15ins diam. £62

Three early German pewter lidded flagons. £340

A Brittania metal coffee pot on four feet. £8

A French pewter circular plate with reeded and wave border, the centre with a crown and fleur de lys, 10½ins diam. £20

A pewter baluster pint measure. £10

A Victorian Britannia metal vase-shaped winejug.   £7

A pewter plate with scroll border, the centre with embossed crest and motto, 9ins diam.   £9

A 19th century baluster shaped pewter quart measure.   £16

Alms dish, inscribed 'the Upper Door 2', and on reverse 'St. Olaves Ch, 1718', 9¾ins diam, by John Boult.   35gns

An Oriental pewter circular spice jar and cover, 7½ins high.   £13

18th century Continental charger, with moulded rim, 14ins diam.   25gns

A Victorian Britannia metal, vase-shaped coffee pot. £8

An oval Britannia metal meat cover, stamped James Dixon and Sons, Sheffield, 10ins long.   £9

A pewter oviform four gallon jug, 16½ins high.   £32

A 19th century pewter quart measure.   £20

Mid 18th century Alms dish, rim inscribed St. Olaves, 1757, Southwark, 12ins diam.   50gns

A pear shaped Britannia metal coffee pot, by Dixon & Sons, Sheffield, 10ins high.   £48

515

PIANOS

Grand piano by Broadwood in a rosewood case, 7ft long. £50

19th century Broadwood japanned boudoir grand piano. £550

A Steck pianola piano in mahogany case with a few rolls of music and a box seat piano stool. £200

Superb harpsichord by Jean Antoine Vaudry, 1681. £18,500

A Bechstein (C.) boudoir grand pianoforte in rosewood case, No. 61450, 6ft 9ins long. £470

A semi grand pianoforte by Ed Seiler, Liegnitz, in a rosewood case. £190

Single manual harpsichord by Burkat Shudi and John Broadwood, London, 1775, 82½ins long. £4,725

Semi grand pianoforte by Bluthner, Leipzig, in an ebonised case. £260

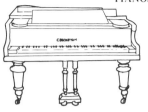

A semi-grand pianoforte by C. Bechstein in rosewood case, No. 106037.   £340

Late 17th century Spanish spinet, the interior of the lid decorated with a scene representing 'Moses in the Bullrushes'.   £1,600

Square pianoforte by Wm. Townsend and Son, in a mahogany case, 5ft 10ins wide. £30

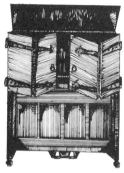

Art Nouveau piano by Broadwood. £420

An upright grand piano by C. Bechstein, in a mahogany case, No. 139370.   £220

An upright grand pianoforte by Vyner in a mahogany case.   £20

English spinet by John Harrison, London, 1781, 73½ins wide.   £2,310

A semi grand piano by Collard and Collard in a rosewood case.   £60

PISTOLS

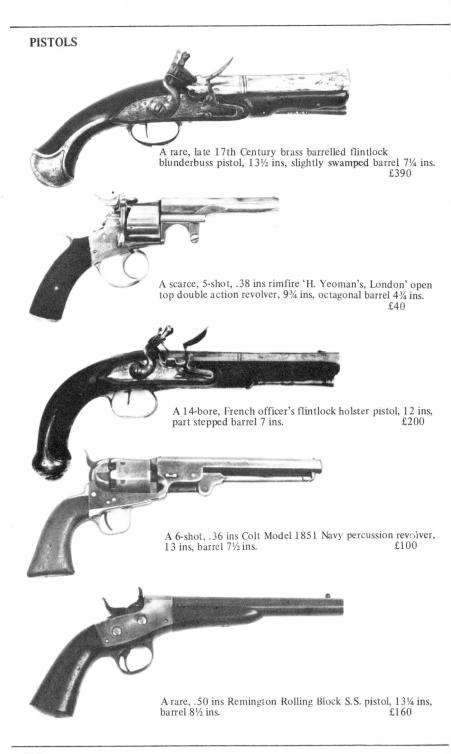

A rare, late 17th Century brass barrelled flintlock blunderbuss pistol, 13½ ins, slightly swamped barrel 7¼ ins.
£390

A scarce, 5-shot, .38 ins rimfire 'H. Yeoman's, London' open top double action revolver, 9¾ ins, octagonal barrel 4¾ ins.
£40

A 14-bore, French officer's flintlock holster pistol, 12 ins, part stepped barrel 7 ins.
£200

A 6-shot, .36 ins Colt Model 1851 Navy percussion revolver, 13 ins, barrel 7½ ins.
£100

A rare, .50 ins Remington Rolling Block S.S. pistol, 13¼ ins, barrel 8½ ins.
£160

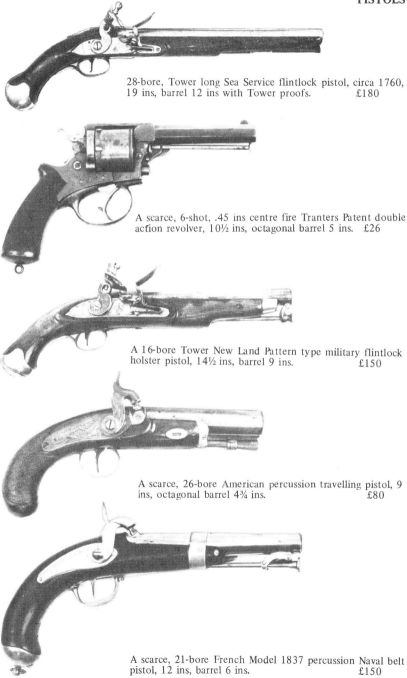

28-bore, Tower long Sea Service flintlock pistol, circa 1760, 19 ins, barrel 12 ins with Tower proofs. £180

A scarce, 6-shot, .45 ins centre fire Tranters Patent double action revolver, 10½ ins, octagonal barrel 5 ins. £26

A 16-bore Tower New Land Pattern type military flintlock holster pistol, 14½ ins, barrel 9 ins. £150

A scarce, 26-bore American percussion travelling pistol, 9 ins, octagonal barrel 4¾ ins. £80

A scarce, 21-bore French Model 1837 percussion Naval belt pistol, 12 ins, barrel 6 ins. £150

PISTOLS

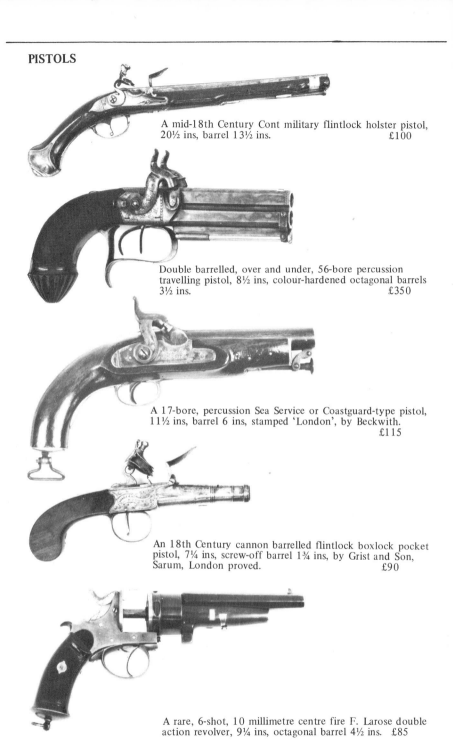

A mid-18th Century Cont military flintlock holster pistol, 20½ ins, barrel 13½ ins. £100

Double barrelled, over and under, 56-bore percussion travelling pistol, 8½ ins, colour-hardened octagonal barrels 3½ ins. £350

A 17-bore, percussion Sea Service or Coastguard-type pistol, 11½ ins, barrel 6 ins, stamped 'London', by Beckwith. £115

An 18th Century cannon barrelled flintlock boxlock pocket pistol, 7¼ ins, screw-off barrel 1¾ ins, by Grist and Son, Sarum, London proved. £90

A rare, 6-shot, 10 millimetre centre fire F. Larose double action revolver, 9¼ ins, octagonal barrel 4½ ins. £85

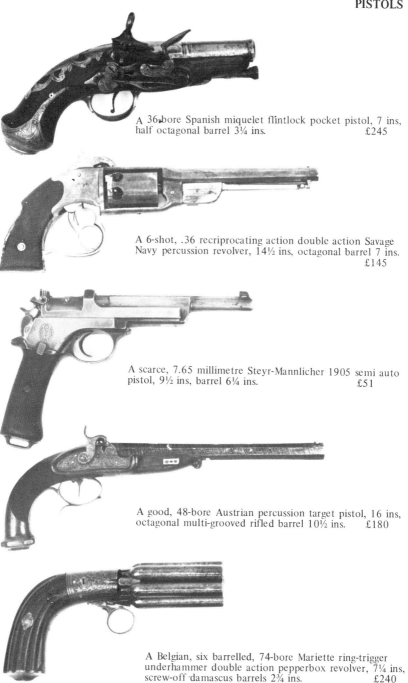

A 36-bore Spanish miquelet flintlock pocket pistol, 7 ins, half octagonal barrel 3¼ ins.   £245

A 6-shot, .36 recriprocating action double action Savage Navy percussion revolver, 14½ ins, octagonal barrel 7 ins.
                                                                                    £145

A scarce, 7.65 millimetre Steyr-Mannlicher 1905 semi auto pistol, 9½ ins, barrel 6¼ ins.   £51

A good, 48-bore Austrian percussion target pistol, 16 ins, octagonal multi-grooved rifled barrel 10½ ins.   £180

A Belgian, six barrelled, 74-bore Mariette ring-trigger underhammer double action pepperbox revolver, 7¼ ins, screw-off damascus barrels 2¾ ins.   £240

RIFLES

A scarce, mid-18th Century Danish 16-bore flintlock sporting gun, 54ins, good quality Persian barrel 38½ ins. £270

A 34-bore Kurdish miquelet flintlock 48½ ins, octagonal damascus twist rifled barrel 35 ins. £150

An interesting, French 100-shot, 52-bore repeating self cocking percussion saloon chain gun. £400

A rare, 9-shot, 64-bore Porter's Patent repeating percussion turret rifle, 43 ins, heavy octagonal barrel 22½ ins. £280

An early 18th Century brass barrelled flintlock blunderbuss, 31½ ins, stepped barrel 16½ ins. £260

A 12-bore, Herzogovanian miquelet flintlock sporting gun, 53 ins, barrel 40 ins. £120

A 24-bore continental military flintlock musket (probably Austrian), 49 ins, barrel 33 ins, fullstocked.   £95

A rare, .66 ins Paget flintlock Cavalry carbine, 31 ins, London and military proved sighted barrel 16 ins.   £410

An interesting, 70-bore walking stick air gun, 37½ ins overall.   £199

A Belgian brass barrelled flintlock blunderbuss, 26½ ins, pronounced swamped barrel 13½ ins.   £210

A good, rare, 16-bore Elliot's-pattern volunteer Cavalry flintlock carbine, circa 1800, 44 ins, barrel 28 ins.   £450

A rare, .577 Storm's Patent breech-loading percussion rifle, 48½ ins, barrel 30½ ins, fullstocked.   £150

RUGS

A Turkoman rug, 84ins x 48ins.
£390

A splendid example of a Hatchli, or prayer rug, 5ft 6ins x 4ft 3ins. £550

Ispahara rug, with multi-coloured floral design on white ground, 7ft 5ins x 4ft 10ins. £290

A Tekke rug of classical design, 4ft x 3ft 3ins. £180

A Turkoman storage-bag face with simple geometric design, 2ft 8ins x 4ft 1ins. £220

One of a pair of Kashan silk rugs, 6ft 10ins x 4ft 6ins. £2,520

A bag face by the Ersari Bshir tribe with chevron design, 4ft 8ins x 3ft. £220

A small Turkoman Beluch saddle bag. £60

A Tekke Bokhara rug, 100ins x 55ins. £170

A Beluch prayer rug, 3ft 6ins x
2ft 4ins.   £75

Turkish Bergama prayer rug,
3ft 10ins x 3ft 6ins, circa
1800.   £1,250

Persian Kurdistan rug,
7ft x 4ft 3ins, circa 1930.
                          £95

A Tabriz rug, having rose and
ivory field with a large pole
medallion to the centre, 6ft
9ins x 4ft.   £290

A Yomat animal trapping, 4ft
3ins wide.   £550

Early 19th century Armenian
Kazak rug, 6ft 10ins x 5ft 1ins.
                          £700

A complete storage bag with an
unusual skirt, made by the Tekke,
5ft 4ins x 3ft 7ins.   £125

A Saryq entrance hanging in
wool and silk with elaborate
tassels.   £450

Persian Kerman rug,
7ft 6ins x 5ft, circa
1890.   £750

RUGS

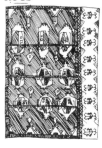

An interesting Tekke Choval
(tent bag) 4ft 2ins x 2ft 10ins. £55

Early 20th century Shiraz,
5ft 11ins x 5ft.   £40

A good Gashgai Shiraz rug,
9ft 8ins x 7ft 1ins.   £210

A Tabriz rug with rose and ivory
field, 6ft 9ins x 4ft.   £290

Early 20th century Tekke rug,
4ft 6ins x 4ft 3ins.   £150

A magnificent Shirvan rug,
the field with a geometric
version of the Fakteh
Jamshid, circa 1910. £360

19th century Oriental bordered
rug, 6ft 10ins long.   £50

A Bessarabian Kilim rug,
9ft 9ins x 7ft 7ins.   £140

A fine Kashan picture rug, the
central medallion depicting a
middle Eastern landscape, 6ft
8ins x 4ft 6ins.   £360

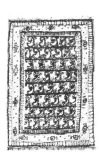

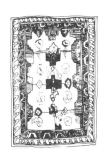

Early 20th century Sehna rug, 6ft 9ins x 4ft 4ins. £50

19th century Caucasus Kazakstan rug, 7ft 7ins x 4ft 1ins. £90

Early 20th century Afshari double ended prayer rug, 5ft 11ins x 4ft 4ins. £42

20th century Gashgai rug, 6ft 11ins x 5ft. £90

An early 19th century Manuluka rug, 6ft x 4ft. £150

An Ispahan rug, the central rose pole medallion edged in blue strapwork, 7ft x 4ft 7ins. £300

19th century Kirman Afshar rug with three typical Afshari borders, 6ft 5ins x 5ft. £70

Early 20th century Kashan rug with a classical Isphanan design, 6ft 5ins x 4ft 1ins. £220

Qum hunting rug, 6ft 5ins x 4ft 6ins. £230

RUGS

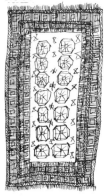

Early 20th century Afghan rug of the Chub Bash, 7ft 6ins x 5ft 3ins. £95

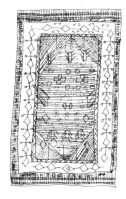

19th century Gashgai rug, 8ft 10ins x 5ft 4ins. £90

Asia Minor rug with 17th century design on a predominantly ivory ground, 8ft 7ins x 5ft. £1,500

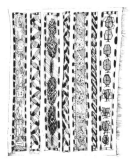

An old Beshir Chival, the field of ersari guls laid in horizontal stripes (damaged) 4ft 10ins x 3ft 10ins. £16

An interesting Lur tribal rug, circa 1800, 4ft x 3ft 5ins. £50

Persian Tribal Afshar, 5ft x 4ft, circa 1880. £195

early 20th century Hamadan rug, 6ft 5ins x 4ft 6ins. £90

19th century Tabriz rug, 4ft 7ins x 3ft 2ins. £120

19th century Genje runner, 9ft 9ins x 3ft 2ins. £38

20th century Kazak Genje rug, 5ft 7ins x 3ft 5ins. £80

Early 20th century Kashan rug, the central field medallion amid interlacing arabesques, 6ft 3ins x 4ft 3ins. £250

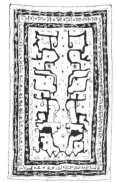

Persian Heroz rug, 7ft 4ins x 5ft 3ins, circa 1850. £1,150

Persian Quash Gai, 5ft 6ins x 3ft 8ins, circa 1870. £1,500

19th century Sehna Rupalani (bride's dowry saddle cover), 3ft 5ins x 3ft 2ins. £200

Persian Herez, 7ft 2ins x 5ft 6ins, circa 1850. £3,250

A rare Armenian Kazak rug, dated 1800, 6ft 9ins x 3ft 8ins. £300

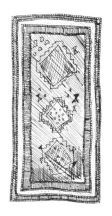

19th century Kazak rug, the field of three stepped medallions, 6ft 7ins x 3ft 11ins. £85

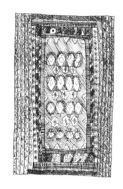

19th century Saryk Choval (tent bag complete with back), 5ft 9ins x 3ft 7ins. £70

RUGS

An old Kazak rug, 5ft 5ins x 2ft 5ins. £60

20th century Kilim rug, the field with three medallions, 4ft 6ins x 2ft. £20

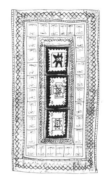

Caucasian Kasak, 6ft 5ins x 3ft 8ins, circa 1880. £285

Early 20th century Afshar rug, 5ft 1ins x 4ft. £90

Caucasian Kazak, 4ft 6ins x 4ft 1ins, circa 1850. £950

Caucasian Soumak, 6ft 11ins x 5ft, circa 1880. £275

Persian Tribal Shiraz, 5ft 8ins x 3ft 5ins, circa 1890. £275

A modern Persian pair of saddle bags. £18

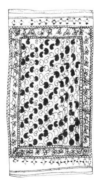

Turkoman Beshire, 6ft 8ins x 4ft, circa 1900. £395

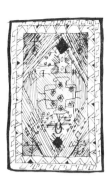

19th century Seichur rug,
4ft 5ins x 3ft 1ins.   £140

A Persian pillow with pile
cover.   £35

19th century Seichur Soumak
rug, the field of three massive
and three subsiduary medallions,
6ft x 4ft 4ins.   £130

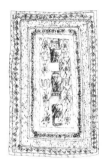

Caucasian Kuba, 5ft 10ins x
3ft 6ins, circa 1850.   £1,450

Belouch Prayer rug, 4ft x 3ft
2ins, circa 1900.   £145

An old Tekke Chuval, 4ft
10ins x 3ft 2ins.   £30

20th century Roumanian copy
of a Tabriz prayer rug, 5ft 8ins
x 4ft 2ins.   £95

A pair of old Persian Belouchi
saddle bags.   £17

Early 20th century Yomud of
good colour, 5ft 2ins x 4ft 7ins.
                        £140

SIGNS

Bovril poster mounted on stretched canvas, 5ft x 3ft 4ins, circa 1940.   £40

One of a pair of cast lead Coats of Arms, circa 1770, 8ins x 6ins.   £56

'The Polecat', a double-sided wooden tavern sign of a black and white polecat, 37½ins wide, 32ins high. £75

An impressive 19th century carved walnut Royal Coat of Arms, from a court house, 48ins overall length, 23ins overall height.   £175

Gargantuan-sized carved wood Hessian Boot covered with gold leaf, circa 1760, originally a boot shop sign, 39¼ins high.   £280

A very fine wrought iron bar grill, 5ft long, 3ft high, circa 1840.   £200

One of a set of ten posters and cut-outs, circa 1930.   £68

Tavern sign, "The Wagon and Horses", double-sided on sheet tin with black wood frame, 46ins x 38ins.   £45

Decorative Inn sign "Sir John Barleycorn', single-sided sheet metal, with wrought iron band around, 50ins x 42ins wide. £75

Copyrighted gouache drawing, probably between 1955-56, 6½ins x 9½ins.　　　£35

Tole shop sign of gold leafed horses head, 24ins high, circa 1830.　£225

"The Rose and Crown", Tavern sign painted on wood, 33ins wide, 40ins high.　　£55

A very fine and heavy door porter of Royal Coat of Arms with Lion and Unicorn supports, circa 1840, 11ins long, 9ins high.　　£38

Shop window sign of a monkey, made entirely of French pipe briar-wood, 27ins wide, circa 1850.　　　　£165

Brass heraldic Coat of Arms, circa 1830.　　　£68

A finely painted double-sided tavern sign, 'The Falcon', 42ins x 33ins.　　£85

19th century advertising plaque by Mayer of Longport.　£440

Colourful and well-painted Old Tavern Sign, 'The George and Dragon', double-sided on board, 37ins wide, 33½ins high.　£75

Pair of Charles II plain circular shallow bowls with covers, maker I.H., 3½ins high, London 1677, 31ozs 10dwt.   £1,700

(Henry Spencer & Sons, Retford)

A fine antique silver Monteith bowl, embossed with a continuous design of flowers, leaves and two hunting dogs, and with a detachable rim. London 1700, by Benjamin Pyne, 82ozs 10dwt.   £750

(King & Chasemore, Pulborough)

BASKETS

A Sheffield circular cake basket with fluted and chased border.   £18

Victorian silver sugar basket with a blue glass lining, Sheffield 1868.   £215

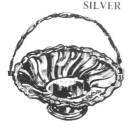

A Sheffield circular plated cakestand.   £20

George III silver swing handle wire-work cake basket, by A.S., London, 1762, 31ozs.   £250

A two tier plated cakestand.   £3

George III silver sweetmeat basket by William Plummer, 1762, 6¼ins long.   £395

BOWLS

Heavy Scottish two-handled bowl, W.M., Edinburgh, 1835, 99ozs, 17¾ins wide.   £850

Circular Edwardian double-handled pierced silver bowl, 7½ins diam., 12ozs 15dwts, with glass liner.   £28

George III circular silver fruitbowl by Philip Grierson, 1825, 49ozs.   £1,060

19th century Chinese silver punch bowl, 84 ozs.   £210

Oriental chased plated bowl.   £9

A late Victorian silver Monteith, Sheffield, 1897.   £1,300

BOWLS

A Russian gilt kovshe in silver gilt and enamel, circa 1900, 10½ins long. £900

George III circular sugar bowl with embossed garlands of flowers, Edinburgh 1784, 7ozs 10dwts. £75

Circular silver rose bowl with chased border, 7ins diam., 13ozs 5dwts. £40

BUTTER KNIVES

A fine Victorian silver butter knife. £9.50

Silver fish slice by William Kingdom, London 1819. £32

Butter knife by R. Gray & Son, Glasgow, 1831. £16

CADDY SPOONS

Caddy spoon with floral engraved bowl, by Yapp and and Woodward, Birmingham, 1850. £30

Caddy spoon, engraved with ivy leaves, makers C & Sons, London, 1899. £29

Shovel caddy spoon, by Samuel Pemberton, Birmingham, 1813. £37

Waisted bowl caddy spoon, 1860. £25

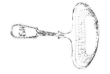

George III kidney shaped caddy spoon, Birmingham 1873. £37

Apostle caddy spoon by George Adams, London 1868. £25

A fine caddy spoon with diamond engraved bowl, by John Bettridge, Birmingham, 1817. £48

Victorian caddy spoon. £25

Caddy spoon with vine decorated handle, by William Davenport, Birmingham, 1904. £17

Pair of George III silver candlesticks with gadrooned borders, on square bases. £540
(Bradley & Vaughan)

Set of four George II cast table candlesticks by George Hindmarsh, 7½ins high, London 1735, 68ozs,   **£2,300**
(Henry Spencer & Sons, Retford)

CANDLESTICKS

Two of a very fine set of four George II cast, table candlesticks. £2,300

Two of a set of four George III silver baluster candlesticks, on rectangular bases, George Cadnam & Co., Sheffield, 1807, 6½ins high. £350

Pair of cast silver candlesticks by William Cafe. £400

Pair of dwarf table candlesticks on square chased bases. £15

Pair of octagonal based silver candlesticks, London 1823. £95

Georgian baluster circular silver candlesticks. £310

A pair of Corinthian column plated candlesticks. £26

Two of a set of four early George III cast, table candlesticks by Ebenezer Coker, one pair 1762, the other 1769, 10ins high, 68ozs. £1,200

Pair of 19th century dwarf candlesticks on fluted pillars and square bases, 5¼ins high. £44

Two of a set of four George III table candlesticks by Samuel Kirby, Sheffield, 1805/6, 12¼ins high. £680

Pair of Sheffield plate table candlesticks on rococo 'C' and 'S' scroll bases, 8ins high, circa 1845. £45

Victorian Adam style silver candlesticks. £320

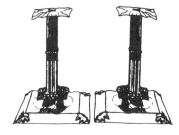

Pair of silver candlesticks by Jacob Bodenick, 1669, 31.1cm high, 84ozs 12dwt. £38,000

George II cast candlesticks by John Pollock, London, 37ozs. £320

Pair of Victorian plated table candlesticks on tapering stems, 10½ins high. £26

George III taper sticks by Ebenezer Coker, 1769, 6ins high. £1,100

A Queen Anne silver sugar caster of cylindrical form, 3¾ins high, London 1709, possibly by Phillip Roker.

(King & Chasemore, Pulborough)

£68

CASTERS

Mid 18th century silver sugar caster.   £205

Victorian cylindrical silver sugar caster, heavily chased with flowers and scrolls, 6½ins high, London 1896, 6ozs, in case. £75

One of a pair of Victorian silver, pear-shaped sugar casters by F.S. and J.H., London, 1889, 12ozs. £145

Silver sugar caster by Samuel Wood, 1752, 6½ins high.   £350

George IV silver pepper by Thos. Jenkinson, London, 1824.   £45

Sugar caster by Crispin Fuller, 1796, 6ins high.   £165

Caster by Henry Brind, London, 1742.   £225

CENTREPIECES

A parcel gilt epergne by Elkington & Co., 1875, 141ozs.   £950

One of a set of three oval boat-shaped silver centre-pieces, each embossed with acanthus scrolls of fruit and flowers, by Sorley, Glasgow, 1897, 285ozs.   £1,300

A large Victorian silver centre-piece.   £3,700

CHAMBERSTICKS

One of a pair of George III chamber candlesticks by John Eames. £330

Victorian silver chamberstick by F.H., 1846. £200

Silver chamberstick by Emes and Barnard, London 1822. £270

A pair of silver chamber candlesticks by Henry Wilkinson & Co., Sheffield, 1845, 5½ins high. £625

Victorian plated chamberstick and snuffer. £18

COASTERS

Sheffield circular wine coaster with pierced border. £12

One of a pair of circular wine coasters with chased borders. £13

Silver wine coaster, Charles Chesterman, London, 1810. £18

One of a pair of Sheffield circular wine coasters with oblique fluted and chased borders. £16

One of a fine pair of early Victorian coasters by Charles Fox. £220

Pair of Edward Barnard & Sons wine coasters, 7ins diam, 1832. £220

Baluster coffee pot by Robert
Hennell, London 1844, 23ozs,
8dwr.   £348

Silver coffee pot by Thomas
Bolton, Dublin, 1706, 25.4cm
high, 25ozs 8dwt.   £2,600

An 18th century pear shaped
Maltese coffee pot, by Manuel
Cinto, on cloven-hoofed feet.
£575

A plated vase shaped
coffee pot.   £14

Edwardian two-piece silver coffee set, 20ozs. £48

Silver coffee pot with later
Victorian moulding. £240

A fine silver coffee pot, by
Joseph and Albert Savory,
London, 1849, 9ins high.
£375

George I coffee pot of tapering
cylindrical form by Benjamin
Pyne, 10½ins high, London
1716, 29ozs.   £2,200

A fine George II plain tapering coffee pot and cover with scrolled spout, acanthus mounted, with 'C' loop handle, London 1742, maker Gabriel Sleath, 21ozs. £530

(M. M. & Bavistock)

CUPS

Edwardian silver double handled prize cup, 5ozs 5dwt.   £9

Gilt cup and cover in the rococo style, by Paul de Lamerie, 1739.   £700

James I silver gilt steeple cup and cover by H.B., London 1621, 13½ins high.   £5,500

Silver racing cup by Barnard, 1873, 31ozs.   £85

Pair of late 17th century German enamelled silver gilt cups, 7.7cm high.   £1,200

Plated double handled prize cup, 10ins high.   £1

An exceptionally fine sterling silver cricketing trophy, by Martin Hall & Co., 1863/4, 20ozs, 9½ins high.   £135

Circular silver double handled prize cup with engraved inscription, 5ozs 5dwt.   £9

Two handled silver cup by Paul Crespin.   £190

545

SILVER DISHES

Plated oblong shaped entree dish and cover with chased borders. £26

A plated circular vegetable dish and cover with divider and side handle. £32

George IV shell butter dish with gilt interior by W.E., 1828. £145

A ware oval dish with plated cover and stand. £13

One of a pair of silver entree dishes, Sheffield 1902, 115ozs. £400

A pyrex dish stand. £1

One of a pair of oval plated entree dishes with beaded borders. £30

Butter shell by Mappin and Webb, Sheffield, 1903. £24

An oval plated entree dish with double handled cover. £11

A Sheffield plate entree dish and cover, on a double handled warming stand. £42

One of a pair of circular sweetmeat dishes, 5¾ins diam., 5ozs 5dwt. £30

A circular plated muffin dish with liner and cover. £4

One of a pair of circular shaped French vegetable dishes and a matching pair of plated warmers, Paris, circa 1845, 125ozs. £500

Oval plated, double handled breakfast dish with revolving cover. £44

Silver sweetmeat dish, Birmingham 1907, 7ozs. £33

James II large porringer and cover by W.I., London 1685, 54ozs, 9ins high, 12ins wide. £9,700
(Henry Spencer & Sons, Retford)

A cut glass oval centre dish with pierced silver collar and detachable silver base, 11ins high, by
W. Comyns & Sons, London 1910. £240
(King & Chasemore, Pulborough)

An exceptionally fine Russian niello silver travelling cutlery set by V. Soloniew, with a fitted case. £400
(King & Chasemore, Pulborough)

A child's Victorian knife, fork and spoon with chased handles, Sheffield 1841.   £24

Set of four George III fruit spoons, engraved with crest, Dublin 1783, maker John Shields, 8ozs.   £64

19th century plated bread knife, fork and cheese scoop with ivory handles.   £13

Six silver coffee spoons and pair of sugar tongs in fitted case.   £16

FLATWARE

Six Victorian teaspoons, Glasgow 1842, in velvet lined case. £18

Twelve fish knives and twelve forks with white handles. £32

Pair of Victorian plated servers in case. £9

Twelve plated fish knives and forks with partly fluted handles. £11

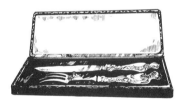

Victorian carving knife and fork with chased handles. £19

Plated fish knife and fork in velvet lined case. £8

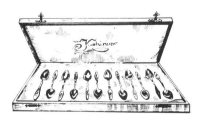

Twelve Norwegian silver coffee spoons with varying coloured enamel handles. £26

Twelve plated dessert knives and twelve forks in oak case. £26

SILVER FLATWARE

George III gravy spoon by Eley, Fearn and Channer, London 1808, 4ozs.   £22

Silver sifter spoon by John Lautier, 1782. £29

Silver tablespoon by Carden, Terry and John Williams, Cork 1805.   £20

A fine Charles II trifid spoon, London 1684. £95

An Apostle spoon of St. Mathew, Exeter 1653.   £200

A rat tailed silver trifid spoon with lace backed bowl, 1684.   £95

Tablespoon by Hester Bateman, London 1766.   £33

Irish rat tail teaspoon, maker S.G., Dublin, 1833.   £5.50

George III fish slice by Ward S. Kingdom, London 1810, 4ozs 5dwt.   £22

Bright cut tablespoon, 1787. £33

One of a set of three George III prize spoons, London 1815/16, by Eley and Fearn, 7ozs.   £12

One of a pair of shell bowl salt shovels by Walter Tweedie, London, circa 1782.   £20

Set of six table spoons, dessert spoons and forks, London 1908/9, 44ozs 5dwt. £115

Part of a 73-piece service of Elizabethan-pattern tableware, by G.W. Adams, 1872, and Francis Higgins, 1881.   £580

FLATWARE

A fine Apostle St. Mathew spoon, Exeter, circa 1653. £200

Jersey feather edge tablespoon by J. Quesney, circa 1800. £20

One of a pair of William III trifid spoons, London 1696, maker probably John Spackman, 3ozs 15dwt. £135

Silver teaspoon, 1790. £14

Bright cut teaspoon, 1781. £15

George III fish slice by Robert Hennel, London 1782. £26

A pair of Scottish teaspoons by William Aytoun, Edinburgh, circa 1790, with pointed terminals. £11

Bright-cut Perth teaspoon by Robert Keay, circa 1800. £15

One of a set of twelve silver-gilt spoons, made in 1592. £70,000

Sifter spoon by Edward Hutton, London 1883. £18

One of a set of six 'Cymric' silver and enamel spoons by Liberty & Co., 1903. £250

Silver dessert spoon by Chas. Murray, Perth, circa 1816. £17.50

Twelve old English fish knives and forks, in case. £16

Fiddle and shell pattern part suite of table appointments, London 1900, 48ozs, 20pieces. £120

SILVER FRAMES

A Victorian silver mounted
photograph frame.   £12

Edwardian silver mounted
photograph frame.   £14

Heart shaped photo frame,
by William Devenport,
Birmingham 1900.   £9

Victorian silver mounted table
mirror, 12ins high.   £42

Silver gilt Louis XIV toilet
mirror, Paris 1660, (a wedding
present from James II to the
Duchess of York).   £50,000

An upright table mirror in
Art Nouveau silver frame.
£34

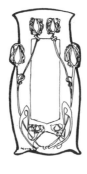

Silver and enamel mirror
frame by Liberty and Co.,
18¾ins high.   £2,400

Silver photo frame by Horton
and Allday, Chester 1887.
£40

Victorian silver framed
standing mirror, 10ins high.
£22

ICE PAILS

A George III silver ice pail of tapering form, with pierced swivel handle, by Thomas Heming, London 1766, 6¾ins high, 59ozs.   £1,050

One of a set of four William IV ice tubs by Paul Storr, 1835.   £2,000

A George III silver sugar pail, by Burrage Davenport, London, 1780.   £160

INKSTANDS

Square shaped plated inkstand, with chased border and glass inkwell.   £7

A Sheffield oblong double handled inkstand with two glass bottles, 14ins wide.   £50

Edwardian silver inkstand, on four ball feet with glass bottle, 4ozs 15dwt.   £13

Oblong silver inkstand with fluted border and glass inkwell, 6ins wide, 3ozs'10dwt.   £28

Victorian capstan design silver inkwell.   £7

An ornate early Victorian double inkstand with two pots, central well and chamberstick with snuffer.   £230

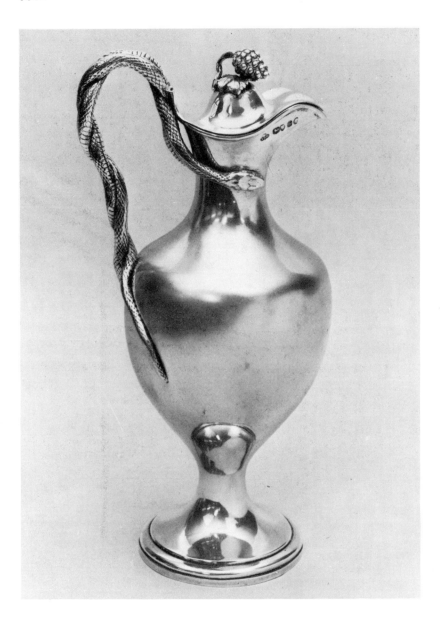

A Victorian silver wine ewer with oviform shaped body, the handle of entwined snakes. Hallmarked London 1858, weight 32ozs. £320

(King & Chasemore, Pulborough)

Cream jug by Richard
Hennel, London, 1862.
£75

Victorian silver cream jug with
chased flowers and scrolls,
London 1839, 3ozs 5dwts. £44

A silver hot water jug on a
stand, part of a three piece
silver semi-fluted melon shaped
tea set by Messrs. Barnard,
London, 1892, 88ozs. £390

19th century Russian silver gilt
and cloisonne enamel cream jug
decorated with formal floral
design, dated 1896, 3ins high.
£270

Pair of covered jugs, maker's
mark T.I. between escallops,
1685, London, 186ozs,
35.5cm high. £18,000

Silver milk jug, Newcastle,
circa 1800, by Thomas
Watson. £66

Victorian silver claret jug by
George Fox with classical
decoration, London 1872, 28ozs.
£300

A silver ewer by E & J.
Barnard, 1853, 12½ins
high. £310

Victorian red glass claret jug
with plated mounts. £56

SILVER
KETTLES

Georgian silver tea kettle on stand, London 1913, 74ozs. £370

George II kettle and stand by Paul Lamerie, London 1734, 690zs. £3,300

An oval plated hot water kettle on stand with two spirit lamps. £30

Victorian silver hot water kettle on stand with spirit lamp, Edinburgh 1898, 24ozs 5dwt. £85

A circular plated plain kettle. £15

George II tea kettle and stand complete with burner. £700

LADLES

One of a pair of King's pattern sauce ladles, by William Bateman, London, 1824. £60

Canadian silver soup ladle by Lewis Hulsman, Halifax 1790, 6ozs. £48

Silver sauce ladle, William Chawner, London, 1820. £18

One of a pair of sauce ladles, maker PP, London, 1827. £36

Silver toddy ladle, with coin inset bowl, circa 1756. £34

Silver ladle by James Erskine, Aberdeen, circa 1796, mailed list mark. £30

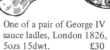

Continental silver soup ladle with chased handle, 3ozs. £6

One of a pair of George IV sauce ladles, London 1826, 5ozs 15dwt. £30

George III toddy ladle by Charles Murray, Perth, 1816. £60

MARROW SCOOPS & SKEWERS

Marrow spoon, by George Smith, London, 1779. £39

SILVER

Thread border marrow scoop, Paul Storr, London, 1820. £85

Meat skewer by Wallis and Hayne, London, 1819.
£55

MINIATURES

Silver knife-grinder, by Willem van Strant, Amsterdam, 1737. £500

Silver field-gun, Amsterdam, 1776, maker's mark AV.
£300

Oblong silver table, the raised sides pierced with hearts, Amsterdam, circa 1735, maker's mark, a shell. £300

A Continental silver toy jug, circa 1900.
£14

Victorian silver miniature cradle, 1896. £48

Plain square coffee-grinder, Amsterdam, circa 1750, maker's mark ES. £320

Octagonal tobacco box, with cover and inside cover, Amsterdam, 1755. £290

French silver miniature tea service in a coromandel wood case with brass mounts, dated 1793 and 1819. £600

Four-wheeled carriage and pair with driver and passenger, Amsterdam, 1749, maker's mark TB in script. £140

Silver printing press, on four baluster supports, with screw-top and three detachable plates, by Arnoldus van Geffe, Amsterdam, 1766. £480

SILVER
MISCELLANEOUS

One of a pair of George I silver chamber pots, 53ozs, 1722.   £6,800

A plated shell design biscuit box on pierced end supports.   £40

A heavily chased and embossed plated bread bin and cover.   £48

An electroplated electrotype card case by Elkington, Mason & Co., circa 1865, 4¼ ins long.   £75

Collector's example of a Georgian silver baby's rattle and comforter, maker's mark GU on whistle mouth piece, Sheffield, 1818, 5ins long.   £65

Gentleman's silver calling card box, 1902.   £10

Georgian silver spectacles by E.T., London 1823.   £20

Continental silver gilt knight in armour, the face in ivory.   £400

Pair of 19th century silver cased field glasses.   £12.50

Victorian silver plate lemon tea or Irish coffee holder, by Mappin & Bros., 3ins high.   £3

A plated cocktail set of six pieces on a wooden stand.   £10

Dutch 19th century silver model Nef, in the form of an 18th century three-masted square rigged ship on rockers, 4ins high, 3½ins long, 1oz 1dwt.   £58

MISCELLANEOUS

A Victorian silver model of an owl, London 1869, 36ozs. £650

Victorian semi-fluted silver jardiniere, with lion mask and ring handles, London, 1891, 30ozs. £125

Model of a standing hen, with detachable head, probably German, sponsor's mark B.M., Chester, 1903, 7¾ins high, 13ozs. £100

"Ye Dragon of Wantley" — silver mounted horn smoker's companion by Walker & Hall, Sheffield, 1916. £76

Mid 19th century fish incense-burner, fashioned in enamelled silver with gilt mounts, 20ins tall. £480

A plated cocktail shaker. £6

Set of three late 19th century Russian silver gilt and enamel items. £900

Silver gilt egg by Stuart Devlin, London 1968, 2¾ins high. £115

Superb 17th century velvet and silver belt, set with turquoise and pearls. £220

An early 19th century campaign box in mulberry wood. £110

A Victorian cigar-lighter in the form of a standing bear, maker's mark JBH, 1876, 6ins high. £260

SILVER MISCELLANEOUS

Continental plated nef in the form of a galleon. £290

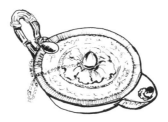

Silver gilt lamp by Benjamin and James Smith, 1809. £1,200

George III wine funnel with fluted border, by George Fenwick, Edinburgh, 1817, 3ozs 10dwts. £46

Oblong silver cigarette box with hinged cover, 8½ins wide. £22

Asprey travelling clock in leather case with eight day movement. £8

Hexagonal silver tea bottle and cover, 3½ins high, 2ozs 15dwts. £13

A fine Dutch engraved silver beaker, 1656, 8¼ins high. £3,200

Victorian silver crumb scoop with ivory handle. £14

Victorian circular silver napkin ring with chased border, in case. £7

A large plated mirror plateau of rock design. £13

17th century South German Mason guild flagon, 52cm high. £1,909

A large silver egg-shaped box, Chester, 1902. £65

MISCELLANEOUS

Sterling silver stamp envelope, Chester 1907.   £9.50

George IV lemon strainer with lyre design handles, Glasgow 1828, makers W.M. & A.M., 4ozs.   £70

Pair of Duck menu holders by C and N, Birmingham 1906.   £40

Victorian leather and silver mounted stationery case.   £38

Georgian folding fruit knife, Sheffield, circa 1800, with case.   £8

A German oval shaped silver biscuit box with hinged cover, 8ozs, 5dwts.   £40

19th century silver-handled desk seal.   £10

Presentation trowel with ivory handle.   £10

Art Nouveau silver canister, Elkington, London, 1901.   £48

Plated sugar skuttle complete with scoop.   £6

Victorian silver gilt table candelabrum by Benjamin Smith, London 1838. £1,050

Silver pin cushion in the form of a chick, Chester, 1906.   £24

Large oval plated dish cover
with fluted corners.   £5

Motoring mascot by
Joe Descompo, circa
1915.   £120

One of a pair of 19th century
Sheffield plated wine coolers.
£230

Cupid motoring mascot by
Norman Eastaugh, circa 1915.
£200

Fitted dressing case with 13
cut glass jars and bottles with
Victorian silver tops.   £140

Dancing figure motoring
mascot.   £140

A George III tea urn in
Adam style, by A.
Fogelberg & S. Gilbert,
London, 1780, 94·5 ozs.
£500

Mid 19th century Continental
silver nef standing on an
ebonised base, 3ft 6ins high,
2ft 6ins wide, probably by
Bernard Muller, 382ozs.
£7,500

Continental, 925 sterling, silver
gilt model of a medieval knight
in armour.   £370

MUGS

A Victorian christening mug
decorated with chased and
embossed flowers by Chas.
Fox, London, 1839.   £80

Victorian silver mug,
5 ozs, London, 1856.
£75

A child's Victorian set of mug,
knife, fork, spoon and napkin
ring, London 1884-6, 10ozs.
£76

George III barrel shaped mug
by P & W Bateman, London
1805, 3ozs.   £40

Continental silver gilt
enamel mug, 3 5/8ins
high, with matching
spoon.   £320

Child's silver mug by James
le Bass, Dublin, 1813.   £85

George III circular child's silver
mug by Samuel Hennel, London
1807, 5ozs 15dwts.   £60

Lowestoft blue and white two-
handled loving cup, circa 1757-
60.   £600

George III silver mug of
classical baluster shape, maker
J.E., London 1732, 8ozs.
£145

One of a pair of ornate standing salts in the form of Nautilus shells, foreign silver with an English hallmark of London 1901, 20ozs.   £180

(King & Chasemore, Pulborough)

George IV salt cellar with heavily chased flowers and scrolls by J. McKay, Edinburgh 1823, 3ozs 15dwts. £40

Continental silver mustard pot, 2ozs. £11

Victorian plain drum, silver mustard pot, 1893. £25

One of a set of four 19th century silver salts on hoof feet, 6ozs. £50

One of a set of four Victorian tripod salts, 1890. £38

One of a pair of salts by Robert Harper, London, 1875. £48

One of a pair of salts by W.R. Smiley, London, 1852. £48

Pair of Victorian 'Golf Ball' condiments, 1890. £22.50

One of a set of four circular salt cellars on hoof feet, London 1863, 8ozs 10dwts. £55

Triangular silver salt-cellar by Floris Bontekoning and Hester de Weer, Amsterdam, circa 1725. £220

Mustard pot by Martin Hall, Sheffield, 1888. £57

Victorian circular mustard pot with hinged cover and four ball feet, 3ins high, Edinburgh 1871, 5ozs. £25

Silver mustard pot by E.E.J. and W. Barnard, London 1844, 6ozs. £85

Dutch silver mustard pot with glass liner. £20

Victorian pierced silver mustard pot, London 1890, 3ozs, with blue glass liner. £13

SILVER
SCISSORS & TONGS

Silver grape scissors, by Mappin & Webb, Sheffield, 1902.   £48

Pierced silver sugar tongs by William Tant, 1764.   £12

George III fiddle pattern salad tongs by Ward S. Kingdom, London 1813, 4ozs 5dwts. £42

Victorian silver sewing scissors by Levi & Salaman, Birmingham, 1895.   £10

Pair of silver sugar nips, circa 1760.   £18.50

Scottish silver sugar tongs, maker J.G., Edinburgh 1804.   £15

Shaped bright cut sugar tongs with incuse head, circa 1784.   £32

George III silver sugar nippers by John Shields, Dublin 1770.   £26

Silver sugar nippers by George Wicks, London, circa 1735. £36

Silver sugar tongs, 1780. £17

SAUCEBOATS

Victorian silver sauceboat by John Hunt, London 1844, 11ozs. £140

A pair of sauceboats decorated with figures of Hebe and Jupiter, circa 1824, Garrard. £4,200

Plain plated sauceboat on three hoof feet. £6

Silver sauceboat by Louis Herne and Francis Butty, 1764. £175

Pair of George III silver sauceboats. £980

George III plain sauceboat with escalloped border, on three claw feet, Newcastle 1776, 2ozs. £17

SNUFF BOXES

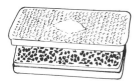

Georgian oval table snuffbox with onyx set hinged cover, and horn support, Dundee, circa 1830. £115

Victorian oval snuff box with inset agate hinged cover, 2ins wide, Birmingham 1857. £30

Late 18th century German gold snuff-box, inset with hardstones, by Christian Neuber, 7.3cm diam. £1,750

Silver snuff box by Ed Edwards, London, 1840. £45

Swiss gold snuff box, 3¼ins long. £550

Vinaigrette, Birmingham, 1832. £64

SILVER
TEAPOTS

A nicely shaped plated teapot. £16

Edwardian silver teapot, Chester 1908, 26ozs. £135

A fine engraved oval straight-sided silver teapot and stand, by R & D Hennel. £320

George IV embossed silver teapot, 1825. £130

A Canadian silver teapot by Francois Sasseville, circa 1850. £2,000

An oval plated teapot with fluted sides. £10

Silver teapot, 20ozs, Sheffield, 1925. £70

Silver gravy Argyle by C. Aldridge and H. Green, 1779, 5ins high. £550

Part of a three-piece silver teaset by Jonathan Hayne, London 1834, 46ozs. £420

A circular engraved Victorian teapot. £5.50

Plain circular teapot, Amsterdam, 1784, maker's mark AV in monogram. £60

A plain oval plated teapot with ebony handle. £9

A George III silver teapot and stand, London 1795, Maker I.R.   £140
(King & Chasemore, Pulborough)

A George III silver teapot with matching stand, Newcastle 1805, probably by Dorothy Langlands, 21ozs.
£200
(King & Chasemore, Pulborough)

A pair of George III silver tea caddies and a silver mounted mahogany case, London 1767, maker Ed. Darvill, 18ozs. £490

(King & Chasemore, Pulborough)

TEA CADDIES

A fine George III tea caddy, London 1791, by James Young. £190

A pair of George III silver bombe shaped tea caddies and rosewood casket. £700

George III oval shaped silver tea caddy with beaded edges and urn finial, by Ang Le Sage, London 1779, 11½ozs. £300

Silver tea caddy by I.P.G., 1762. £310

A Continental silver, square, tapering tea caddy and cover, 5½ins high, 7ozs. £40

Set of three George III tea caddies in case. £1,585

TOASTERS

An attractive silver toast rack by William Eaton, London, 1836, 11ozs, 1¾ins long. £115

Edwardian seven bar plated toast rack. £8

Georgian six-compartment oval toast rack by Peter and Ann Bateman, London 1799, 5ozs. £68

SOVEREIGN CASES

Gilt metal double sovereign case. £4.50

Gilt metal sovereign case. £3.75

Victorian metal sovereign case. £3.50

William IV four piece tea and coffee service by E.E.J. and W. Bernard, 1832/4, 95ozs. £900

An oblong shaped silver teaset with gadrooned border, 43ozs 10dwt. £120

American silver tea set by Salisbury & Co., New York, circa 1830, 72ozs. £575

Edward Barnard & Sons tea and cofee set, 1872, 69ozs. £680

A hand-made art nouveau five-piece silver teaset, Birmingham 1919, maker's mark DMW, 70¾ozs. £380

Three piece silver tea set with matching hot water jug, by Messrs. Barnard, London, 1892, 88ozs. £390

An oblong teaset with fluted borders, 33ozs 5dwt. £130

An oval plated teaset of three pieces. £15

A three piece oval plate teaset comprising teapot, sugar and cream.   £20

George III silver tea service by Peter and Anne Bateman, 1795, 117ozs.   £2,900

Victorian circular silver three piece teaset with chased flowers, scrolls and shells, by Wm. Reid, London 1844, 46ozs 10dwt.   £420

A small Victorian ornate silver teaset with matching tray, Birmingham 1877, 70.9ozs.   £300

Late Victorian four piece silver tea and coffee service.   £480

Three piece Edwardian silver coffee set with chased borders, 16ozs 15dwt.   £62

TEA & COFFEE SETS

Edwardian three-piece silver teaset with fluted panels, 20ozs. £48

George IV silver teaset with boars head motifs on the feet, London, 1822, 48ozs. £825

Five piece silver teaset, 70ozs, Sheffield, 1905. £400

Three-piece cymric silver tea service by Liberty, Birmingham 1902, 25ozs. £80

William IV three-piece silver tea-service. £270

A Russian gold-plated lidded tankard, the body and lid with incised enamelled scroll decorations and two
pictorial panels in Niellio black enamel, marked 1886 and 84, 25ozs.   £355

(King & Chasemore, Pulborough)

Baluster tankard by
W.B., London 1794.
£160

German parcel-gilt tankard,
by Melchior Gibb, circa
1620, 9½ins high.   £10,000

A fine George III domed
tankard of tapering form with
sea scroll handle, London
1778, 24ozs 10dwt.   £500

Queen Anne silver lidded
tankard, London 1712, 33ozs.
£640

Silver lidded tankard marked
Thomas Wynne, London, 1773,
24½ozs.   £480

Small tankard by Thomas
Whipham, London 1783.
£105

Baluster tankard by
I.K., London, 1787.
£155

A fine George III domed
tankard of tapering form by
John Schofield, London 1779,
22ozs.   £500

Victorian small tankard inset
with 1901 halfcrown, 3¾ins
high, 6ozs 5dwt.   £20

A fine George III silver
tankard by Hester
Bateman.   £925

William and Mary bulbous lidded
tankard engraved with the Coat
of Arms of Richard Lassells,
London, 27ozs.   £4,000

George III tankard with scroll
handle, London 1767.   £145

SILVER
TRAYS & SALVERS

George III circular salver
by Thos. Wallis and
Jonathan Hayne, London,
1818, 19ozs.   £95

George III circular silver
salver by M & R, Edinburgh,
1817, 20ozs.   £120

William IV circular shaped
card tray by William
Marshall, Edinburgh, 1835,
11ozs.   £56

A plain circular plated
salver.   £16

Oval, plated, double-handled
tea tray with gadrooned border,
24½ins wide.   £28

Decorative silver salver, London
1832, 105ozs.   £570

George III oval silver tray,
by John Crouch & Thos.
Hannam, London, 1781,
12.5ozs.   £140

George III circular silver
waiter, by John Kidder,
London, 1784, 4ozs. £78

Silver tray engraved with
insignia of the Knight Garter
and inscribed '25 December
1896, 180gns.   £680

Continental silver salver, 11½ins
wide, 21ozs 5dwts.   £26

Edwardian plated oblong tray
with pierced border, 25ins
wide.   £24

One of a pair of James II
octagonal footed silver
waiters.   £7,100

TRAY & SALVERS

George II silver salver by Paul Crespin, dated 1730, 56½ozs, 14ins diam. £1,200

A large oblong shaped double handled tea tray with heavy shell and scroll border, 32ins wide, 182ozs. £460

Victorian chased silver salver, with applied scroll and floral border, on four leaf feet, by Garrard, London, 1852, 22ins diam, 124ozs. £250

One of a set of four George III silver dishes by William Hall of London, 1802. £766

Sheffield plated oval wine tray with pierced gallery, 14¼ins wide. £30

A George III silver salver by John Carter, London 1771, 76ozs, 17ins diam. £700

Late 19th century gold and silver Damascenes steel dish by Placido Zuloaga, 16ins wide. £1,150

Silver salver by Paul Crespin, London 1730, 35.5cm diam, 56ozs 10dwt. £1,200

19th century plated ashet with gadrooned border. £14

George II square silver waiter, by John Tuite, London, 1727, 8.5ozs, 6ins high. £120

Oblong shaped plated double-handled tea tray with rail border, 20½ins wide. £8

A Victorian decorated silver salver by J. Hunt and Roskell, London 1883, 17ozs. £64

SILVER
TANTALUS

Mid 19th century gilt-topped, three-bottle scent tantalus with leather case. £28

A Victorian oak tantalus spirit case with three cut glass decanters and stoppers. £20

A mahogany tantalus spirit frame with plated handles and mounts, and three cut glass decanters. £80

Victorian three bottle tantalus with silver mounts. £90

TUREENS

An Electroplated decanter stand with bottles, and three silver wine labels, by Roberts & Belk, Sheffield, 1867, 15¼ins high. £110

Victorian silver plated tantalus with three cut glass decanters. £55

One of a set of four silver sauce tureens by William Grundy, London, 1776, 76ozs. £2,000

An old Sheffield plate soup tureen and cover, circa 1820, 13¾ins wide. £248

One of a pair of silver sauce tureens, 1775, 28ozs. £320

An oval plasted double handled soup tureen with liner, cover and bead border. £54

Silver tureen by Benjamin Smith, London, 1824, 37ozs. £250

Plated oval double handled soup tureen and cover, with beaded border. £28

Art Nouveau large circular
double handled silver flower
vase, 12ins high, 18ozs 10dwt.
£58

Pair of ornate silver vases
embossed with flowers, leaves
and fruit, London 1882, 19ozs.
£165

One of a pair of Art
Nouveau double handled
flower vases, 8¾ins high.
£38

Circular plated flower epergne
with four vases.   £15

Victorian silver vase embossed
with fruit and flower decoration,
London 1878, 30ozs.   £250

Triangular shaped plated flower
epergne with four vases.   £10

Victorian Persian silver vase
with black cloisonne enamel,
8ins high.   £9

Pair of silver fluted flower
vases, 6½ins high.   £12

Art Nouveau silver flower vase
with pierced and chased
flowers, 9¾ins high, 8ozs. £46

SILVER
WINE LABELS

A silver wine label 'Hermitage' a French Rhone Valley wine, circa 1785. £18

Silver White wine label, circa 1785, 'Hock'. £13

Silver wine label 'White Champagne', circa 1785. £22

Silver wine label, Birmingham 1847. £18

George III spirit label and chain. £16

A pair of Bilston decanter labels, circa 1790. £80

George II wine label by Sandylands Drinkwater, London 1755. £20

A silver wine label with unrecorded name 'Morachez', circa 1785. £24

Unmarked silver wine label, circa 1785, 'Champagne — Red'. £24

An unmarked silver wine label, circa 1785, 'Grave'. £12

An unmarked silver wine label 'Hermitage', a French Rhone Valley wine, circa 1785. £18

19th century elm spinning
wheel.   £38

An early pine and oak
spinning wheel, in need
of repair.   £15

18th century spinning
wheel.   £95

An early oak spinning wheel.
                          £20

18th century upright fruitwood spinning wheel, 31ins
high.   £65

18th century oak spinning
wheel.   £35

An 18th century pine spinning
wheel.   £25

18th century oak spinning
wheel.   £45

An 18th century stained
wood spinning wheel.   £25

SWORDS

A cut steel-hilted court sword, triangular tapering, hollow-ground blade 31 ins.
£30

A good, Indian shamshir hilt sword, slightly curved blade 28 ins. £35

A good quality Persian sword shamsir, mid-18th Century, curved watered blade 32½ ins.
£26

A good, mid-18th Century European hunting sword, plain, straight single edged blade 21½ ins. £48

A French Curassier broadsword, straight single edged blade 38 ins. £75

A mid-18th Century Scottish basket-hilted horseman's broadsword, blade 32½ ins.
£125

A good, Georgian officer's Spadroon, circa 1770, straight single edged blade 28½ ins.
£40

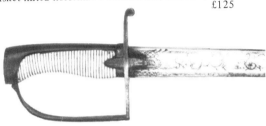

A fine, Georgian 1822-pattern general officer's sword, clipped-back blade 33 ins.
£150

A good, United States society sword by Horstmann, Philadelphia, double edged blade 31 ins.
£36

A good Nazi police officer's sword, straight blade 33½ ins.   £80

A good Japanese Katana, blade 30 ins. £190

A good Turkish sabre, Kilij, curved blade 27½ ins with broad clip-back. £230

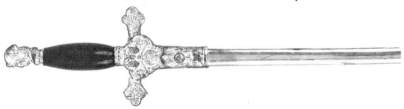

A good United States society sword, by Lynch and Kelly Utica, double edged blade 28 ins. £26

A large, old Ceremonial Executioner's Tulwar, broad, curved blade 24 ins. £160

A Georgian cut steel-hilted smallsword, circa 1800, plain triangular tapering blade 32 ins. £52

A good, Japanese Katana, blade 23 ins. £190

A Japanese Katana, blade 26 ins, solid iron tsuba.   £155

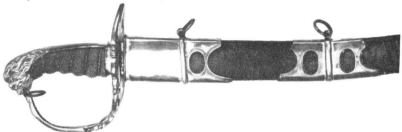

A rare, Georgian officer's sabre of the Royal Regiment, plain curved blade 29½ ins.
£120

A fine Chinese sword with straight double edged blade 27 ins long.   £65

A very fine Georgian Naval officer's dirk, curved fullered blade 13¾ ins.   £85

A United States society sword, straight blade 28 ins.   £26

A fine, late 18th Century Wakizashi for presentation to a temple, 19 ins hira zukuri.
£1,100

An unusual French toy in mahogany and glass case, circa 1900, 1ft 6ins wide. £65

A late 19th century English painted wooden rocking horse on trestle rocker with baluster supports, 4ft 6ins long. £120

Victorian childs' push along horse with original dapple grey paint, 31ins long. £68

An early childs' pedal car by Chas. Boardman and Sons. £85

A wooden dray and pair with driver, 15ins high, 27½ins long, signed Gregory Ivory, 1892. £95

A painted wood model of Noah's ark, and a large collection of the carved wood animals and birds. £75

A German Laterna Magica Lantern with a quantity of slides in case. £23

Substantially built doll's house, with two reception rooms, hall, staircase, landing and two bedrooms. £95

Early Edo period iron tsuba depicting Shoki. £500

A good Japanese iron tsuba, possibly 18th century mito-work. £31

19th century Ishigura school tsuba depicting a cockerel strutting through some flowers. £2,600

Mid 18th century tsuba chiselled in the round with a dragon amidst foliage and waves. £55

Iron tsuba decorated with tangs. £160

A good Japanese openwork iron tsuba, pierced with stylised bamboo and foliage, signed "Coshu No Ju Massasaba". £50

A large iron tsuba, chiselled in low relief with a man bearing a sword Ken who has frightened an oni. £44

A Japanese oval silver dagger tsuba, engraved with a simple pattern in katakiri. £21

A good Japanese iron tsuba showing a chidari perched on a twig, possibly 18th century goto work. £21

De Dion-engined two seater tandem cyclecar, circa 1899. £2,535

Rolls-Royce 40.50 h.p. Phantom II four-door, six-light Sports saloon, 1930. £5,352

Renault type - AX 9h.p., two-seater, circa 1909. £3,943

De Dion-Bouton 3½ h.p. Vis - A - Vis, circa 1900. £4,225

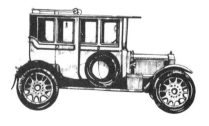

Super 10 h.p., two-seater tandem cyclecar, 1913. £1,830

Rolls-Royce 40.50 h.p. 'Silver Ghost' seven-seater, fully enclosed limousine, circa 1910. £30,986

Ford model - T, 20 h.p. tourer, 1926.
£1,690

De Dion-engined 1¾ h.p. Light two-seater
car, circa 1897.   £3,380

Lion-Peugeot 6/7 h.p., Type - VA Sporting
two-seater, circa 1907.   £3,943

Renault 9 h.p. type AG two-seater, 1912.
£2,676

Fiat 50-60 h.p. Tipo 5, six-seater Torpedo
Tourer, 1912.   £5,634

Darracq 15.9 h.p., type - PRX, four-seater
Double Phaeton, circa 1910.   £5,634

A 1936 Rolls Royce. £3,200

Bugatti Brescia, type 23, 1½ litre Sports, three-seater, Cloverleaf, 1923. £7,746

Motor cycle by Wearwell Stevens, with original rams horn handle grips, made in 1903. £660

Dumont single-cylinder, rear-entrance Tonne A U, circa 1901. £2,394

A 1926 series, speed model, three litre Bentley, finished in racing green. £8,100

Lorraine-Dietrich B3/6, 20.9 h.p., four-door fabric saloon, 1923. £2,817

Graf und Stift 40-45 h.p., six-seater Tourer, 1913. £26,760

Excelsior 16.20 h.p., four-seater Tourer, circa
1911.   £5,634

Isotto Fraschini 20-30 h.p., type OC4, four-
seater Sporting Tourer, 1913.   £7,042

A 19th century penny-
farthing bicycle.   £170

An interesting 18th century
Dutch sleigh.   £520

Early 20th century Reading
caravan painted red, blue and
beige.   £875

Aston Martin, 1½ litre Twin Overhead Camshaft
Racing two-seater, 1924.   £5,634

De Dion-Bouton 6 h.p., type De 1., two-
seater, circa 1911.   £3,943

TRAYS

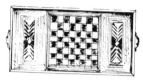

A walnut and parquetry inlaid oblong tray with chess board and brass handles, 20½ins wide. £22

Victorian papier mache oval tray with painted flowers and inset with mother of pearl. £28

A mahogany sectioned oval tea tray with pierced brass gallery. 33ins wide. £24

Pontypool tray with Napoleonic battle scene, circa 1820, 30ins x 21ins. £95

A 19th century butlers' mahogany oblong tray with folding sides, on folding stand. £85

A 19th century Toleware tea tray with floral pattern in the centre, 26½ins x 20½ins. £28

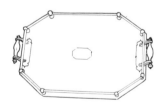

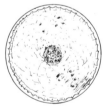

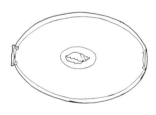

Edwardian oak double handled octagonal tea tray. £10

A large circular 17th century mother of pearl tray possibly Persian. £5,760

Mahogany inlaid oval tea tray with brass handles. £12

INDEX

INDEX

SPECIALIST INDEX

ANTIQUES

Angel Antiques, 16 Church Road, Hove, Sussex BN3 2FL
(Telephone Brighton 737955)

Ashurst Antiques, Granary Cottage, Ashurst, Steyning, Sussex
(Telephone Partridge Green 710256)

J.W. Blanchard,Ltd., 12 Jewry Street, Winchester, Hampshire
(Telephone Winchester 4547 or 2041)

P.M.J. Capewell, Antique Corner, 99 St. George's Road, Brighton, Sussex
(Telephone Brighton 682741)

Martin Christopher Antiques, Cowfold, Sussex
(Telephone) Cowfold 573)

D.D. Antiques, 53 Northfield Road, London W 14
(Telephone 01 567 3655)

Iain Downe Antiques, 3 Prince Albert Street, Brighton, Sussex
(Telephone Brighton 25383)

Christopher George Antiques, 217 Preston Road, Brighton, Sussex
(Telephone Brighton 500481)

Gorski Antiques, 201 Westbourne Grove, London W.11
(Telephone 01 229 8903)

Harris and Son, 40-41 Castle Street, Brighton, Sussex
(Telephone Brighton 29947)

David Hawkins (Brighton) Ltd., 4 Frederick Place, Brighton, Sussex
(Telephone Brighton 28106)

South Coast Antiques, 11 Boundary Road, Hove, Sussex
(Telephone Brighton 411115)

Sutton Valence Antiques Ltd., Sutton Valence, Kent
(Telephone Sutton Valence 3333)

Terry Antiques, 175 Junction Road, London N 19
(Telephone 01 263 1219 or 01 889 2398)

Town Antiques, 48 Surrey Street, Brighton BN1 3PB
(Telephone Brighton 29544)

Woburn Abbey Antiques Centre, Woburn Abbey, Bedfordshire
(Telephone Woburn (052525) 350)

ANTIQUE BEDSTEADS

...And So To Bed Ltd., 7 New King's Road, London SW6
(Telephone 01 731 3593/4)

ANTIQUE CLOCKS

Adrian Alan Ltd., 51 Upper North Street, Brighton, Sussex
(Telephone Brighton 25277)

Derek Roberts Antiques, 24 Shipbourne Road, Tonbridge, Kent
(Telephone Tonbridge 5286)

Wheelhouse Antiques, 59 Middle Street, Brighton, BN1 1AL
(Telephone Brighton 28944)

ANTIQUES AND FINE ART

G.A. Key, 8 Market Place, Aylsham, Norwich NOR 07Y
(Telephone Aylsham 3195)

ANTIQUES PERIODICALS

Antiques Yearbooks, 29 Maddox Street, London W1R 9LD
(Telephone 01 629 8532 - Advertising, 01 629 8667 Editorial & Production)

ANTIQUE SERVICES, including upholstery, picture framing, restoration, etc.

The Baron Group, Highgate Gallery, Highgate High Street, Highgate Village, London N6
(Telephone 01 348 8088)

Art & Antiques Weekly, 181 Queen Victoria Street, London EC4
(Telephone 01 248 3482)

ANTIQUES WAREHOUSES

Derek Boston's Salisbury Antique Warehouses, 223 Wilton Road, Salisbury, Wiltshire
(Telephone Salisbury 22682)

Peter Marks Warehouse, 1-11 Church Road, Portslade, Sussex, England
(Telephone Brighton 415471)

ARMS AND ARMOURY

Wallis and Wallis, 210 High Street, Lewes, Sussex
(Telephone Lewes 079 16 3137)

ART CONSULTANTS

Alfred W. Franks Ltd., 16 Hillbrow, Dyke Road Avenue, Hove, Sussex
(Telephone (0273) 777050 - day or (0273) 500678 - night)

AUCTIONEERS AND VALUERS

Boulton & Cooper Ltd., Forsyth House, Malton, North Yorkshire
(Telephone Malton 4051 - three lines)

Fox and Sons, Rivoli Salerooms, Chapel Road, Worthing, Sussex
(Telephone Worthing 30121)

John Francis, Thomas Jones & Sons, King Street, Carmarthen, Dyfed.
(Telephone Carmarthen 6465 - ten lines)

Peter Francis (Auctioneers) Salerooms, 2-5 Marsh Lane, Preston, Lancs
(Telephone)Preston 52098)

Raymond P. Inman, The Auction Galleries, 35 & 40 Temple Street, Brighton, Sussex BN1 3BH
(Telephone Brighton 774777)

King and Chasemore, Pulborough, Sussex
(Telephone Pulborough (07982) 2081

John Stacey & Sons, 86/88/90 Pall Mall, Leigh-On-Sea, Essex
(Telephone Southend 77051)

Sussex Auction Galleries, Perrymount Road, Haywards Heath, Sussex
(Telephone Haywards Heath 50333 - 7)

BAROMETERS

Mitre Antiques, 17 Sadler Street, Wells, Somerset
(Telephone Wells 72607)

COINS

S.N. Lane (Coins) Ltd., 178 New Bond Street, London W1
(Telephone 01 493 9841)

COINS AND MEDALS,

L.A. Kaitcer (Antiques) Ltd., 16 Castle Lane, Belfast
(Telephone Belfast 44505/4)

COLLECTORS' ITEMS

The Antiques Centre, 22 Haydon Place, Guildford, Surrey
(Telephone Guildford 67817)

DECORATIVE FURNITURE
Joyce Ruffell, 189 - 191 Highland Road, Southsea, Portsmouth, Hampshire
(Telephone Portsmouth 31411)

DOLLS
Somersham Antiques, 97 High Street, Somersham, Cambridgeshire
(Telephone Somersham 487)

EARLY OAK AND FINE FURNITURE
Brecon Antiques, Free Street, Brecon, Wales
(Telephone Brecon 3857 day or night)

EXPORT AND SHIPPING GOODS
Timperley Antiques, 190 Stockport Road, Timperley Village, Altrincham, Cheshire
(Telephone 061 980 3700)

EXPORTERS
Victor M. Gunn, 372 Brighton Road, Shoreham, Sussex
(Telephone Brighton 691474)

EXPORT SHIPPERS AND PACKERS
British Antique Exporters Ltd., New Road Industrial Estate, Newhaven, Sussex
(Telephone Newhaven (07912) 5561 - eight lines)
Cosmo Antiques, The Old Telephone Exchange, Vicarage Road, Lingfield, Surrey
(Telephone Lingfield 833024)
Mike Deasy Ltd., Partridge Green, Sussex
(Telephone Partridge Green 710631)

Lewis Belt Shipping, 24 Middle Street, Brighton, Sussex
(Telephone (0273) 23546)

FINE ART AUCTIONEERS
Dowell's, 65 George Street, Edinburgh EH2 2JL
(Telephone 031 225 2266/8)

D.M. Nesbit & Company, 7 Clarendon Road, Southsea, Hampshire
(Telephone Portsmouth (0705) 20785/6)

Russell, Baldwin and Bright, 38 South Street, Leominster, Herefordshire
(Telephone Leominster 2363)
Henry Spencer & Sons, 20 The Square, Retford, Nottinghamshire
(Telephone Retford 2531 or 3768)

FORTHCOMING AUCTION LISTS
Romeike & Curtice Ltd., Hale House, 290 - 296 Green Lanes, London N13 5TP
(Telephone 01 882 0155)

18TH AND 19TH CENTURY FURNITURE
Manker (Antiques) Ltd., Lion House, 79 St. Pancras, Chichester, Sussex
(Telephone Chichester 85956)

FRENCH STYLE FURNITURE PRODUCTIONS
Meubles Francais (Reproductions) Ltd., Albion House, Southwick, Brighton, Sussex
(Telephone Brighton 592983 or 593001)

HARPSICHORD AND PIANO MAKERS AND RESTORERS
Robert Morley and Company Ltd., 4 Belmont Hill, London SE13
(Telephone 01 852 6151)

LUSTREWARE AND GARDEN ORNAMENTS
Albany Marketing Services, Upper Emmott House, Laneshawbridge, Colne, Lancashire BB8 7EQ
(Telephone Colne 5838)

OAK AND WALNUT COUNTRY FURNITURE
Laughton of Farnham Ltd., Willey Mill, Alton Road, Farnham, Surrey
(Telephone Farnham 23480 or 21422)
PAINTED AND GILDED FURNITURE
Antique Restorations, 211 Westbourne Park Road, London W11 1EA
(Telephone 01 727 0467)
POT LIDS
Beckford Antiques, P.O. Bob 26, Sutton Coldfield, West Midlands B72 1TP
(Telephone 021 308 1498)
REMOVALS
K. and F. Transport, 3 Victoria Road, New Barnet, Hertfordshire
(Telephone 01 440 8974)
REPRODUCTIONS
Martell's of SuttonLtd., 71 - 74 Westmead Road, Sutton, Surrey
(Telephone 01 642 9551)
RESTAURANTS
Talk of the Town, 124 - 125 St. James's Street, Brighton Sussex BN2 1TH
(Telephone Brighton 63773)
RESTORATION
John Hartnett, 20 Church Street' Brighton, Sussex
(Telephone Brighton 28793)

Tontine Antiques Ltd., 75 - 81 Tontine Street, Folkestone, Kent
(Telephone Elham (0303 84) 357)
RESTORATION AND UPHOLSTERY
Chas. Lowe & Sons Ltd., 37, 38 & 40 Church Gate, Loughborough,
Leicestershire Le11 1UE
(Telephone Loughborough 2554)
ROLLS ROYCE AUTOMOBILES
T. and J. Davis, 22 & 23 Battersea Rise, London SW11
(Telephone 01 228 1370)
SILVER
The Antique Centre, 22 Haydon Place & 25 Chertsey Street, Guildford, Surrey
(Telephone Guildford 67817)
STATELY ANTIQUES
Woburn Abbey Antiques Centre, Woburn Abbey, Bedfordshire
(Telephone Woburn (052525) 350)
TRANSPORT
M. Dawes, 31 Upper Gardner Street, Brighton, Sussex
(Telephone Brighton 61259)
WHOLESALE AND SHIPPING GOODS
Timperley Antiques, 190 Stockport Road, Timperley Village, Altrincham,
Cheshire
(Telephone 061 980 3700)